Mapping the West European Left

MAPPING

This series of readers, edited by *New Left Review*, aims to illuminate key topics in a changing world.

Mapping the
West European Left

Edited by

PERRY ANDERSON

and

PATRICK CAMILLER

PUBLISHED IN ASSOCIATION WITH
new left *review*

VERSO

London · New York

First published by Verso 1994
© This collection New Left Review 1994
All rights reserved

Verso
UK: 6 Meard Street, London W1V 3HR
USA: 29 West 35th Street, New York, NY 10001–2291

Verso is the imprint of New Left Books

ISBN 0–86091–213–2
ISBN 0–86091–927–7 (pbk)

British Library Cataloguing in Publication Data
A catalogue record for this book is available from the British Library

Library of Congress Cataloging-in-Publication Data
Mapping the West European left/edited by Perry Anderson and Patrick Camiller.
p.   cm.
Includes bibliographical references (p.   ) and index.
ISBN 0–86091–213–2.—ISBN 0–86091–927–7 (pbk.)
1. Socialism—Europe.   I. Anderson, Perry.   II. Camiller, Patrick.
HX239.M367   1994
320.5'31'094 – dc20

Typeset by Type Study, Scarborough
Printed and bound in Great Britain by Biddles Ltd, Guildford and King's Lynn

Contents

Introduction

Social Democracy in Western Europe has traditionally enjoyed a placid image. The parties of the Socialist International have seemed stable fixtures of the postwar scene, vehicles of a rather uneventful – not always effective, but eminently respectable – politics of reform. A sudden series of shocks has recently held up an eerie mirror to this identity. In February 1993 the Italian Socialist leader Bettino Craxi – the dominant political figure of his country in the eighties, when he was twice prime minister – resigned under an avalanche of charges of corruption. He now escapes arrest in Tunisia. In May 1993 Pierre Bérégovoy, Socialist prime minister of France, queried by the press over his private finances and discouraged by his party's rout at the polls, shot himself on Labour Day. Two weeks later the leader of the German SPD, Bjorn Engholm, resigned after confessing he had lied over the downfall of a Christian Democratic rival in Schleswig-Holstein, later a suicide. Within another month Germany's most powerful trade-union leader, Franz Steinkühler, secretary-general of IG Metall, was forced to quit after revelations of insider trading in a company on whose board he sat as a labour representative. In the same period, meanwhile, accusations of widespread corruption were mounting against the government of Felipe González in Spain. Eventually, in the spring of 1994, two of its highest officials – the heads of the Central Bank and of the Guardia Civil – were charged with illegal enrichment. One is now in prison, the other in hiding. In Britain, the Labour Party – unlike its counterparts in Italy, France, Germany and Spain – has enjoyed neither national nor regional power for over a decade. But even here, the party's leading press patron and benefactor Robert Maxwell – a former Labour MP, whose control of the *Mirror* empire was sealed by the Labour leadership – dropped to his death from a luxury yacht after the largest financial fraud in British history.

1

Sensations pass. The spate of scandals that has swept West European social democracy in the nineties is not necessarily a sound guide to its future. But the coincidence of such events in the five major states of the Union is unlikely to lack all significance. What they suggest is a wider moral crisis in the identity of the major organizations of the West European left. In the past, of course, it would not have been possible to speak in a single breath of social democracy throughout the region. For the western half of Europe was traditionally divided into two distinct zones.[1] Historically, the mass parties of the Second International arose in the Northern countries. In this zone, where there was either a numerous working class based on major concentrations of heavy industry (Britain, Germany, Belgium), or a small-farmer class ready to ally with labour (Scandinavia), classical social democracy took root. Mass parties, strong trade unions, and early electoral advance marked this Northern reformism. Despite some experience of office in the inter-war period, however, it did not become a normal governing force throughout the area until after the Second World War. It was then, during the long postwar boom, that the British, Benelux, Nordic and Germanic parties, with no significant rivals to their left, came into their own. Although selected industries were nationalized in a number of countries (Britain and Austria were the most significant), public ownership was not among their primary objectives. The hallmark of Northern social democracy was rather the construction of welfare states with full employment and wide social services. The forms and scope of these varied from country to country, and the results were seldom due only to social-democratic initiative. But the political success of these parties always rested on their ability to secure popular identification with those two achievements. The fund of political support so created proved cumulative. The fortunes of Northern social democracy as a whole reached their zenith, not in the early fifties or sixties, but in the early seventies. In the years 1974–75, for the first and only time in postwar history, there were social-democratic prime ministers in every state of the region: Britain, West Germany, Austria, Belgium, Holland, Norway, Denmark, Sweden and Finland.

More or less as this political crest was reached, however, the economic conditions underlying the success of Northern reformism gave way. By the mid seventies, growth rates had fallen, inflation was accelerating, and unemployment rising: it was clear that the world capitalist economy was moving into a long downswing. In the new conjuncture social democracy not only lacked effective policies to meet the crisis. It suddenly found itself associated with it, when the

---

1. For a more extended discussion of this contrast, see Perry Anderson, 'The Light of Europe', *English Questions*, Verso, London 1992, pp. 307–25.

ideological revival of monetarism picked out excessive state spending and over-mighty trade unions as the key causes of stagflation. The result was a wave of reaction against the welfare consensus over which social democracy had presided, which brought governments of the right to power throughout the region. Starting with the election of Thatcher's regime in Britain in 1979, the movement spread to West Germany, the Low Countries, and then, more unevenly, to Scandinavia. Only Austria and Sweden resisted the trend in these years. The dominant pattern of the eighties was clear-cut. In Northern Europe the left lost political and intellectual ground everywhere to a reinvigorated right on the attack against its whole postwar record.

In Southern Europe, the growth of the left had taken a quite different path. In France, Italy, Spain, Portugal and Greece, industrialization on the whole came less completely or later, typically in the setting of a backward agriculture, in which clerical or seigneurial influence was often strong. Here anarcho-syndicalism was a major current in the heyday of the Second International; while in the inter-war period, the Third International formed Communist parties that by 1945 had become the leading force in the labour movement. But if the left in the South was politically more radical than in the North, it was also structurally weaker. In less modern societies, the balance of postwar forces was for most of the time heavily weighted to the right. In Italy, Christian Democratic hegemony was unbroken for thirty years after the onset of the Cold War. In France, de Gaulle's erection of the Fifth Republic ensured stable conservative rule for two decades. In Spain and Portugal, dictatorships persisted from the prewar period; as late as the sixties, officers took power in Greece. Over time, however, the long boom had its effects in the Mediterranean belt too, as economic development and social change gradually eroded the foundations of the dominant order. By the second half of the seventies, the regimes of Franco, Salazar and Papadopoulos had finally come to an end. In France, Giscard's capacity to maintain the continuity of the Gaullist heritage was visibly declining. In Italy, Andreotti had to enlarge the area of his parliamentary support to informal consultations with the PCI.

Belated liberalization of the political order opened up obvious opportunities for the left, as the bearer of long-denied alternatives. In the major trio of states, the Communist parties attempted to position themselves as the natural candidates for a change of power by adopting a conciliatory constitutionalism, in keeping with Western – as opposed to Soviet – traditions. But the Eurocommunist attempt to adjust to new conditions everywhere misfired. Presenting themselves in a range of colours, all of them social democratic by the standards of the Third International, the Italian, French and Spanish parties had to confront competition from genuinely social-democratic rivals, that were initially much weaker, but without the same handicaps of internal bureaucracy and external association with the regimes in Eastern Europe. All were rapidly outflanked by the rise of these Eurosocialist formations – PS, PSOE, PSI – to the centre of the national stage. In Portugal and Greece, where the Communist parties remained unreconstructed, the result was the same: the PSP and PASOK – the latter an entirely new creation – soon overtook them.

When national power finally changed hands, it was thus a new social democracy, not a renovated Communism, that was the beneficiary. In a reversal of postwar roles, just as Northern Europe turned to the right, Southern Europe moved to the left. By the early eighties, Mitterrand was President of France, and González, Craxi, Papandreou and Soares were prime ministers of Spain, Italy, Greece and Portugal. The political composition of these governments was far from uniform. In France, Spain and Greece there were large Socialist majorities in the Chamber, while in Italy and Portugal the Socialists were only the pivot of a ruling coalition. Nor were the policies initially pursued by the Eurosocialist parties all that similar. In France, and to a lesser extent in Greece, an ambitious programme of nationalization, redistribution and reflation was undertaken, without counterpart elsewhere. In Spain financial orthodoxy was pursued from the start, never practised to the same extent in Italy. But by the end of the decade, the elements of a common balance-sheet stood out. Southern social democracy has not reproduced the original Northern pattern of mass working-class parties linked with strong union movements – to a leadership typically composed of upwardly mobile professionals, there has corresponded a more heteroclite electorate, and a decline rather than growth in the size and strength of the trade unions. Nor was it able to repeat the Northern achievement of full employment in the postwar period: the number of jobless remained high throughout the eighties. Spain, where Socialist rule has lasted longest, holds the European record for mass unemployment.

On the other hand, modest social reforms were typically introduced, if no major creation or extension of a welfare state; together with some civic modernization, where legal systems were particularly archaic or democratic procedures still insecure. The overall performance of these administrations was tightly limited by the international conjuncture. The same pressures from the world market that helped to bring the right to power in the North inhibited any radical impulses by the left in the South. Once the initial French attempt at counter-cyclical expansion failed in 1982–83, Eurosocialism for the most part simply floated with the tide of the global economy. After the middle of the decade it became a passive beneficiary of the speculative fever set off by Reagan's deficit financing, which spread high-consumption drives among the more prosperous layers of the electorate, while doing little for the poor and unemployed: a pattern most pronounced in Italy, with the flowering of the *ceti rampanti* under Craxi, and during the second González administration in Spain.

However far from the classic model of welfare reformism, the performance of the Southern version of social democracy – ratified by re-election in France, Spain and Greece, and relative advance in Italy – could still be held to compensate for the setbacks of the Northern movements in the eighties. In a West European balance, the survival of SAP rule in Sweden, still resistant to the neo-liberal turn, and of an Austrian coalition under SPÖ dominance, also had to be counted. The overall picture might be thought mixed, but not unduly dark. Such is in fact the conclusion of the major comparative synthesis on European social democracy in these years. Wolfgang Merkel's *Ende der Sozialdemokratie?* traces the performance of social-democratic parties in the sixteen principal countries of Western Europe with admirable care and detail up to 1990. Original political science at its best, Merkel's study is not only an impressive work of scholarship. It is also a reasoned polemic.[2] Arguing against a wide range of critics – neo-conservatives, liberals, marxists, regulation theorists, rational-choice analysts – who have suggested from different standpoints that social democracy is in historical decline, Merkel undertakes to show with statistical precision that if the period 1974–1990 is compared with that of 1945–1973, European social democracy as a whole suffered loss neither of electoral strength nor of governmental power. Even policy retreat, in so far as it occurred, has – he contends – been overstated. In a spirit of sober loyalty to progressive ideals, Merkel ends on a note of optimism. Despite altered conditions, social democracy has in fact weathered the change of international conjuncture fairly well, and as a 'new demand for regulation beyond the market' develops, there is no reason why it should not flourish anew.

Such could look the balance-sheet, to a committed but scrupulous observer, in 1990. Events have not been kind to it since. In the North, the Swedish attempt at a 'Third Way' disintegrated; the SAP lost office in 1991 to the first Conservative-led government since the twenties, and by the summer of 1994 the number of jobless was about 14 per cent of the labour force – one of the highest rates in the OECD. In the South, French socialism was routed in the elections of 1993, which gave the right the largest parliamentary majority in the history of the Fifth

---

2. Wolfgang Merkel, *Ende der Sozialdemokratie? Machtressourcen und Regierungspolitik im westeuropäischen Vergleich*, Frankfurt 1993. Merkel had earlier written studies of Italian and Spanish socialism.

Republic. In Italy the PSI – caught at the centre of *tangentopoli* – has been obliterated, its list failing to elect even a single deputy in the elections of spring 1994, which brought to power a more radical coalition of the right, much of it recently fascist. A few months later, the European elections offered a bleak snapshot of the state of the left throughout the EU. In Spain the Socialist Party was for the first time decisively beaten by its conservative opponents. In France the PS vote fell to less than a sixth of the electorate, forcing Michel Rocard to resign as party leader. In Italy, the largest residual party of the left, the newly converted PDS – former Communists become social democrats – was reduced to less than a fifth of the electorate, obliging Achille Occhetto to quit. In Germany, after twelve years of Kohl's rule, the SPD vote fell to its lowest level since the fifties. In Britain alone Labour scored major gains as the traditional party of the left, but on a turn-out so low – scarcely more than a third of the electorate – as to afford little security for the future. Statistical comparisons from the mid nineties, when Southern Europe has shifted sharply to the right, without the left so far making any convincing comeback in Northern Europe, would be less comforting than at the close of the eighties.

National electoral cycles come and go. The diversity of states in Western Europe makes them unlikely ever to coincide completely. There will continue to be governments led by social-democratic parties – as at the time of writing in Norway, Denmark, Austria, Spain and Greece – and future elections won by them, as no doubt probably soon in Sweden. But an underlying crisis of direction is unmistakeable. It has not been alleviated, but if anything deepened by the collapse of Communism in Eastern Europe, which sanguine observers often held would be a tonic for social democracy, vindicating *a contrario* its historic option for the road of moderate constitutional reforms. In the event, the ideological triumph of the market has been so complete in the East that it has ricocheted against any use of the state for economic regulation or social welfare in the West. How long this fall-out will last is hard to say. At present its effect is striking. For it has occurred at a time when Western Europe has yet to recover from the worst recession since the War. Today mass unemployment is not only far above levels in the USA or Japan. It is actually higher than in the thirties, without any prospect of long-term improvement.[3] There are now about twenty million people – more than the entire population of Scandinavia – out of work in Western Europe. Yet far from strengthening the appeal of social democracy as a remedy against the ills of capitalism, the return of the scourge that provided so much of its original *raison d'être* has only

3. For comparative figures, see Andrea Boltho's powerful article, 'Western Europe's Economic Stagnation', *New Left Review* 201, September–October 1993, p. 62.

weakened it further. Once the major champion of programmes to resist widespread unemployment, it now seems reduced to a helpless onlooker as the tide of the jobless steadily rises, from one business cycle to another. Social democracy may not be at an end. But who can doubt that it is at an impasse?

Historically, there have always been other forces to the left of it in Western Europe. The principal of these, of course, was Communism. Today, with the collapse of the Soviet bloc, the rationale of descent from the October Revolution has all but disappeared. In Italy the largest Communist movement of the West has become a much smaller social democratic party, of very moderate cast, taking the place of the PSI. Elsewhere the Communist tradition persists in an uncertain after-life. Typically, it still musters a minority of voters more radically opposed to established arrangements than the electorates of the Socialist International. The degree to which these parties have broken with orthodox doctrine and discipline varies widely. At one extreme, Swedish Communism democratized itself as early as the seventies into an independent, open party of the left. At another, the outlook of Greek or Portuguese Communism remains largely unaltered. French Communism, despite much internal dissidence, is still something like a shrunken version of its former self; whereas Spanish Communism has reshaped its image within a coalition of the United Left. Italian Communism itself did not wholly dissolve into the PDS, but left a lively residue in Rifondazione. Even in Germany, the Communist tradition has survived in defence of the identity of the Eastern population. All these parties currently poll within a range of 5 to 10 per cent of the electorate. Their overall constituency remains larger than that of the Green parties, which in most countries now compete with them on the left flank of social democracy. Elsewhere, in Denmark or Norway, left-socialist parties of a populist character, born from earlier revolts within the Communist or the social democratic tradition, have established themselves as durable features of the political landscape. In Western Europe as a whole it is everywhere the rule that, under conditions of minimally equitable representation of political opinion, there is another left beyond the boundaries of the Socialist International. Nowhere, however, does it have any chance of forming a government: its only hope of office is in coalition with a dominant social democracy. Nor, for all the greater sharpness of its rejection of post-Reaganite capitalism, is its stock of solutions much richer. For the moment, at any rate, the existence of this political area does little to modify the programmatic dilemmas of the left.

In these conditions, there is plainly a need for comparative reflection on the experience of the recent past. This volume offers one kind of inventory. Its origins lie in a series of essays published over a decade by

New Left Review, a journal published in Britain but international in its contributors and readership, which – in reaction to the parochialism of political culture in the UK itself – took an early interest in the varieties of the West European left. The book marks a new approach to its subject in a number of ways. Traditionally, the literature on the European left has tended to fall into two categories: studies of the classical parties of social democracy in the North, and works on the Communist or – more recently – Eurosocialist parties of the South. There were good reasons for this division, but it makes little sense today. Merkel's comparative survey overcomes it with a quantitative analysis of elections and 'power quotients' across the OECD half of the continent. But Merkel's actual accounts of the performance of social democracy in office, acute though they often are, remain much more selective. Here a representative regional balance has been sought, that tries for the first time to give equal attention to the Scandinavian North, the Anglo-Germanic Centre, and the Latin South. The result is not exhaustive. On the edges of each of these bands, Finland and Iceland, Austria and Ireland, Portugal and Greece have been omitted – as also the religious and linguistic mosaics of the Low Countries and Switzerland. Priority has been given to the major states of the three tiers of West European capitalism.

A second distinctive feature of these essays lies in the particular way they focus on the national cases under view. Most serious writing on parties or movements today is the product of a modern political science that has specialized in quantitative research and statistical correlation. Indispensable for an understanding of electoral systems, voting patterns or rules of coalition, this style of analysis tends to put less emphasis on the longer-term dynamics of social and ideological conflict. Without forgoing the insights it provides, this collection typically seeks to reconstruct the development of the left in each country with a historical narrative going back further in time. In the case of Denmark or Norway, societies little known abroad, the political landscape of the country is traced from the nineteenth century. More usually, the beginnings of the current institutional order – the Cow Deal (Sweden), the Liberation (Italy), the Cold War (Germany), the Fifth Republic (France), the Transition (Spain) – provide the relevant starting-points. In none of these accounts is history given a stamp of necessity. Parties are taken to be collective actors making discretionary choices. Rather than reducing their path to any preordained fate, a historical retrospect will usually disclose possibilities that were not realized, opportunities missed as often as errors avoided, which form part of their record. The essays here are written from an independent but unsectarian standpoint on the left, critical of official orthodoxies. Nearly all of them suggest some counter-factual reflections on the facts effectively accomplished.

At the same time, they seek to respect the spirit of Gramsci's dictum that 'to write the history of a party is to write the general history of a country from a monographic point of view'.[4] Thus each chapter tries to situate the evolution of the left within the overall field of force of the nation in question – including, notably, the configuration of the right, as well as the broader range of allies or adversaries bearing on its development. Within this general setting, the angles of vision vary widely as each essay highlights what it takes to be the salient features of the particular national scenery. It is striking that the two opening chapters on Sweden and Norway do not give primary attention to the welfare states that are the most common object of foreign interest in them, but to the economic models of their postwar growth. For these, Jonas Pontusson and Lars Mjøset and his colleagues argue, were the material condition of the social reforms for which the two countries are better known; the key to the fate of the left in each has always been its macroeconomic management. The record here, they show, has differed significantly. Swedish labour-market regulation, followed by the defeat of wage-earner funds, the temporary success and then the ultimate failure of the Third Way, is one pattern. Norwegian 'credit socialism', dismantled in a liberalization softened by oil rents, is another – currently with less unemployment. The originality of each experience remains striking. In Denmark another kind of drama has dominated, the trailer for significant developments elsewhere. There, Niels Finn Christiansen explains, a distinct class configuration in which a radical petty bourgeoisie was originally much stronger in the countryside – transmitting important traditions to urban society, generated the first major tax revolt against the welfare state by a populist right in the West. Here too there emerged perhaps the first clear-cut division within the left between traditional industrial and new public-service constituencies, refracted in the contrast between the Social Democratic and Socialist People's Party: another theme with a future.

It is in Germany that the dilemmas posed by this kind of divergence have since been staged in most obsessive form. There the deepest cultural and generational revolt of the late sixties paved the way for the emergence of the Greens, in much sharper antithesis to the official politics of Social Democracy than the SPP had been in Denmark. Stephen Padgett and William Paterson trace the tensions that have increasingly paralyzed the SPD as it tries to hold onto old and new electorates, of increasingly different outlook, in the face of avowedly 'post-materialist' competition – often immobilizing it in the posture of Buridan's ass. In no other European country has political and intellectual debate on the left been so dominated by the problem of the

4. *Quaderni del Carcere*, vol. III, Turin 1975, p. 1630.

strategic composition of the majority to be won. If similar issues have arisen in Britain, they have been posed less acutely, in part because of the absence of any comparable political counter-culture, but also because of the nature of the electoral system. It is the latter that provides the focus of Peter Mair's contribution to the volume. In the English-speaking world, the Labour Party has attracted such an extensive literature that familiar ground could be taken for granted here. The electoral misfortunes of the party, which from 1979 to 1992 suffered the worst set of defeats of any social democracy in Europe, have been well tracked by Ivor Crewe, in particular; while its political vicissitudes have been the object of renewed attention in Gregory Elliott's spirited *Labourism and the English Genius*.[5] In this context, it seemed preferable to spotlight the least discussed, but arguably most important determinant of the special character of Labourism, its position within the peculiar British electoral structure. Here Mair's comparative analysis of the relationship between voting systems and radical politics contains lessons of general significance to the left.

The relevance of these in Italy, where in 1993 the PDS campaigned behind a referendum to abolish proportional representation in favour of first-past-the-post rules, scarcely needs emphasis. Historically, it is the European right that has – with good reason – typically favoured systems of disproportional representation since the time of Versailles.[6] In Italy Mussolini was the first to introduce them in the inter-war period, and it is no surprise that Berlusconi has been the first to benefit from them in the present era. Here electoral engineering has been part of a wider theme unifying the major Latin states: the politics of 'modernization'. Given the genuine archaism of so many of the institutions of these societies, any pursuit of a mandate for change by the left could not but make appeal to ideals of modernity. But no signifier is so quicksilver. In France, George Ross and Jane Jenson show how suicidal was the refusal of the Communist Party, when it still had time, to abandon anachronistic traditions, to which it clings *in extremis* even today – a refusal which cost the Common Programme, in principle the boldest single attempt to alter the limits of advanced capitalism since the war, its popular dynamic and hence any realistic chance of success. But they also show how self-defeating was the

5. For Crewe's analysis of Labour's position on the eve of the last elections, see his trenchant essay, 'Labour Force Changes, Working-Class Decline, and the Labour Vote', in Frances Fox Piven, ed., *Labour Parties in Post-Industrial Societies*, Oxford 1992; Elliott's *Labourism and the English Genius*, Verso, London 1993, includes a sharp retrospect of the party's history up to the end of the seventies, as well as an overview of its development since.

6. For the comparative pattern, see 'The Light of Europe', *English Questions*, pp. 340–45.

conversion of the Socialist Party, in the wake of that failure, to an idolatry of the firm and the market as the titans of modernization. In Spain, nearly forty years of centralist dictatorship left the right isolated from the regional industrial elites of the country, giving Socialist modernization a longer leash. But, although extended by belated concessions to the labour movement, in the nineties this too has become very frayed, as Patrick Camiller makes clear. The principal reason is one common to all three countries, but on most comprehensive display in Italy. Modernity voided of any content beyond market adjustment has dangerous anagrams. Its nemesis has everywhere been corruption. While the scale on which money lubricated government was exceptional in the heyday of Craxi, the starting-point of the PSI's rise to prominence was not untypical – an attunement to real processes of secularization in Italian society, to which the PCI gave a cold shoulder. If the outcome of the eighties has been so disastrous for the Italian left, ending not merely with the complete extinction of the PSI but the demoralized exit of the PCI, Tobias Abse argues that the main single cause was the consistent failure of Italian Communism to respond creatively to popular aspirations and upsurges against the old order, from the sixties onwards.

Macroeconomic management; social aggregation; electoral justice; popular rapport; cultural modernity – these have been some of the central questions confronting the West European left, in a time when hopes of socialism have been struck off its agenda. Behind them lies a double change in its strategic situation. First, there has been a fragmentation of its constituencies. There was never a time when the parties of the Second or Third International, or their postwar successors, rested on a homogeneous social base. Pure labour movements were always a legend. But up to the sixties, at any rate, the manual working class formed the magnetic centre of every social coalition that the leading parties of the left could muster, in Northern or Southern Europe alike. The industrial proletariat was numerically the largest component of their electorates, structurally the best organized, morally the most authoritative. The political leadership of these parties might come from professional or intellectual groups, their voters include contingents from the lower middle class or peasantry; while often, of course, large numbers of workers also voted for conservative parties. Nevertheless, it was what Italian theorists termed *centralità operaia* – the 'centrality' of the working class – that welded together an array of forces around the left. Typically, this is no longer so today.[7] Over the past twenty years wage-labour has generally

7. The best discussion of this change is to be found in Gerassimos Moschonas, *La social-démocratie de 1945 à nos jours*, Paris 1994, pp. 37–52 and 75–83. This excellent book by a Greek scholar working in Crete, although shorter in length, rivals Merkel's study in

continued to spread, as traditional peasants, craftsmen, shopkeepers have lost their independence, and housewives have entered the labour force, even if there have been some recent enclaves of growth in the newly self-employed. But the divisions within the ranks of wage-earners have greatly increased.

Five axes of differentiation now make any united movement for radical change more difficult. The first of these is an old one, whose distribution has shifted. In Europe there was always a more significant contrast of status and income between manual and clerical labour, reflected in levels of collective organization and political outlook, than in the United States or Japan. Today the proportions of each in the West European labour force as a whole have changed places. The manual working class has declined to an average of little more than a quarter of the economically active population, and has been overtaken everywhere by the number of employees in the tertiary sector. Even where white-collar workers have achieved very high levels of unioniz-ation, and traditionally identified with objectives of the labour move-ment, as in Sweden, the objective change in their relative weight has loosened past ties of solidarity with industrial workers. At the same time the span of skills, income and security *within* the manual working class itself has steadily widened.[8] At one end, the material position of skilled workers in high-technology sectors, prospering through the boom of the Reagan years, has never been so favourable – often with marked effects on their voting patterns, as in Britain at the height of Thatcher's success.[9] At the other, the pool of unskilled and casualized labour – at the limit sweated or depressed into the long-term unemployed – has swelled. Between the two, the semi-skilled oper-atives of classic manufacturing industry have dwindled in numbers and influence. The result has been a social polarization of manual labour itself, with growing conflicts of interest between its most exposed and its privileged groups.

Meanwhile another kind of stratification has become increasingly important, as entry into the labour force starts later and retirement

quality and range. The two works, written in ignorance of each other, form an interesting contrast. Moschonas does not attempt to analyse the policies of social-democratic governments, which form the main focus of Merkel's book, but gives closer attention to the social basis and organizational structures of social-democratic parties.

8. Historically, there is no precedent for the increase in wage dispersion that occurred in Britain between 1976 and 1990: see Amanda Gosling, Stephen Machin and Coastas Meghir, *What Has Happened to Wages?*, Institute for Fiscal Studies, June 1994, p. 3. It was even higher in the USA in the eighties, but lower in most other European countries.

9. One of the themes of Moschonas's work is that after 1973 social democracy in general lost more support within the working class than the class itself decreased in size. The SPD was an exception, holding its proletarian vote, but losing much of its white-collar and civil-service electorate.

from it lasts longer. Age now divides wage-earners in new ways. On the one hand, adolescence is no longer a sharply drawn preamble to adulthood. The worlds of late schooling (or what passes for it) and early working have merged into a largely self-contained youth culture that – except at moments of high political tension – tends to cut each new generation, as it passes through it, off from the common concerns of class or locality. On the other hand, the fall in birth rates and extension of life-expectancy have transformed the weight of the elderly in the population at large. About a third of the average adult's life is now spent after retirement from the labour force. The welfare state is now overwhelmingly a system of public support for this group, whose pensions and health care absorb about two-thirds of all social expenditure.[10] The result is a logic of segmentation – both fiscal and cultural – that makes the 'second age' of wage-labour, caught between the needs of the 'third age' above it and the drives of a 'first age' below it, potentially the political pressure-point.

If these changes have tended to pull apart constituencies that could once be readily brought together, the effect of the feminization of the work force has been more ambiguous. The traditional electorates of the left always revealed a sexual deficit. Under the influence of customary belief or domestic isolation, women invariably voted in greater numbers for conservative parties than men. The gap between the two was, for example, on its own large enough to keep the British Labour Party out of power between 1951 and 1964. The steady growth of female participation in waged work – to an average of about 60 per cent of the male rate in the EU, and 70 per cent in Scandinavia – could have been expected to weaken this pattern. Signs of a historic reversal have in fact occurred: in a number of national elections, women have outnumbered men in voting for the left. But the shift remains scattered and episodic. So far, the potential enhancement of political strength from the relative decline of the housewife has probably been out-weighed by the actual difficulty that male-dominated trade-union movements have had in adjusting to the multiplication of the female worker. The wage gap between the sexes remains high in most of Western Europe; and even where it is lower, in the Nordic countries, job segregation continues to be pronounced. Net indices of labour-market inequality have probably increased rather than diminished, as more women have entered it.

Lastly, the transformation of Western Europe from a traditional zone of emigration into one of immigration has – more notoriously

10. For these data, see Göran Therborn's majestic panorama of social and cultural changes in Western Europe since the War: 'Modernità Sociale in Europa (1950–1992)', in *Storia d'Europa*, vol. I, Turin 1993 (ed. P. Anderson, M. Aymard, P. Bairoch, W. Barberis, C. Ginzburg), pp. 467–8.

than any other factor of differentiation – eroded a culture of solidarity
in the working population of most of its nations. If ethnic diversification has enriched the life of its big cities, the political price has been
an erratic but unmistakeable rise in symptoms of racism and xenophobia. The total number of immigrants from Asia, Africa and the
Caribbean in the European Union is now about 13 million. In
Germany, France, Britain, Sweden and Belgium ten per cent or more
of all school-children are now of non-European origin. The experience
of the United States is a reminder of what the consequences of racial
and ethnic division can be for a labour movement, indeed for any wider
sense of social interdependence. The working-class catchment of new
parties of the anti-immigrant right – in France, Italy, Flanders, Austria,
Denmark – is a warning of fractures that could become much deeper.
The politics of national identity is unlikely to offer terrain favourable
to the left.

Differences in work, income and security, age, gender, origin – so far
the effect of all these has been to unstitch the collective agencies
required to challenge the status quo. The unravelling of constituencies
makes the task of *subjective* mobilization for any radical change
inherently harder. But this is only one side of the new difficulties facing
the left in Western Europe. The other is more intractable. It is the
tightening of constraints that reduce the *objective* space for its traditional policies. If the primary achievements of the postwar left were
the creation of welfare systems and maintenance of near-full employment, its means of steering the capitalist economy to deliver these were
essentially two: monetary policy and fiscal policy. The basic instruments of macroeconomic management were, on the one hand, setting
of interest rates and exchange rates, and on the other, control of
taxation. In the most favourable cases these were supplemented, but
never substituted, by corporatist wage accords. In the course of the
eighties each has been critically weakened. Incomes policies, always a
patchy phenomenon, were marginalized as employers lost interest in
national agreements and trade unions the power to enforce them –
even in countries like Sweden, let alone Britain. The more important
changes, however, have come elsewhere. The internationalization of
capital flows released by the deregulation of financial markets has
made it increasingly difficult either to devalue to restore trade
balances, or lower interest rates to stimulate demand. In the past these
were the two most frequent weapons in the arsenal of social-democratic
crisis management. Today the mobility of speculative transactions,
instantly sensitive to fears of inflation, undermines the effects of each.
In the early eighties the failure of French reflation was often contrasted
with the success of Swedish devaluation. But by the end of the decade
the effects of the latter had worn off, and could not be repeated:

subsequent depreciation by the SAP was a prelude to electoral disaster. In Western Europe today the loss of national autonomy over monetary policy, though in no case absolute, is in general becoming steadily more pronounced.

Fiscal policy has been less directly affected by the globalization of capital, since most individual tax-payers do not enjoy the option of exit from their national setting – even if high rates of corporation tax are vulnerable to reactions of institutional withdrawal. Here it is domestic political opinion, in Hirschman's terms the expression of voice, that has become the key constraint. Historically the pattern of taxation has tended to be rather inertial in most West European countries, its respective national forms varying little over time. But for thirty years after the War its overall level rose in the OECD, as the share of public expenditure in GNP steadily increased. Starting in Denmark in the early seventies, and triumphing in the USA and UK in the early eighties, tax revolts led by the radical right have since halted the trend. The result has not been any significant reduction in public spending as such – its average level in the OECD actually increased from 46 to 48 per cent during the eighties, as the weight of existing entitlements grew heavier, with larger numbers of pensioners and unemployed. Rather, public borrowing has grown, and taxes have become more regressive. But while indirect levies on consumption have risen, direct taxes on income have generally been cut, in the name of incentives. The ideological effect of this lowering of the most visible form of taxation has far exceeded its practical consequences, except for the very well-off. A new social consensus has been created, in which it has become difficult for any party of the left to propose measures that run the smallest risk of appearing to raise taxes on most citizens, no matter how neutral or redistributive their actual effect, without courting electoral suicide.[11] The fate of the Labour Party in 1992, and more recently of the SPD's programme in the spring of 1994, are vivid illustrations of this bottleneck. The limits of fiscal initiative have drastically narrowed for the left. The new tax aversion has everywhere put it on the defensive.

Trapped between a shifting social base and a contracting political horizon, social democracy appears to have lost its compass. In such altered conditions, is it likely to undergo a new mutation? Once, in the founding years of the Second International, it was dedicated to the general overthrow of capitalism. Then it pursued partial reforms as

11. This was certainly one factor in the extreme reluctance of Eurosocialist governments to alter the fiscal systems of their countries, no matter how unjust or deficient. Merkel, inclined towards a lenient view of their spending programmes, which he thinks were more generous than often given credit for, is severe on their failure here: *Ende der Sozialdemokratie?*, pp. 209–301.

gradual steps towards socialism. Finally it settled for welfare and full employment within capitalism. If it now accepts a scaling down of the one and giving up of the other, what kind of a movement will it change into? In the judgement of one of its shrewdest and most sympathetic observers, no particular pessimist, 'the only certainty about the future of the new social democracy *in statu nascendi* is that socially and culturally it will be *more composite*, organizationally it will be *weaker*, and *more dependent* on the personality of the leader, and politically and electorally it will be *more unstable* than the "old" social-democracy'.[12] This is scarcely a reassuring prediction. But it speaks only of the probable solidarity or strength of the parties of the Socialist International. What of their rationale or purpose? Historically, social democracy has been a governing force only in Western Europe. Neither the United States nor Japan, the two other core zones of advanced capitalism, has known it. There labour never achieved the same political independence or salience. For long, it could seem that these alternative versions of capitalist civilization were anomalies, that might be expected sooner or later to align themselves with the classical model of the Old World. Today, the opposite looks more likely. The population of the EU is a little less, and its production far less, than that of the USA and Japan combined. The larger reality of contemporary capitalism lies outside Europe. This is the dominant environment, registering consistently faster growth than the EU, and exercising a downward cost pressure on its social models. In the official rhetoric and – increasingly – policy of the European Commission, not to speak of the Council, the need to compete becomes the obligation to adapt. In this logic it is social democracy that becomes the anomaly to be pared away, as the legacy of an unaffordable past.

Such a scenario, now quite widely canvassed by business opinion, does not spell the end of the parties of the Socialist International as we know them: simply the loss of the distinctive role that once set them apart from, say, the Democratic Party in the United States, as a force straightforwardly committed to capitalism without social trimmings. A farewell to the substance of social democracy need not mean a disappearance of the term, which could persist indefinitely into the next century – rather in the way, as Dahrendorf has suggested,[13] that 'Liberal' parties of every stripe survive in many parts of Western Europe, without any meaningful connection to liberalism as a political ideal of the last century. Such an analogy could allow for one difference. Today's Liberal International accommodates a wide spectrum

12. Moschonas, *La social-démocratie de 1945 à nos jours*, p. 151.
13. See his famous essay, 'Das Elend der Sozialdemokratie', *Merkur*, December 1987, p. 1022, one of the targets against which Merkel directs his fire.

of parties, from the mildly progressive (Denmark or the UK) through the staunchly conservative (Belgium or Italy) to the shrilly reactionary (Austria). The ranks of Socialist International, even if social democracy should become as notional for them tomorrow as socialism is today, are more likely to continue to define themselves as parties of the left.

For many who are inclined to accept the victory of capitalism as final, subject only to local variations, the latter is anyway a preferable category – historically older and morally less compromised. The left is here conceived, in one of its most attractive theorizations, as a tradition born from the Enlightenment whose mission is to repair successive kinds of inequalities weighing on the less advantaged – the *sinistrés de la terre* – as history renders them amendable.[14] This work of 'rectification' requires no general theory of an alternative society, and accepts the need for a right as a perpetual counterweight to itself, in meta-consequence of its own principle of parity. The appeal of such a vision, abandoning the idea of 'socialism' while retaining the notion of a 'left' – so to speak, dispensing with the literal for the allegorical vocabulary of opposition – is likely to grow. But, honourably enough, it suggests its own limits. Politically, the terms 'left' and 'right' are as inescapable as they are untransfixable. Since each acquires its meaning only from the other, their values are always relative. Historians speak intelligibly of a left and right not merely within, say, the Labour Party, but in Christian Democracy, or for that matter even fascism. A 'left' could survive within an all-capitalist system that was to the right of anything now considered in the centre. Beyond the problem of this topographic mobility, however, lies the logical subordination that a politics of rectification implies – as the etymology of the term itself, involuntary homage to the enemy, indicates. In such a conception, the social fabric is always woven on the right: the left does no more than stretch or mend it. The modesty of the proposal may seem a token of realism. In many ways it speaks to the current mood of social democracy. Beyond it, however, lie systematic changes in European society.

The postwar success of social-democratic politics rested on a set of structures distinctive of the period. It was based on the normalcy of full employment, within national economies amenable to fine-tuning of demand; the provision of social services to single-earner households, composed of traditional families headed by a male wage-worker; the extension of universal education through adolescence; the operation of a mixed economy with a public sector accountable to government; the vitality of a parliamentary democracy sustained by mass parties and

14. See Steven Lukes, 'What is Left? Essential Socialism and the Urge to Rectify', *Times Literary Supplement*, 27 March 1992: a richly compressed text, which the remarks above may force, certainly only skim.

high turn-out. Today, all of these elements of the postwar order are in eclipse or decline. The two deepest changes are those which have overcome the worlds of work and of home. Full employment has vanished. Perhaps twenty million West Europeans have no work at all, and many more only part-time employment. In some countries, no more than a third of the adult population may now be in full-time jobs. National regulation appears helpless in the face of a crisis that has worsened with every downturn since the seventies. Meanwhile, most women – from 60 to 80 per cent, according to country – have ceased to be housewives. Maternity has for its part come loose from marriage – half of all births are now out of wedlock in Scandinavia, and a third in France, where only twenty years ago the respective figures were 20 and 7 per cent.[15] Increasing numbers of children – one out of five in Greater London today – are brought up by a single parent, and still more are mainly looked after outside the home: in Denmark, about half of all mothers with infants under two are in the labour market. With ever larger retired and marginal populations, part-time workers and poverty-trapped parents, even neo-liberal regimes have found it difficult to contain an escalation of welfare costs.

Nor, in many countries, has the spread of universal education borne the fruits expected of it. Rather than state schools offering a free culture to all, capable of rendering private schools a pointless expense as the general stock of intellectual skills levelled up, they have all too often become impoverished battle-grounds, deserted by middle-class parents once cast as an enlightened support of them. Beset by new tensions of ethnic division and commercial distraction, public schooling has become an endemic source of dissatisfaction in the big cities of England or France, as it has long since been in the United States. In the economy itself, of course, public enterprise of any kind – stigmatized as inherently inefficient – has receded. In Western Europe, the wave of privatization launched by the Thatcher governments in Britain is far from spent. Currently France, Germany and Italy are all the scene of major asset sales, whose scope has progressively broadened – from mining and manufacturing to utilities, and now to functions like postal delivery and tax collection which even nineteenth-century liberalism assigned to the nightwatchman State. Finally, the authority of parliaments has been weakened as power has passed to inter-governmental Councils of Ministers, or extra-territorial capital markets, and voter participation has declined. Ideologically, the space of political conflict has shifted from mass parties to television shows, speeches to sound-bites, policies to personalities.

15. Hervé Le Bras, 'La Popolazione', *Storia d'Europa*, vol. I, p. 89, who suggests that most European countries will probably move towards the Scandinavian norm of 50 per cent of 'illegitimate' births.

The new social democracy has so far yielded few responses to any of these problems: at most, here and there, adaptations to them. Traditionally, from the thirties onwards, this was a movement that tended to acquire many of its leading ideas from outside its ranks – from liberals like Keynes or Beveridge, or mavericks like Wicksell – rather than within them. The same might come to be true again, were Rawls to have the influence sometimes forecast for him. For the moment, however, there continues to be an impressive contrast between the intellectual efficacy of the right and left in their respective periods of opposition. In the heyday of social-democratic government, neo-conservatism was an engine-room of theories and proposals for regaining the political initiative, ready for implementation when power returned. Financial resources, of course, were always more available for this work; and the policies advocated more congenial to the natural order of a capitalist society. But even granting these advantages, the difference in energy of research remains striking. It is only very recently that this has started to change.[16] Beyond the mainstream of the established parties themselves, however, the culture of the left has not been asleep. It is here, on the margins of day-to-day politics, that creative reflection is still mostly to be found.

Significantly, perhaps, no plausible programme for a restoration of full employment has yet to be framed, from any quarter, in the nineties[17] – as if the limits of this mode of production, now uncontested, preclude any chance of it. Within the bounds of actually existing capitalism, however, two alternative – not necessarily incompatible – kinds of remedy for the dislocation of the jobless have been explored in increasing practical detail. The first envisages a generalized reduction of working time, to allow more equitable sharing of employment[18] – an approach already receiving some test in the largest auto plant in Germany, and more airing in national forums in France. The second argues for the replacement of archaic systems of unemployment insurance and supplementary benefit, with their characteristic stigma and inefficiency, by the right to a basic income guaranteed to all citizens, whatever their position on or off the labour market. In origin going back to the time of Condorcet and Paine, proposals along these

16. In Britain, the work of the Institute for Public Policy Research represents a very important departure.

17. The use of wage subsidies, now advocated as a way of reducing levels of unemployment in Britain by (perhaps) half, was proposed as a means of securing a universal right to work, of which no public figure now speaks, in the eighties: see Michael Rustin, *For a Pluralist Socialism*, London 1985, pp. 147–72.

18. The most eloquent advocate of this strategy has always been André Gorz: see *Critique of Economic Reason*, Verso, London 1989, pp. 183–215.

lines have recently acquired new economic and philosophical sophistication.[19] Elements of them have reached the stage of official recommendation in the Netherlands.

By definition, such schemes remain gender-neutral. They address the crisis of work rather than of the family. For the asymmetry of the sexes poses a different set of problems. Maternity has always meant some kind of withdrawal – partial or total – from the labour market, which has lain at the root of sexual inequality. In the past the male wage tended both to codify and cushion female dependence within the conjugal unit. With the destabilization of the nuclear family, the burdens of procreation tend to fall even more heavily on women, left to rear children on their own. A specifically female poverty has been a marked trend of recent years. In the long run, it is only when maternity ceases to be an economic handicap that equality of the sexes will be possible.[20] A range of measures could contribute to this end. The most advanced existing arrangements are to be found in the social provision of childcare widespread in Sweden and Denmark. But the logic of free choice points beyond these, to a guaranteed income for reproduction of society's next generation, to be spent at the recipient's discretion.[21] The other side of such reproduction, of course, is the task of the school system. Here the direction of progress could be straightforward: acceptance of the simple principle that every child ought to have equal resources devoted to it. Wherever private education subsists, its advantages can normally be taken as a benchmark of standards to be generalized.[22] The structure of public education, in other words, should aim at a levelling up rather than a levelling down. It is no accident that this is one area – despite the scale of investment it represents – where there are no calls from the right for sweeping privatization.

Production, of course, is another matter. Public enterprise has not been eliminated by the neo-liberal turn of the eighties. However diminished, it remains a residual element of the economy in most countries of the European Union. But politically there is no sign of its rehabilitation. 'Nationalization' – always a guilty euphemism – was not invariably inefficient, but it brought no meaningful increase of either

19. See the different essays, based on an international conference in Louvain, in Philippe Van Parijs, ed., *Arguing for Basic Income*, Verso, London 1992, which includes a critique of the limits of the idea by André Gorz: pp. 178–84.

20. The general argument is most powerfully put by Nicky Hart, 'Procreation: the Substance of Female Oppression in Modern Society', *Contention*, nos 1–2, fall 1991–winter 1992.

21. For persuasive comments on the limits of childcare, see Patricia Hewitt and Penelope Leach, *Social Justice, Children and Families*, IPPR, London 1994, pp. 24–6.

22. This is the case made by Paul Auerbach, 'On Socialist Optimism', *New Left Review* 192, March–April 1992, pp. 31–3.

democracy or equality to the enterprises under public management. If existing property relations are ever to be altered, it is clearly not by this route. Two alternative lines of attack on the current settlement are available. The first of these focuses on the structure of corporate decision. Ideas of industrial democracy have a long and variegated history. Recent years have seen a burst of new proposals across quite a wide political spectrum, running from moderate advocacy of the German model of 'stakeholder' companies, in which workers, suppliers and bankers are all represented on supervisory boards above management, to more radical conceptions of labour-managed firms as such – LMFs of the American type, or cooperatives along Basque lines.[23] A second strategy, by contrast, would accept the internal hierarchy of the firm, on grounds of relative efficiency, but alter the pay-out of profits by giving all citizens a social dividend from them.[24] Here the priority is a more egalitarian distribution of income, rather than democratic organization of the enterprise. But in either case, the historically realistic premiss is that the present configuration of corporate property is mutable.

The same holds true, no less eminently, of the familiar institutions of constitutional democracy. The United Kingdom is no doubt an extreme case of the gap between the claims and realities of representative government. Here, where in the past social democracy never challenged the arbitrary powers of an untrammelled executive, vested with royal legitimacy above and a docile legislature below, without pretence of either equitable reflection of political opinion or legal protection of fundamental rights, an independent movement within civil society – Charter 88 – has forced Labour to take up issues of democratic reform, of which it is itself famously in need. The results are still timid enough.[25] Elsewhere in Western Europe, democracy is at least nominally conceived as popular sovereignty. But which is the state where liberty has reached its natural limit? There was a time, in the late sixties, when the SPD adopted as its motto *Mehr Demokratie wagen*: 'Dare more democracy'. Thereafter, its own contribution to political reform became the *Berufsverbot*; and no call has been so thoroughly buried in the collective memory of the International since. The decay of the public sphere charted by Habermas thirty years ago, when he still

---

23. For a fine description of the German model, see David Goodhart, *The Reshaping of the German Social Market*, IPPR, London 1994, pp. 17–32; the idea of the LMF is explored in Jacques Drèze, *Labour Managements, Contracts and Capital Markets*, Oxford 1989.

24. John Roemer, *A Future for Socialism*, Verso, London 1994, is now the central work here.

25. By contrast, the radical critique behind the Charter is best gauged from Anthony Barnett's remarkable essay, 'The Empire State', in *Power and the Throne*, London 1994, a volume based on a conference the Charter organized on the British monarchy.

hoped parties and assemblies could revitalize it, has proceeded unchecked. The further 'structural transformation' he did not foresee, of course, has been the by-passing of national legislatures by financial markets and ministerial conclaves, in a European space devoid of even the semblance of responsible government. The Treaty of Maastricht, promising a central bank and a single currency without a sovereign parliament or elected executive, has only deepened this abyss. Reclamation both of the basic principles of representative democracy, and of any prospects of effective macroeconomic policy, requires the construction of a true federal framework in Europe. The left has on the whole been no more clear-sighted or imaginative about this than the centre or right. Indecision and confusion are still the norm. But as the essays in this book demonstrate, the issue of Europe already dominates the domestic politics of country after country – from Norway to France, from Denmark to Britain, from Sweden to Italy. Purely national strategies are vanishing, for every part of the political spectrum. The West European left will acquire new contours only when this crux is resolved.

July 1994

Sweden: After the Golden Age

Jonas Pontusson

Among the advanced capitalist countries, Sweden stands out as the country with the highest rate of unionization (today roughly 85 per cent) and the longest experience of left government. From 1932 to 1976, Sweden had but three prime ministers, and they were all Social Democrats. Following an interlude of bourgeois coalition governments (1976–82), the Social Democrats restored their claim to be Sweden's 'natural party of government' by scoring three successive election victories in the 1980s, but then suffered a defeat of historic proportions in the election of September 1991. From 1932 through 1988, the Social Democrats' share of the national vote never fell below 41 per cent. In 1991, they received only 37.6 per cent of the national vote and, for the first time since 1928, the leader of the Conservative party became prime minister.[1]

The Socialdemokratiska Arbetarpartiet (SAP) went down to defeat amidst Sweden's most severe postwar recession. The rate of unemployment doubled in 1990–91, reaching the 4 per cent mark by the time of the election, and has nearly doubled again since the election. By the summer of 1993, the rate of unemployment stood at 7 per cent, with an additional 4–5 per cent of the labour force engaged in retraining and other government labour-market programmes, and many observers expect the rate of unemployment to rise above 10 per cent in the next year. Though hardly extraordinary by comparative standards, these are staggering, almost unbelievable, numbers from a Swedish perspective.

Yet as economic conditions have further deteriorated since the election, the popularity of the four-party coalition government headed by Carl Bildt has plummeted, and the ratings of the Social Democrats in opposition have recovered. Indeed, two separate polls conducted in

23

the spring of 1993 gave the SAP about 50 per cent support among voters with a clear party preference (the highest level in any poll or election since 1968).[2] It seems likely, then, that they will regain office in the elections scheduled for September 1994. But it is very unlikely that the Social Democrats will ever regain the hegemonic position they once held in Swedish politics. The election of 1991 cannot be seen as simply a temporary setback for the SAP: it was a landmark in a reconfiguration of Swedish politics that is still continuing.

It is thus an opportune moment to take stock of the experience of Swedish Social Democracy over the last two or three decades. One way of doing this would be to draw up a balance-sheet of what the Swedish Social Democrats did (and did not) accomplish during the postwar era, and to assess the extent to which their reformist achievements have held up in the face of economic and electoral difficulties since the mid 1970s. This is an important task.[3] But the precondition of the Swedish model of welfare has always lain in the ability of the Social Democratic Party to reconcile the imperatives of capitalist growth in an open, trade-dependent economy with the interests of the labour movement. Economic management has historically been the foundation of the social reforms the SAP has achieved, and still remains the key to the future of the party in Sweden. To understand the crisis of Swedish Social Democracy today, the analytic priority is to look at the path of its long-term economic strategies, as these have evolved in three distinct phases, since the 1950s. It is here that the secret of the past success and present impasse of the SAP lies.

Labour's Postwar Strategy

The origins of the unique role of Social Democracy in Sweden go back to the interwar period.[4] In the course of the 1920s, the party in practice abandoned its commitment to large-scale nationalization as a primary or immediate objective. Its reformist ambitions were not, however, restricted to 'consumption politics'. Rather, the Social Democrats conceived the public-works programme for which they campaigned in 1932 as part of a broader strategy to extend democratic control of the economy through macroeconomic planning and state intervention in the restructuring of industry. Selective nationalizations were not repudiated, but envisaged as just one means among others to this end[5] – which was to include not only public control from above, but some form of codetermination from below, at the enterprise level.

In the 1930s the SAP became a stable governing party by securing a parliamentary coalition with the farmers, and an extra-parliamentary accommodation with organized business.[6] Each of these deals ruled out any measures that would have significantly curtailed the autonomous prerogatives of private enterprise. In particular, the Basic Agreement signed by the Landsorganisationen (LO), the confederation of blue-collar unions affiliated to the Social Democrats, and the Svenska Arbetsgivarföreningen (SAF), the employers' federation, at Saltsjöbaden in 1938 rested on the unions' tacit acceptance of paragraph 32 of the SAF statutes, which stipulated that any collective bargaining agreement entered into by an SAF affiliate must expressly acknowledge the rights of management to hire and fire workers and to control the labour process.

Partly in response to the gains made by the Swedish Communist Party during the War, the Postwar Programme adopted by the SAP and LO in 1944 strongly emphasized the need to extend public control over the economy (but did not challenge the terms of the industrial relations settlement of 1938). However, while most of the social reforms in the Programme were passed by large parliamentary majorities, the spectre of planning united organized business and the opposition parties – now including the Agrarians – against the Social Democrats. The SAP was put on the defensive. In the 1948 elections, it managed to hold its own, but the combined vote of the Social Democrats and Communists, which had risen from 43.4 per cent in 1928 to 57.0 per cent in 1944, now dropped to 52.4 per cent. Unwilling to rely on the Communists, the SAP retreated from the more radical ideas of the Postwar Programme, and subsequently formed a new coalition government with the Agrarians. Though planning retained an important place in party ideology, the concept was now redefined to mean essentially counter-cyclical spending, coordination of public investment, and long-term economic forecasting.

The strategic reorientation of the labour movement in the late 1940s may be characterized as a move away from production politics, towards a more strictly welfarist strategy for reforming society.[7] But this did not mean that Social Democracy had lost interest in the evolution of industry. It was in this period that the LO's newly established research department, led by Gösta Rehn and Rudolf Meidner, began to develop a highly original approach to economic management, which rejected the conventional efforts of the time to check inflationary pressures by freezing wages. By the late 1950s, the strategy they had worked out was being more or less consistently pursued by Swedish Social Democracy. The premise of their thinking was that rising productivity was an essential precondition for real-wage growth and welfare-state expansion. Perhaps because of the country's exposure to international competition, this belief was already deeply ingrained in the Swedish labour movement. Their other key notion was that the LO unions should coordinate their wage bargaining, in such a way as to give collective support to the wage claims of the weakest unions. This too was an idea dating back to the interwar period. The ingenuity of the Rehn–Meidner model was to combine these different strands of Swedish tradition, in a way that legitimated the short-term redistributive pressures of low-wage unions by identifying them with the long-term interests of the labour movement as a whole.

The central axiom of the model was that wages should be determined by the nature of work rather than the ability of employers to pay. The principle of equal pay for equal work would enable the labour movement to side-step the tangle of an incomes policy. For it would dampen wage rivalries by creating a more 'rational' earnings structure – workers would more readily accept differentials based on the nature of work. At the same time, the compression of wage differentials would promote productivity growth by squeezing corporate profits in selective fashion. On one hand, a concerted union effort to increase wages for the low-paid would put pressure on the profit margins of less efficient firms and sectors, forcing them to rationalize production or go out of business. On the other hand, wage restraint by the well-paid would promote the expansion of more efficient enterprises and industries.

The institutionalization of peak-level wage bargaining between the LO and the SAF in the 1950s was a result of employer and government efforts to restrain wage increases rather than LO efforts to redistribute them, but it nevertheless facilitated subsequent LO efforts to implement the kind of solidaristic wage policy Rehn and Meidner had advocated. Although the equalizing effects of central agreements were partly offset by wage drift at the local level, a significant compression of wage differentials among blue-collar workers did indeed occur in the 1960s and 1970s.[8]

Rehn and Meidner stressed from the outset that the promotion of economic rationalization through solidaristic wage bargaining required the active support of the government. For the unions could not take on the role that the model assigned to them unless the state compensated workers adversely affected by restructuring and helped them adjust to changes in the demand for labour. This was well understood by the SAP. From the recession of 1957–58 onwards, government spending on labour exchanges, retraining programmes and relocation subsidies increased steadily throughout the 1960s and 1970s. The purpose of such supply-side measures was not only to lessen worker resistance to ongoing rationalization. They were also designed to accelerate the pace of restructuring itself, by subsidizing the recruitment costs of 'advanced' sectors, and to reduce wage drift by removing bottlenecks in the supply of labour.

What, however, was to prevent firms that were squeezed by a solidaristic wage policy from defending their profits by passing on higher labour costs to consumers? The answer was to expose them to international competition. The Rehn–Meidner model thus provided a further rationale for the Swedish labour movement's long-standing commitment to free trade. But what if more efficient firms used the 'excess profits' granted them by a solidaristic wage policy to bid up the price of labour, instead of investing in new capacity? Here the government had to act. If some wage drift was acceptable, a restrictive fiscal policy was necessary to prevent it getting out of hand. As Rehn put it, the model prescribed an 'unsolidaristic profits policy . . . within the framework of a general policy of low profits'.[9]

But if the profits of efficient firms were also to be restrained, wouldn't this undermine their expansion? Rehn and Meidner had an answer for this difficulty too. The solution was to transform the public savings generated by restrictive fiscal policy into new investment. In essence, the state would absorb corporate profits through taxation and then lend public savings to the corporate sector. Low interest rates would offset whatever negative effects the combination of wage solidarity and fiscal frugality might have on the propensity of firms to invest. The 'recycling' of profits via credit markets would not only act to check undue concentration of wealth, it would also promote capital mobility, by increasing the supply of finance to more efficient firms. The build-up of public pension funds in the 1960s functioned more or less in the manner prescribed by Rehn and Meidner.

In sum, postwar Social Democratic strategy promoted productivity growth by accentuating profit differentials among firms and removing obstacles to factor mobility. Under the market conditions that prevailed from the 1940s through the first half of the 1970s, the policies pursued by the SAP favoured large export-oriented firms and promoted the concentration of capital. They also encouraged companies to substitute capital for labour.

The Socialist Offensive of the 1970s

The labour movement's postwar acceptance of private control of investment rested on the assumption that the sectors of industry that benefited from solidaristic wage bargaining would generate new employment at roughly the same rate as the sectors squeezed by solidaristic wage bargaining would shed labour. From the mid 1960s onwards, this premiss became increasingly shaky. The decline of more backward industries accelerated while the growth of advanced sectors no longer translated into much, if any, employment growth. Full employment now came to depend increasingly on the expansion of the public sector.

While these trends were becoming apparent, the rank and file of the labour movement were growing restive on their own account. A wave of wildcat strikes in 1969–70 took the LO leadership by surprise. In part a reaction by high-wage workers to the implementation of solidaristic wage policy, these stoppages also featured new 'qualitative' demands, and were widely interpreted as an expression of discontent with the working conditions and managerial practices of Fordist mass production.

In response to the new economic trends and social pressures, the labour movement launched a series of initiatives that challenged the terms of the postwar settlement between labour and capital. In 1968–70 the SAP government introduced a number of institutional reforms designed to extend public control of investment and make possible an 'active industrial policy'. In 1971 the LO congress endorsed an ambitious legislative programme to democratize working life. This rejected the German model of codetermination rights vested in works councils (separate from the unions and without the right to strike), advocating instead the extension of collective bargaining to non-wage issues. The aim of the LO leadership was to canalize rank-and-file militancy and to revitalize local union organizations, without re-linquishing central control of wage bargaining. It also conceived the issue of industrial democracy as a bridge to the Tjänstemännens Centralorganisation (TCO), the Swedish white-collar federation, which had grown rapidly in the 1960s, and quickly came out in support of LO's main proposals.[10]

The TCO membership, long an electoral mainstay of the Liberal Party, had recently become a prime target of the renamed Agrarian – now Centre – Party's efforts to expand beyond its traditional rural constituencies. Competing with each other as well as the SAP, neither of these parties could ignore the TCO's interest in industrial democracy. The result was that large parliamentary majorities passed an impressive series of pro-labour laws from 1972 to 1976, including minority representation on company boards, enhanced powers for safety stewards, much tighter rules on lay-offs and firings and, most importantly, the Codetermination Act of 1976, which effectively annulled paragraph 32 of the SAF statutes by requiring management to negotiate with unions over any corporate decisions that would affect the workforce.

Emboldened by the political success of its campaign for industrial democracy, the LO now endorsed the idea of gradually changing the ownership structure of the economy through collective profit-sharing, set out in a report drafted by Rudolf Meidner for its congress in 1976. This explosive document launched the 'great wage-earner funds debate'. Meidner's scheme proposed that legislation be passed requiring companies above a certain size (50 or 100 employees) to issue new shares corresponding to a certain proportion of their annual profits (perhaps 20 per cent) to wage-earners as a collective group.[11] The share of equity capital acquired by wage-earners each year would be determined by the relationship between a corporation's profits and its net value. The higher the rate of profit, the more rapid the transfer of ownership would be.[12]

The Meidner Plan stipulated that this new form of collectively owned capital remain as working capital in the firms that had generated it. Voting rights and other ownership prerogatives would be exercised by local unions until wage-earner shares represented 20 per cent of equity capital. Above that threshold, ownership rights would be vested in fund boards appointed mainly by national unions but also including representatives of other social interests.

Rejecting the idea of individual share distributions, the Meidner committee provided three basic justifications for its plan. First, the scheme would help to enforce wage solidarity by neutralizing 'excess profits'. Second, it would counteract concentration of wealth and reconcile the need to improve the financial balances of firms with the redistributive ambitions of labour. Finally, wage-earner funds would complement the industrial democracy reforms of 1972–76 by giving employees and their unions direct ownership-based influence in corporate decision-making.

Uncharacteristically, the LO leadership approved the Meidner Plan without any prior consultations with the SAP leadership. In the election campaign that began shortly after the LO congress, the Social Democrats sought to sidestep the issue of wage-earner funds, stating repeatedly that legislative action would have to await the results of a public commission of inquiry, which would not complete its work prior to a subsequent election.

In 1976, however, for the first time in over forty years the SAP was defeated at the polls, and a coalition of the three bourgeois parties – Centre, Liberal, Conservative – took office. Now in opposition, the SAP formed a joint working group with the LO, which drafted an amended scheme for wage-earner funds in 1978, and yet another proposal in 1981.[13] The new versions shifted the argument for wage-earner funds from redistributing wealth and power to increasing the rate of investment, and retreated from the most radical features of the Meidner Plan. Linking collective stock ownership directly to wage restraint, the 1978 and 1981 proposals scaled down the scope of profit-sharing, and stipulated that wage-earner funds should partly be built up through payroll taxes. In the 1981 proposal, obligatory share issues were replaced by a tax on excess profits. The revenues generated by payroll and profit taxes would be transferred to regionally based wage-earner funds, to invest in corporate equity. Thus the collectivization of ownership would occur entirely through market transactions. While reaffirming the Meidner committee's rejection of individual ownership claims, the WEF proposal of 1981 sought to give wage-earners a personal stake in the proposed reform by requiring the funds to contribute to the pension system.

The motivation for these changes was political. Both the business community and the bourgeois parties had attacked the Meidner Plan ferociously, and the intention of the new variants was to broaden the popular appeal of the WEF initiative. In the event, however, public support for wage-earner funds actually declined with each new proposal, as can be seen from Table 1.1. The shift of mood after 1979 was especially pronounced among white-collar union members. The TCO leadership, after initially taking a positive view of the idea of collective profit-sharing, was forced to retreat to a neutral attitude in 1979–80, and this in turn undermined Social Democratic efforts to reach a compromise on the issue with the Liberals and/or the Centre Party. A public commission was appointed to investigate the whole question, but in pointed contrast with the traditional pattern of Swedish politics, it resulted in a deadlock, and failed to produce any legislative recommendations at all.[14]

As Leif Lewin noted, 'the Social Democrats won the 1982 election despite and not thanks to wage-earner funds'.[15] The bourgeois coalition had not been a success – the jobless total had reached what was then a postwar record of 3.5 per cent by 1982. Many voters who opposed wage-earner funds were more concerned with this failure to keep unemployment in check. In office, the Social Democrats tried once more to reach a compromise on wage-earner funds with the Centre and Liberal Parties – without any greater success. Under pressure from LO, and with the support of the Communist parliamentary group, the Palme government finally enacted a much watered-down version of wage-earner funds in December 1983. The new law provided for the build-up of five regionally based funds from special payroll and profit taxes over a seven-year period (1984–90), at the end of which no further revenues would be transferred to them. It stressed that the funds were to behave as portfolio investors, avoiding

Table 1.1 Voters' views of wage-earner funds (in percentages), 1976–82

	For	Against	Undecided
All voters			
1976	33	43	24
1979	32	45	23
1982	22	61	17
SAP voters			
1976	55	18	27
1979	58	15	27
1982	43	29	28

Source: S. Holmberg, *Väljare i förändring*, Stockholm 1984, pp. 170, 186.

any responsibility for employment or industrial policy, and stipulated that no fund could exceed 8 per cent of shareholder votes in any one company.

The modesty of this scheme can be seen from the fact that by the end of 1987 the total securities held by wage-earner funds were worth less than half of the liquid assets of Volvo as a single company.[16] By the end of 1990, when transfers to them were complete, the funds accounted for a mere 3.5 per cent of the total value of corporate shares listed on the Stockholm exchange. The gulf between labour's reformist ambitions in 1976 and the legislative outcome of 1983 was yawning. Not only was the social change insignificant. It was bought at a high ideological cost, since the inability of the SAP to defend the original principles of the Meidner Plan had made the whole idea of wage-earner funds a political liability for the Swedish labour movement by 1982–83. While the bourgeois parties continued to rally public opinion with thunderous attacks on surreptitious collectivization, the Social Democrats tried to get voters to forget the issue in the election campaigns of 1985 and 1988.

The fate of wage-earner funds can be seen in retrospect as a turning-point in postwar Swedish politics. The SAP's adoption of the Rehn–Meidner model had given it a coherent economic strategy, designed to reconcile equality and efficiency, full employment and price stability, through a combination of solidaristic wage bargaining and active labour-market policy. The success of this model provided the basis for the impressive record of social reforms achieved under Erlander. When the first strains in it surfaced, the labour movement kept the initiative with a series of radical reforms in the 1970s, that challenged the systemic power of capital more directly. Measures to increase industrial democracy were successfully introduced, with strong popular – white- as well as blue-collar – support. The Meidner Plan for wage-earner funds projected a bold move. Its thrust was to give Swedish Social Democracy a second economic strategy, capable of creatively addressing the dilemmas left by the first. Why did this 'socialist offensive' fail?

A common explanation is that wage-earner funds aroused little enthusiasm because they promised no direct or immediate benefits to wage-earners. There is an important element of truth in this, but it is insufficient to account for the defeat of the plan, for the industrial democracy reforms of the early 1970s had also involved no instant material gains for workers. Popular support for measures to redistribute power will rest on different premises from measures to redistribute income, but there is no reason to doubt that it can be forthcoming. Wage-earners are capable of perceiving long-term collective interests, as well as making short-term individual calculations. They can also perfectly well respond to considerations of social justice, which are always a dimension of reformist politics.[17]

In fact, as Table 1.1 reveals, a third of all voters welcomed the idea of wage-earner funds in 1976 and 1979. It was not until the early 1980s that public support for them plummeted. The reason for this change is not hard to seek. The bourgeois parties and organized business unleashed a massive ideological campaign against the LO's proposals, and the reduced versions adopted by the SAP. Swedish employers, convinced they faced a real threat to their economic position, demonstrated a political muscle they had never flexed so overtly before. In 1982 alone, organized business spent as much money on propaganda against wage-earner funds as all five parliamentary parties put together on their election campaigns. Still more decisive was the role of the press – newspapers affiliated to the bourgeois parties commanding well over 80 per cent of total circulation. Michael Gilljam's careful study of the formation of public opinion demonstrates conclusively that political arguments against wage-earner funds dominated in the mass media after 1979, and that the public's understanding of what the issue was about coincided closely with its presentation by the media: as he puts it, 'everything indicates that the strong resistance of business and the bourgeois parties to collective wage-earner funds had great importance for the Swedish people's views on the question.'[18] On the other side of the battle, divisions among the Social Democrats – in the first instance, between the LO and the SAP leadership – played into the hands of their opponents. The succession of different schemes created confusion among voters over the institutional form and aims of the contemplated reform, while party leaders – not least Palme himself –

defending proposals that they did not really believe in, often did so with a great deal of ambiguity. When asked about the details of the funds, many voters gave wrong answers, and the number without a firm opinion on the issue remained high through the entire debate.[19] It is difficult to avoid the conclusion that the struggle over what became of the Meidner Plan was lost in large measure because it was so little fought.

This is not to say the strategy of wage-earner funds was without difficulties. But it is important to see what these were. The Norwegian theorist Jon Elster has argued that wage-earner funds failed because they did not embody a simple and universalistic conception of social justice. In this view, it was 'perverse' to 'give employee voting rights only to workers in firms which for some reason happen to be chosen as investment objects for the funds', and 'ridiculous' to 'argue that "the working class" as a whole would have control over the firms through trade-union representatives in the funds', since 'real power would be vested in the trade-union bureaucracy.'[20] This is a cavalier judgement, more germane to the diluted proposals of 1978 and 1981 than to the original Meidner Plan. For there was nothing arbitrary about the investment of wage-earner funds in the 1976 scheme: the shares owned by the funds would remain as working capital in the firms where the profits had been generated, and ownership rights were to be vested in *local unions*, not the 'trade-union bureaucracy' at the national level, until the funds owned 20 per cent of the equity in a firm. Elster fails to explain why the industrial democracy reforms of the 1970s were not similarly vulnerable to the charge that they would give power to trade-union bureaucrats.

Nonetheless, his critique does point towards a serious political problem in the design of wage-earner funds in all their incarnations. The intended empowerment of employees (or unions) through profit-sharing would have been as unevenly distributed as are profits in a capitalist economy. In particular, and crucially, public-sector employees and unions, naturally inclined towards the SAP on many other issues, had nothing to gain from the reform. By contrast, the industrial democracy measures of the 1970s promised to enhance the opportunities for participation throughout the economy, and thus provided a powerful motive for all unions to mobilize their members behind them. Significantly, the shift of public opinion against wage-earner funds in 1979–82 was most dramatic among public-sector employees.[21] Here lay the real Achilles' heel of the strategy. The LO leadership had initially conceived it as a technical solution to the problem of wage drift, not as a hegemonic project that would demand a mobilization of public opinion. That course would have required a different institutional design, providing public-sector employees and unions with a stake in collective capital formation.

The Third Road of the 1980s

The quiet burial of wage-earner funds in 1983 was in reality a side-show of the SAP's return to power. For by then the party had adopted a quite new direction. The economic strategy pursued by the Social Democrats in the 1980s not only abandoned the radical ambitions articulated by the labour movement in the 1970s; it also diverged from labour's traditional approach to economic management of the 1960s. The architects of the new approach called it the 'Third Road', in favourable contrast to both a reflationary course of traditional Keynesianism, as attempted at the time by the French Socialists, and a deflationary course of neo-liberalism, as practised by the British Conservatives. This description conveniently avoided the question of its relationship to the Rehn–Meidner model, which itself had been conceived as an alternative to Keynesianism. In fact, the difference between the two was fundamental. For whereas the Rehn–Meidner model rejected the notion of a necessary trade-off between efficiency and equality, the premiss of the Third Road was that renewed growth required a substantial increase of corporate profit margins, in other words, a significant redistribution of national income from labour to capital. The apparently innocuous slogan of the Social Democratic government of 1982, 'first growth, then redistribution', expressed a major shift in Social Democratic thinking.

Behind the new course lay an altered constellation within the counsels of the labour movement itself. Since the War, the most influential source of ideas for the Swedish left had been the research department of the LO. Its intellectual ascendancy was in good measure due to the stature of its two leading theorists, Rehn and Meidner, themselves. But it was also partly a function of the fact that ambitious Social Democratic intellectuals without organizational ties to the trade unions were more or less automatically drawn into the machinery of government, and absorbed by its day-to-day activities. In these conditions, the LO's research department came to form a unique site for thinking about long-term strategy. After its electoral defeat in 1976, however, the SAP formed its own research unit, staffed by personnel who had previously worked in government ministries. These policy intellectuals typically came from an academic background in economics, and were united by aversion to the Meidner Plan. Their patron was Kjell-Olof Feldt, the SAP's chief economic spokesman in opposition, who became minister of finance in 1982, and in many ways the strong man of the regime after Palme's death.[22]

The centrepiece of Feldt's strategy to boost corporate profit margins was an immediate and massive devaluation of the Swedish currency by 16 per cent, on the new government's first day in office. The bourgeois coalition had itself already cut the value of the krona by 10 per cent in 1981, after several smaller depreciations in 1977–78. The continuity was no accident: like the bourgeois governments before it, the Social Democrats now identified labour costs as the key to international competition. A year earlier, by contrast, the LO congress had rejected devaluation as a solution to Sweden's problems, calling instead for selective demand stimulation at home by increased public investment in transport and infrastructure.

There was no immediate conflict between government and unions. The LO accommodated the devaluation of 1982 by demanding average wage increases of 2.5 per cent in the ensuing wage-bargaining round. The Palme government kept its promises to restore welfare entitlements cut by the bourgeois parties, and to spread the burden of austerity by increasing taxes on wealth, inheritance, gifts, and stock-market transactions. It also launched a public investment programme and, as we have seen, went through the motions of creating wage-earner funds. The SAP could thus claim to have incorporated elements of the LO's programme. But the dominant thrust of its policies now pointed in a very different direction. Feldt and his advisors were determined to give priority to private-sector growth, profits and market forces. The macroeconomic kick-start of 1982 was to be complemented by a series of supply-side measures that became central to the Third Road. Five of these were of special signficance:

1. The new government moved quickly to cut subsidies to ailing industries, and to restructure firms that had come under state ownership in the 1970s, when the bourgeois parties had nationalized more industry than the Social Democrats in the previous forty-four years. Once state-owned firms became profitable again, the government encouraged them to raise new capital by issuing shares in the stock market, and some firms were simply sold off to private interests. This partial and pragmatic privatization served not only to relieve fiscal pressures on the government, but also to insulate corporate decision-making from politics.

2. While the SAP eschewed privatization of public services, it launched a major programme to rationalize the public sector, and to enhance its responsiveness to consumer demands through

decentralization and 'corporatization' (the hiving off of auxiliary services to companies owned by local governments). The idea that the public sector should learn from the private sector defined much of this change.[23]

3. Conforming to international trends, the government deregulated financial markets in 1985–86, and phased out all exchange control in the second half of the 1980s.

4. With the support of the Liberals, a major tax reform was pushed through in 1989–90, sharply reducing marginal income-tax rates and creating a single income-tax bracket for most wage-earners. Explicitly modelled on Reagan's tax reform of 1986, it was financed by the elimination of many deductions, the extension of VAT, and an increased levy on capital gains.

5. Finally, the Carlsson government announced in late 1990 that Sweden would apply for membership of the European Community, and tied the currency to the ecu. The application to Brussels was a complete reversal of the Social Democrats' previous stance. Indeed, every one of the structural reforms listed above can be seen as overturning or redefining traditional priorities. On each count, the Social Democrats moved in a neo-liberal direction.

The Contradictions of the Third Road

The inception of the the Third Road coincided with the Reaganomic recovery of the US economy. Sheltered by the international boom that followed, the new course appeared at first to be a stunning success. From 1983 to 1988, the Swedish economy grew at an annual rate of 2.7 per cent, the balance-of-trade deficit turned into a substantial surplus, and the rate of unemployment fell from 3.5 per cent to less than 2 per cent. By 1988, the Social Democrats had eliminated the huge budget deficit they had inherited from the bourgeois parties (13 per cent of GDP in 1982), without cutting welfare entitlements. Flourishing this record before the electorate, the SAP won easy re-election in September 1988. Feldt's strategy seemed vindicated. But there was all along a fly in the ointment of Swedish performance. The Social Democrats had never managed to bring the rate of inflation down to the OECD average. By 1989 prices were rising at 6.6 per cent a year, as against 4.5 per cent in the OECD as a whole, and the gap was widening. The effect on export performance was not long in coming. By the end of the year, Sweden had run up a balance of payments deficit larger even than in 1982.

The result was a major political crisis in the spring of 1990. Consistent with his premisses, Feldt – ignoring the credit boom his own deregulation of financial markets had unleashed – identified excessive wage growth as the overriding cause of domestic inflation and declining competitive capacity. To tackle them, the Carlsson government devised a legislative package whose centrepiece was a draconian wage freeze and strike ban for two years. The LO leadership was cajoled into accepting this proposal, but the unions soon showed their discontent, and every other parliamentary party rejected the package. When it became clear the SAP could not force it through, Feldt resigned. Obliged to abandon the wage freeze itself, the Social Democrats instead struck a deal with the Liberals to cut public expenditure – this time including welfare entitlements. Feldt had gone, but his logic had survived him. The options of the previous eight years were now reinforced. The SAP had promised three major reforms in its electoral campaign of 1988: the introduction of a sixth week of paid holidays, the extension of parental leave insurance from nine to fifteen months, and the expansion of public day-care so that every pre-school child above the age of eighteen months would be ensured a place. All were now deferred. Organized business had strongly opposed the first two, as reducing the supply of labour. Conversely, the US-inspired tax reform of 1989–90 was intended to increase the supply of labour. Traditional Social Democratic voters perceived it as regressive, and the SAP's standing slumped at the polls.[24] Unemployment doubled under the impact of the austerity measures, and within a little over a year the SAP went down to its worst defeat in six decades.

Why had the Third Road, after its initial successes, ended in such dramatic failure? What was the underlying cause of its inability to sustain non-inflationary growth? The proximate answer is fairly clear. Swedish productivity remained sluggish throughout the period. From 1980 to 1990, the employment of labour, measured in working hours, increased by 11 per cent, but labour productivity only rose by 9.5 per cent. But what in turn accounts for the slow growth of labour productivity? One frequent explanation points to the expansion of the service sector, which was indeed rapid in Sweden, but this is only part of the story. For in manufacturing industry itself, the annual growth of labour productivity averaged only 2 per cent in 1983–88, as compared to 2.5 per cent in 1975–83 and 6.0 per cent in 1963–75.[25] Despite increased investment and capacity utilization, the deceleration of productivity growth that began in the mid 1970s persisted in the 1980s.

Contrary to its intentions, SAP policy contributed directly to this outcome – one that could have been foreseen from the standpoint of the Rehn–Meidner model. For, as Lennart Erixon has persuasively argued, the Third Road encouraged companies to compete on the basis of labour costs and lessened the pressure on them to engage in process and product innovation. In favouring large, export-oriented engineering firms, it also helped to preserve Sweden's existing industrial structure.[26] At the same time the profits boom of the 1980s stimulated wage drift through plant-level bargaining over piece rates, productivity bonuses and the like – accounting for about half of the increase in relative labour costs in the second half of the decade.[27] Just as the Rehn–Meidner model would have predicted, the government's strategy of a profit-led recovery made it more difficult for the LO and white-collar federations to exercise wage restraint, in effect playing into the hands of employers that wanted to decentralize wage bargaining.

The SAP's incomes policy for the public sector also undermined the position of labour's peak organizations. As part of its efforts to cut public expenditures, the government began to put the squeeze on public-sector unions in 1985–86, specifying wage ceilings for public-sector contracts in advance of private-sector settlements and insisting that public-sector employees would no longer be automatically compensated for private-sector wage drift. At the same time, it sought to address recruitment bottlenecks and promote productivity improvements by decentralizing wage determination in the public sector – that is, allowing more room for variations in pay according to localities and individual performance.[28] Both policies ran counter to the principle of equal pay for equal work and no doubt contributed to the erosion of the normative consensus that underpinned centralized wage bargaining in the 1960s and 1970s.

In other words, the logic of the Rehn–Meidner model provides a ready explanation for the failure of the Third Road: while high corporate profits generated inflationary wage rivalries and weakened the ability of national union leaders to pursue redistributive objectives, the growing importance of market forces in wage determination weakened the pressure on firms to engage in productivity-enhancing innovations.[29] The obvious question arises: why then did Swedish Social Democracy forget the lessons of the Rehn–Meidner model?

Much of the answer lies in a change in the balance of forces within the labour movement. The LO was now much weaker in its relation to the SAP than in the past. Intellectual authority had passed from its researchers to the policy unit of the party. The defeat of the Meidner Plan had meant a sharp fall in its public prestige. At the time of its adoption by the LO congress of 1976, the number of people who thought that unions had too much power was almost exactly the same as the number of people who thought that unions had too little power. By the spring of 1984, after the massive bourgeois campaign against the successor schemes, the first group outnumbered the second by thirty-nine percentage points.[30] In the view of public opinion as well as SAP leaders, the LO had overreached itself in its pursuit of wage-earner funds. Beyond these intellectual and political setbacks, moreover, the LO was losing control over its own industrial territory. The growth of white-collar unions and the outbreak of distributive conflicts between blue-collar unions eroded its ability to coordinate the wage-bargaining practices of its affiliates, and to deliver voluntary wage restraint.

In these conditions, a decline in LO influence over Social Democratic policy choices was only to be expected. After failing to mobilize support for wage-earner funds, the LO had no coherent alternative to the Third Road. It went along with it, because one of its objectives was to maintain full employment − in contrast to Thatcherism, as was regularly pointed out by SAP leaders. Later, there were Social Democrats to remark that the Third Road might have yielded more sustained growth (with less inflationary pressure) if the government had been willing to create more unemployment. But this was never an option considered by the SAP before 1990. The Third Road thus in a sense expressed a stalemate within the Swedish labour movement in the 1980s. The LO remained able to insist on full employment as an overriding goal of government policy, but it lost its ability to inform the SAP's approach to inflation, productivity, and competitiveness.

The Restructuring of Capitalism

It remains, however, to understand why the SAP made the turn it did in the 1980s. Here, it is clear that the politics of Social Democracy cannot be understood in isolation from the politics of capital. In Sweden, as elsewhere, organized business went on the offensive in the 1980s. On one hand, employer organizations launched a sustained campaign to decentralize the system of industrial bargaining and thereby undermine wage solidarity. On the other hand, business became increasingly outspoken in criticism of the Swedish welfare state and advocacy of privatization, deregulation, and entry into the EC. Eventually, under pressure from engineering firms and other foes of centralized bargaining, the SAF simply closed down its negotiation and statistics departments in the spring of 1990. The following winter, it withdrew from the system of corporatist representation on government bodies.[31]

This two-pronged business offensive can be dated back to the period of bourgeois coalition government in the late 1970s, and is often treated as if it were merely an opportunistic response to more favourable political conditions. But the long-term interests of capital were changing in this period, and its new posture reflected alterations in the marketplace. The political economy of postwar Sweden was distinguished from that of the larger European states by its high degree of trade dependence, and its notably institutionalized form of class compromise. It is tempting to attribute the compromise to the dependence, but a historical perspective qualifies the connection. For the ascendancy of Social Democracy and fixture of class compromise in the 1930s coincided with a marked decline in Sweden's dependence on foreign trade. It was not until the 1960s that the Swedish economy regained the level of trade dependence of the 1920s.

It has often been suggested that the historic compromise of the 1930s was first and foremost a pact between labour and firms producing for the home market or, more broadly, that Social Democracy rested on an alliance between workers, farmers, and domestic industry.[32] Peter Swenson has argued that on the contrary the historic compromise should be seen as an agreement between labour and capital in export sectors to curtail the wage demands of unions in sectors sheltered against international competition.[33] The two views are not necessarily contradictory, for the key to the success of the interwar SAP was its ability to pursue several cross-class alliances simultaneously. The same holds true of the postwar epoch too. While the supply-side policies of the Rehn–Meidner model favoured large, export-oriented firms, full employment and welfare-state expansion benefitted firms oriented toward domestic consumer markets. In large measure the postwar growth regime balanced the interests of domestic and of export-oriented industries.

Nevertheless, the conventional distinction between the two misses a crucial feature of the political economy of class compromise after 1945: the rise of consumer durables and the spread of Fordist mass-production principles. Broadly speaking, there had earlier been three main branches of Swedish industry: (1) sectors based on raw materials, processed by very capital-intensive methods (mining, steel, and forestry) for export markets; (2) engineering firms, engaged in labour-intensive 'craft production' (industrial machinery and other mechanical or electrical equipment) for foreign markets; and (3) traditional consumer-goods industries, employing more or less skilled labour (foods, textiles, construction, and printing), and producing for the home market.[34]

In Sweden as elsewhere, new consumer durables – especially auto and white goods – started to spread during the interwar period and their production expanded at a very rapid rate during the postwar

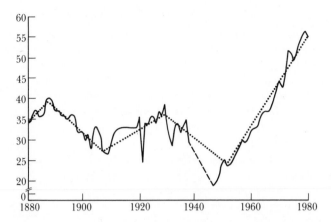

Figure 1.1 Foreign trade (exports and imports) as a percentage of industrial production (at constant prices), 1880–1980

Source: O. Krantz and L. Schön, 'Den svenska krisen i långsiktigt perspektiv' in L. Jörberg, ed., *Ekonomisk historia*. Stockholm 1985, p. 99.

boom. The firms in this sector, typified by Volvo and Electrolux, were less capital-intensive than raw-materials-based industries, but more capital-intensive than older engineering firms. Employing semi-skilled labour, they expanded by catering to domestic demand, but became increasingly export-oriented in the course of the boom. Fordist mass producers thus occupied an intermediary position between domestic- and export-oriented industry, and also between the two traditional types of export-oriented industry. More so than other firms, they benefitted from both sides of the postwar growth regime – that is, from the supply-side measures to promote rationalization and labour mobility *and* the demand-side measures to promote full employment and raise the living standards of working people. It is no accident that Volvo emerged in this period as the principal representative of the 'class-collaborationist' wing of the business community.[35]

Promoted by the policies of the labour movement, the rise of consumer durables and the spread of Fordist mass-production principles to other industrial sectors was a major source of postwar productivity growth – which in turn made possible increasing real wages and expanding welfare services, in a virtuous circle. Fordism had a further consequence: just as it created a new sector of firms occupying a pivotal intermediary position within the business community, so it generated a new stratum of semi-skilled workers with an

analogous position in the labour movement. Attenuating the bifur-
cation of the working class into skilled and unskilled, the integrated
character of the new production system strengthened the bargaining
power of assembly operators, and facilitated the aggregation of worker
interests by national union organizations.[36] Fordism as such was
neither a necessary nor a sufficient condition for centralization of wage
bargaining – Britain had the first without the second, Denmark the
second without the first. But in Sweden an interaction occurred
between the national legacies of export dependence, industrial unionism, struggle for universal suffrage, and the international pattern of
Fordism, which contributed powerfully to the emergence of LO's
distinctive 'class unionism'.[37]

It was this formative context that had started to come undone by the
seventies. Three major changes altered the Swedish economic landscape. The first of these was the growing export orientation of
industry. From the mid 1950s, the trade dependence of the economy
increased steadily. Figure 1.1 shows the trend. As import penetration
rose, and older home-market industries declined, the engineering
sector turned outwards. By the 1960s the leading Fordist producers
were starting to outgrow their domestic markets. In time this was
bound to affect the attitude of business to the welfare state, since the
more export-oriented a firm the less it has to gain from demand
stimulation at home. It also altered the fiscal logic of the postwar
settlement. To keep the lid on corporate profits and wage drift, the
Rehn–Meidner model prescribed taxation of domestic consumption,
rather than direct levies on company profits themselves. But once the
importance of foreign sales passes a certain threshold, corporate
profits require more direct taxation if they are to be controlled –
bringing the model into sharper conflict with business interests.

There was a second change of still greater significance. The
Rehn–Meidner model had rested on the premiss that the 'excess
profits' generated by solidaristic wage restraint would translate into
increased production and employment in firms or sectors with
above-average productivity. From the late 1960s onwards, however,
successful companies – especially large engineering firms – responded
to world-market pressures by increasing their investment abroad. The
ratio of employment by foreign subsidiaries of Swedish corporations to
their domestic employment increased from 12 per cent in 1960 to 26
per cent in 1978 and to 37 per cent by 1987.[38] The acceleration of
multinationalization in the 1980s is graphically depicted in Figure 1.2.
What it suggests is that the Third Road of a profit-led recovery failed to
generate productivity growth because a large portion of the surplus it
created went abroad.

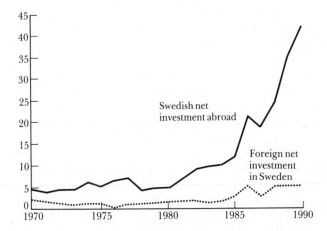

Figure 1.2 Swedish net investment abroad and foreign net investment in Sweden, billion SEK at 1985 prices, 1970–90

Source: Hans T. Soderström, ed., *Sverige vid vändpunkten*, Stockholm 1991, p. 50.

Reduction of labour costs was not the primary motive behind the expansion of foreign operations by Swedish capital. Typically, firms that invest abroad are more profitable than those which do not, and solidaristic wage bargaining has favoured these firms. Moreover, the bulk of foreign investment has been made in other high-wage zones (Western Europe and North America). Its aim is to circumvent barriers to trade and strengthen market position. For during the 1980s Swedish multinationals were acquiring a new configuration – no longer exporters with assembly plants and sales organizations abroad, but global corporations drawing on R&D and other resources from a number of different countries. The increased import content of Swedish exports is a telling index of this development.[39] In the most dramatic development, several large engineering firms have moved their headquarters abroad. Volvo is now based in Brussels and Brown-Boveri in Zurich.

The new cast of multinational corporations, combined with the internationalization of financial markets, has undermined the internal coherence of the Swedish economy and restricts the ability of any government in Stockholm to pursue economic policies that diverge from those of other advanced capitalist states. The SAP's abrupt decision to apply for membership of the EC in 1990, announced as part of an austerity package, was a direct response to the problem of capital outflow. There was also an electoral motivation – public opinion seeming strongly in favour of such a move at the time. In fact, the Social Democrats' reversal backfired, leaving many voters with the sense that the government was no longer in control of its policy agenda.

A third important change of economic setting lay in corporate investment behavior. The Rehn–Meidner model assumed that borrowed capital could readily substitute for equity capital. If a restrictive fiscal policy was necessary to curtail wages, public savings could offset the compression of business margins. The pension reform of 1959 conformed to this logic: business savings fell, and the supply of credit increased sharply. Although the rate of return on investment tended to decline from the mid 1960s onwards, it remained higher than the rate of interest, so borrowing made sense to firms. Measured as the ratio of equity capital to turnover, the financial solidity of industry declined from 44 per cent in 1958 to 21 per cent in 1976.[40]

In the second half of the seventies, however, business became much less willing to finance new investment through borrowing. The result was that a given level of investment came to require a higher rate of profitability. This change in business behaviour has reflected an environment of greater uncertainty, in the new world economy. Outlays on R&D investment have become more important to competitive capacity – and their risk is such that firms prefer to finance them on their own, through savings or equity issues. The new preference for self-financed investment as against borrowed capital has been reinforced by the higher solidity requirements of international creditors, with whom Swedish firms operating abroad have to deal.[41]

The LO recognized that competitive adjustment to world-market pressures demanded an increase in the supply of risk capital to industry. The proposal for wage-earner funds was designed to achieve this objective without redistributing income from labour to private owners of capital. But once it had failed to realize its own project, the LO was obliged to accept the market-led response. The impact on wage bargaining was direct. In the late 1970s, the SAF rejected the way in which the overall room for wage increases had previously been calculated, on the grounds that raising needed equity capital required larger profit margins. The relevant yardstick, it argued, was not productivity increases in those sectors of the economy exposed to international competition, but rather in the economy as a whole. The thrust of the criticism was, of course, aimed at the public sector – by far the largest segment of the sheltered economy, where productivity growth (as conventionally conceived) has always been much lower than in the private sector.

Finally, these years saw a significant reorganization of production within Sweden itself. Confronted by intensified international competition from the 1960s onwards, Swedish industry responded with a wave of mergers and management efforts to automate production and divide the labour process into ever smaller fragments. Conventional rationalization yielded few fruits: often provoking wildcat strikes and other forms of worker resistance (as elsewhere), it proved unable to raise productivity growth.[42] The gains from economies of scale and subdivision of labour were by now generally exhausted in the OECD, with competition focusing increasingly on product quality and customization. The new watchword became flexible production.

This general imperative took a particular direction in Sweden. The combination of full employment and wage solidarity forced Swedish firms towards innovations designed to improve the quality of industrial work.[43] Constrained in their ability to use wages as a means to recruit and keep workers on the assembly line, Volvo and other Fordist mass producers had to contend with very high rates of absenteeism and labour turnover. Programmes of 'work humanization' were in part a response to this problem – in other words, a functional equivalent of wage drift. However, the same firms also spearheaded the employer offensive against solidaristic wage policies in the 1980s. Seeking to use renumeration more actively to stimulate productivity improvements, quality consciousness and worker commitment to the enterprise, they not only sought to decentralize wage bargaining but also introduced profit sharing, bonus systems, and other rewards not formally subject to collective bargaining.[44] Employer efforts to differentiate wages are here thus not an alternative but a complement to job redesign. Many new payment-by-result schemes, in fact, are tied to work teams or other units within the company. Job redesign demands training and endeavour from employees, and employers maintain that assembly operators are not very interested in workplace reform unless they are compensated for their efforts. At the same time, of course, corporate investment in employee training increases the costs of labour turnover.

If employers always have an interest in both wage restraint and wage flexibility, these objectives tend to be contradictory, and the weight assigned to each will vary depending on production strategies and market conditions. Confronted with tight labour markets, large engineering firms in Sweden gave priority to restraint over flexibility in the 1950s and 1960s. Faced with similar labour-market conditions in the 1980s, they preferred flexibility, because their production strategies had changed. The result was to create incentives for national unions affiliated to the LO, and their local organizations, to circumvent LO's coordination of the wage-bargaining process. Organizational rivalries between blue-collar and white-collar unions within the private sector have exacerbated the difficulties of maintaining a solidaristic wage policy. The introduction of new computer-based technologies has generated jobs that might be classified as either blue-collar or white-collar. The Metal Workers Union has consequently had to accept a widening of the wage gap within its ranks in order to avoid losing members to the TCO-affiliated union of salaried industrial employees (SIF).[45]

Local wage bargaining and payment-by-result schemes form part of a broader employer effort to institutionalize a 'firm-level corporatism' that involves direct employee-management consultations as well as codetermination bargaining within parameters set by management.[46] The reform of the system of sick pay introduced by the Social Democrats in 1990 is in effect another step in this direction, as it transfers financial responsibility for the first fifteen days of sick pay to employers. The growing importance of the firm as the point at which the relationship between labour and capital is regulated poses an obvious threat to solidaristic, class-oriented unionism.

What conclusions can be drawn from these changes in contemporary Swedish capitalism? From the standpoint of the Rehn–Meidner model, the basic problem confronting the labour movement since the early 1980s has been the sluggishness of productivity growth, and this problem derives from the policy choices of Social Democratic governments. From a survey of the landscape of capital, these choices look more like political adjustments imposed by long-term changes in the economic structure of the country, which are the real source of labour's problems. The two perspectives are not incompatible. Industrial renewal is not the same as productivity growth. Further research is needed to establish just how far the restructuring of Fordist production went in Sweden, and what its effects were. But it is possible that a great deal of industrial renewal – in the sense of new technologies, job redesign, team work, and so on – did take place, undermining class unionism, without resulting in significant productivity increases. It may have been failure to translate workplace innovations into sustained productivity growth, in fact, that propelled employer efforts to differentiate wages. Alternatively, major renewal may have occurred in some firms or sectors, not only weakening class unionism but also accelerating productivity growth, while most manufacturing enterprises remained unaffected by the movement, apart from its rhetoric.[47]

Whatever the validity of these hypotheses, it is clear from data collected by the research department of the Metal Workers Union that the proportion of blue-collar engineering jobs requiring few skills and involving physically hard work actually increased as a result of the restructuring of the industry in the 1980s. Machine tools and other sectors competing on the basis of worker skills lost ground both to mass producers of consumer durables, and to high-tech enterprises employing disproportionate numbers of unskilled blue-collar workers together with well-educated white-collar personnel.[48]

The Swedish experience may, then, crystallize a dilemma confronting all Social Democratic movements in the 'post-Fordist' era. If it is indeed the case that the Fordist engine of productivity growth has been exhausted, labour must choose between two alternative growth strategies: one based on extraordinary product and process innovations, and the other on wage-cost competition. For Social Democracy, the first strategy is the only acceptable one in the long run, but it may often be that wage-cost reduction represents the most effective means to maintain or restore full employment in the short run.

The dilemma is compounded by the fact that the process of industrial renewal tends to weaken the cohesion of national labour movements. Many workers stand to gain from post-Fordist innovations in the workplace, but such benefits are unevenly distributed, and the process of renewal itself tends to generate decentralization of collective bargaining and greater wage differentiation. According to the logic of the Rehn–Meidner model, unions should be willing to accommodate a wider wage span if it corresponds to an upgrading of worker skills and responsibilities. But they should resist differentials reflecting variations in corporate profitability, which do not erode class solidarity but reduce pressure on firms to innovate. In practice, of course, it is not always easy to distinguish between skill-based and profit-based wage differentiation – and union locals do not have as much incentive to make the distinction as nation-wide unions.

Resilience and Retrenchment

Where does this leave Swedish Social Democracy in the mid 1990s? Paradoxically, its immediate electoral prospects are good. Since the Bildt government took office in late 1991, it has presided over a steadily worsening economic situation, with widespread financial insolvency, large trade deficit, depreciated currency, and – most spectacularly – growing mass unemployment. The Bildt regime has naturally sought to pin the blame for these unprecedented difficulties onto the stewardship of the SAP, as the Thatcher government in Britain so successfully did onto Labour. Yet despite the apparent plausibility of the argument, it has not convinced Swedish voters. On the contrary, the SAP's standing in the polls has recovered to near its all-time high.

The failure of the Third Road has not been converted into a legend like that of the Social Contract. What accounts for this resilience of the Swedish party?

Popular memory of the fiasco of the earlier bourgeois coalitions of 1976–82 has no doubt played a part. The shadow of the policy failures and manifest incompetence in that period lurks around the new government. The severity of the crisis has focused public attention on immediate existential problems, and this short-term outlook appears to have benefitted the Social Democrats. As voters become more and more disillusioned with the ability of any government to pursue a coherent strategy for growth, the SAP's lack of one is not a serious electoral liability for the moment, while its commitment to the welfare state remains popular.[49]

The bourgeois parties, aware of the welfarist strand in Swedish culture, did not argue for cutbacks in entitlements during their successful campaign of 1991. On the contrary they presented their programme of 'structural reforms' as a means to preserve the level of welfare benefits to which Swedes had become accustomed. The tax burden would be cut, the cost of social services reduced, and citizens assured a freer choice of benefits, by elimination of public-sector monopolies and encouragement of private provision. This was a package that might have served as a vehicle of an enduring electoral realignment, which was certainly its intention. But the critical economic situation forced the Bildt government to introduce unpopular austerity measures, overshadowing and to some extent pre-empting its reform programme – in ways reminiscent of the experience of many a left government. The coalition had promised, for example, to introduce a substantial child-care allowance, paid in cash, so as to allow parents who wanted to bring up their children at home, or entrust them to private day-care, to do so without disadvantage. The fiscal crisis has thwarted this scheme. Unwilling to finance the reform by cutting existing entitlements and closing public day-care facilities, the Bildt government has had to put it off indefinitely. Public expenditure was already out of control.

With the budget deficit growing very rapidly, the Swedish currency came under intense pressure during the European monetary storm of autumn 1992. The government had staked its reputation on the maintenance of a hard currency. In order to restore business confidence and avoid a devaluation, it was forced in the emergency to seek a deal with the Social Democrats. Now welfare provision had to be reduced. In return for the SAP's support of major cuts in social entitlements, the government introduced new tax increases, shelved its plans to abolish wealth taxes and to remove the administration of public unemployment insurance from union control, and agreed that it would not undertake any further privatization measures without prior consultations with the SAP. Taking a significant political risk, the SAP thus assumed shared responsibility for fiscal austerity, in exchange for guarantees that secured the organizational strength of the unions (unemployment insurance benefits providing a major incentive for employees to join unions), and pre-empted structural reforms that a future Social Democratic government might find difficult to reverse.[50] In similar circumstances, most parties of the European left would have gladly confined themselves to an oppositional role. The crisis agreement of 1992 is a perfect illustration of the SAP's deep commitment to the idea of being a governing party, which cannot avoid responsibility for the state of the nation, even when it is out of office. Its position was rewarded by a swell of popular support, coinciding with a marked shift of public opinion against EC membership. For many voters, shaken by the new insecurities of their country, the Social Democrats represent the political force most disposed to resist the potential effects of EC integration on the Swedish welfare state.

Beyond the immediate lie of the conjuncture, what explains the durable power of the SAP? The divisions among the country's bourgeois parties have often been emphasized.[51] Rooted in Sweden's pre-industrial social structure, with its independent peasantry, these have been preserved by the electoral system, and remain an important feature of Swedish politics. But a fundamental change has occurred here since the late 1970s. The Conservatives have emerged as the dominant party in the bourgeois bloc, representing a coherent neo-liberal alternative to Social Democracy. Their rise constrains the ability of the SAP to set the terms of political debate. The effects are evident today. Whereas the experience of bourgeois government in 1976–82 abruptly checked the ascendancy of the Centre Party, as the dominant force in the coalition, this time the experience has reinforced the dominance of the Conservatives within the bourgeois bloc. The polls show that it is mainly Bildt's junior coalition partners that have suffered from the unpopularity of his government.[52] In this sense, the election of 1991 looks like a stage in an ongoing reconfiguration of Swedish politics, rather than merely a temporary setback for Social Democracy.

For its part, the SAP has been a formidable historical agent. The extraordinary success of Swedish Social Democracy cannot be explained simply in terms of favourable political and economic conditions. As Göran Therborn has emphasized, the tactical skill and strategic vision of the SAP were indispensable.[53] No less remarkable has been the internal cohesion of Swedish Social Democracy. In any comparative perspective, the political conflicts within the movement that accompanied the socialist offensive of the 1970s, and the turn to the right in the 1980s, were very limited. They did not have the debilitating consequences that similar conflicts have produced in other countries (notably France and the UK); they never undermined voters' perception of the Social Democrats as a coherent force capable of governing the country. An electoral defeat as massive as the downfall of 1991 might have been expected to precipitate internal disputes and leadership changes. In fact the Social Democrats closed ranks without recrimination behind Ingvar Carlsson and the rest of party leadership.

There has been little research on the reasons for the unusual cohesion of Swedish Social Democracy.[54] It seems probable that the survival of the Swedish Communist Party (now known as the Left Party), and its transformation since the mid 1960s into a 'broad church' of left-wing activists, has served to limit the range and intensity of ideological conflict within the SAP. The virtual permanence of the party in government has also helped to stifle factionalism by absorbing career ambitions in public office or the civil service, while focusing internal debate on substantive policy rather than ideological issues. In so far as there was a contrast between left and right within the labour movement as a whole, from the mid 1950s onwards it increasingly came to coincide with the organizational division between the LO and the SAP.[55] While the LO research department harboured innovative intellectuals whose sympathies were on the left, LO congresses articulated radical rank-and-file demands in the 1960s and especially the 1970s. The organizational dualism of the industrial and political wings of the movement seems to have contributed to the pragmatism of Swedish Social Democracy, by concentrating debate on policy questions, and settling disagreements through bargaining. It has also facilitated strategic shifts via redefinitions of the division of labour between the two wings, without any individual having to reverse their positions or leadership changes on either side. The turn to the right in 1980s meant that the LO withdrew to a more narrow conception of union competence. Under the circumstances, many union leaders and activists considered the retreat desirable, because it freed the unions from responsibility for government policy, and enabled them to concentrate on defending the interests of their members.

Nevertheless, despite these enduring strengths, and the current resurgence of support for the SAP, the prospects of Swedish Social Democracy do not seem very promising. Welfare-state expansion no longer provides a viable vehicle for SAP hegemony, and the electoral success of Social Democracy has become increasingly contingent on the vagaries of the business cycle. The internationalization of capital has undermined the government's control of the economy, and the restructuring of domestic industry has eroded the solidaristic unionism that was once integral to Social Democratic success. In the short run, these challenges provide the SAP with certain political opportunities, as it benefits from popular anxieties about the effects of entry into the EC, and pursues swing voters in the centre, who are chary of the LO. However, the issue of EC membership is fraught with political dangers for Social Democracy, as it seeks to steer a narrow path between outright rejection and admission on terms dictated by Brussels. The referendum tentatively scheduled for 1994 could turn out to be as divisive for the Swedish labour movement as it was the Norwegian in 1972. Over the long term, moreover, EC membership and decentralized wage bargaining will render the reconciliation of capitalist growth with labour interests more difficult. If the next election does indeed yield a new Social Democratic government (or a coalition headed by an SAP prime minister), the policies of such a government are likely to resemble those of German Social Democracy, under the leadership of Helmut Schmidt, in the second half of the 1970s. The German experience suggests that this path, paved with acceptance of mass unemployment, will not provide a lasting recipe for Social Democratic success.

Notes

1. For overviews of electoral trends and political developments leading up to the 1991 election, see H. Bergström, 'Sweden's Politics and Party System at the Crossroads', and D. Sainsbury, 'Swedish Social Democracy in Transition', both in *West European Politics*, vol. 14, no. 3, 1991.

2. *Dagens Nyheter*, 22 May and 9 June 1993.

3. For such an analysis, see S.E. Olsson, *Social Policy and Welfare State in Sweden*, 2nd edn, Lund 1993.

4. On most of the topics covered in this part, see Jonas Pontusson, *The Limits of Social Democracy: Investment Politics in Sweden*, Ithaca 1992, for further details and references.

5. L. Lewin, *Planhushållningsdebatten*, Stockholm 1967; cf. also N. Unga, *Socialdemokratin och arbetslöshetfrågan 1912–34*, Lund 1976.

6. The literature on the realignment that enabled the Social Democrats to consolidate control of the government in the 1930s is extensive. For a particularly comprehensive analysis, see G. Therborn, 'Socialdemokratin träder fram', *Arkiv för studier i arbetarrörelsens historia*, vols 27–28, 1984.

7. The distinction between 'consumption politics' and 'production politics' is taken from J. Stephens, *The Transition from Capitalism to Socialism*, London 1979.

8. See D. Hibbs, 'Wage Compression Under Solidarity Bargaining in Sweden', Trade Union Institute for Economic Research, Stockholm 1990. On the politics of solidaristic wage policy, see A. Hadenius, *Facklig organisationsutveckling*, Stockholm 1976; A. Martin, 'Trade Unions in Sweden', in P. Gourevitch et al., *Unions and Economic Crisis*, London 1984; and P. Swenson, *Fair Shares: Unions, Pay and Politics in Sweden and West Germany*, Ithaca 1989.

9. G. Rehn, 'Idéutvecklingen', in LO, *Lönepolitik och solidaritet*, Stockholm 1980, p. 46.

10. A. Martin, 'Sweden: Industrial Democracy and Social Democratic Strategy', in D. Garson, ed., *Worker Self-Management in Industry*, New York 1977; and B. Simonson, *Arbetarmakt och näringspolitik*, Stockholm 1988.

11. R. Meidner, *Employee Investment Funds*, London 1978. E. Åsard, *LO och löntagarfondsfrågan*, Stockholm 1978, provides a detailed account of the origins of the idea of wage-earner funds.

12. The Meidner committee calculated that under its proposal it would take wage-earner funds thirty-five years to acquire 49 per cent of the equity in a firm operating at an average annual rate of profit of 10 per cent.

13. LO–SAP, *Löntagarfonder och kapitalbildning*, Stockholm 1978, and LO–SAP, *Arbetarrörelsen och löntagarfonderna*, Stockholm 1981.

14. E. Åsard, *Kampen om löntagardfonderna*, Stockholm 1985.

15. L. Lewin, *Ideologi och strategi*, Stockholm 1985, p. 356.

16. V. Bergström, 'Party Program and Economic Policy', in K. Misgeld, K. Molin and K. Åmark, eds, *Creating Social Democracy: A Century of the Social Democratic Labor Party in Sweden*, University Park, PA 1992, p. 166.

17. J. Elster, 'The Possibility of Rational Politics', *Archives Européenes Sociologiques*, vol. 28, 1987.

18. M. Gilljam, *Svenska folket och löntagarfonderna*, Lund 1988, p. 232. Cf. also S.O. Hansson, *SAF i politiken*, Stockholm 1984.

19. See Table 1.1 and Gilljam, pp. 82–93.

20. Elster, p. 99.

21. Among public-sector employees, supporters of wage-earner funds exceeded opponents by one percentage point in 1979, and opponents exceeded supporters by forty-one percentage points in 1982. Among private-sector employees, opponents exceeded supporters by ten percentage points in 1979, and thirty-three percentage points in 1982. Gilljam, p. 179.

22. See H. Bergström, *Rivstart? Från opposition till regering*, Stockholm 1987, and Feldt's political memoirs, *Alla dessa dagar . . .*, Stockholm 1991. Walter Korpi also emphasizes the role of academic economists in 'Politik och väljare bakom valutgången 1991', *Sociologisk Forskning*, vol. 1, 1993. He claims that the proportion of academic economists among policy-makers in the ministry of finance increased from roughly 15 per cent prior to the election defeat of 1976 to 50 per cent in the late 1980s. More generally on the conception and policies of the Third Road, see P. Walters, '"Distributing Decline:" Swedish Social Democrats and the Crisis of the Welfare State', *Government and Opposition*, vol. 20, no. 3, 1985; H. Heclo and H. Madsen, *Policy and Politics in Sweden*, Philadelphia 1987, ch. 2; and A. Martin, 'Sweden: Restoring the Social Democratic Distributive Regime', Occasional Papers, Harvard Center for European Studies, Cambridge, Mass. 1987.

23. R. Premfors, 'The "Swedish Model" and Public Sector Reform', *West European Politics*, vol. 14, no. 3, 1991.

24, Cf. Korpi, 'Politik och väljare'. The distributive effects of the tax reform have been a subject of much controversy. If it is true, as its proponents claim, that the reform does not involve a regressive redistribution of income, this can only be because the previous system of taxation was not very progressive. There is certainly no question that the reform represents a retreat from selective state intervention. For the traditional Social Democratic approach to taxation, see S. Steinmo, 'Social Democracy vs. Socialism', *Politics and Society*, vol. 16, no. 4, 1988, and 'Political Institutions and Tax Policy in the United States, Sweden and Britain', *World Politics*, vol. 41, no. 4, 1989.

25. Swedish Ministry of Industry, *Svensk industri i utveckling*, Stockholm 1990, pp. 65–6.

26. L. Erixon, 'Den tredje vägen: inlåsning eller förnyelse?', *Ekonomisk Debatt*, vol. 17, no. 3, 1989. The issue of how Swedish productivity growth compares to that of Sweden's competitors in world markets has been a subject of much contention among Swedish academics. Contrary to conventional wisdom among economists, Korpi argues that the lag of Swedish productivity growth relative to the average for European OECD countries in the 1980s was entirely a function of a higher level of productivity to begin with: see

Korpi, 'Halkar Sverige efter?', *Ekonomisk Debatt*, vol. 18, 1990. Erixon's analysis is not necessarily inconsistent with Korpi's, for neo-liberal supply-side policies, emphasizing wage-cost containment, are scarcely unique to Sweden.

27. H. T. Söderström, ed., *Sverige vid vändpunkten*, Stockholm 1991, pp. 115–8.

28. On public-sector incomes policy in the 1980s, and wage bargaining more generally, see N. Elvander, *Den svenska modellen*, Stockholm 1988; K. Ahlén, 'Swedish Collective Bargaining under Pressure', *British Journal of Industrial Relations*, vol. 27, 1989; P. Swenson, 'Union Politics, the Welfare State and Intraclass Conflict', in M. Golden and J. Pontusson, eds, *Bargaining for Change: Union Politics in Europe and North America*, Ithaca 1992; and A. Kjellberg, 'Sweden: Can the Model Survive?', in A. Ferner and R. Hyman, eds, *Industrial Relations in the New Europe*, Oxford 1992.

29. The basic elements of this critique are articulated by Meidner, 'The Swedish Labour Movement at the Crossroads', *Studies in Political Economy*, vol. 28, 1989.

30. Gilljam, p. 237.

31. The engineering employers' campaign to decentralize wage bargaining was initially resisted by other groups within the SAF. On the business offensive of the 1980s, see A. Martin, 'Wage Bargaining and Swedish Politics', Occasional Papers, Harvard Center for European Studies, Cambridge, Mass. 1991; V. Pestoff, 'The Demise of the Swedish Model and the Resurgence of Organized Business as a Major Political Actor', School of Business Administration, University of Stockholm, 1991; H. De Geer, *The Rise and Fall of the Swedish Model*, Chichester 1992, chs 14–16; and J. Pontusson and P. Swenson, 'Varför har arbetsgivarna övergivit den svenska modellen?', *Arkiv för studier i arbetarrörelsens historia*, vols 53–54, 1993 (English version forthcoming).

32. E.g., G. Olsen, 'Labour Mobilization and the Strength of Capital', *Studies in Political Economy*, vol. 34, 1991, and G. Esping-Andersen and R. Friedland, 'Class Coalitions in the Making of West European Economies', *Political Power and Social Theory*, vol. 3, 1982.

33. P. Swenson, 'Bringing Capital Back In, or Social Democracy Reconsidered', *World Politics*, vol. 43, no. 4, 1991, and 'The End of the Swedish Model in Light of its Beginnings', Working Paper, Wissenschaftszentrum, Berlin 1992.

34. My treatment of the long-term evolution of Swedish industrial structure draws extensively on B. Carlsson et al., *Teknik och industristruktur*, Stockholm 1979.

35. Curiously, there exists no scholarship that explores Volvo's political role or, more generally, the connection between production organization and the political attitudes of different segments of industry in Sweden.

36. Cf. R. Mahon, 'From Solidaristic Wages to Solidaristic Work', *Economic and Industrial Democracy*, vol. 12, no. 3, 1991.

37. See Pontusson, *Swedish Social Democracy and British Labour*, Ithaca 1988, for a more sustained treatment of these variables and their implications for labour politics. On class unionism as a distinctive feature of the Swedish labour movement, see G. Ross, 'What is Progressive about Unions', *Theory and Society*, vol. 10, no. 5, 1981, and W. Higgins, 'Political Unionism and the Corporatist Thesis', *Economic and Industrial Democracy*, vol. 6, no. 3, 1985.

38. Swedish Ministry of Industry, p. 105. The engineering industry alone accounted for 68 per cent of employment abroad in 1987.

39. According to Carlsson et al., p. 69, the import content of engineering exports increased from 24 per cent in 1957 to 44 per cent in 1980. There is every reason to believe that the trend has continued.

40. Ibid., p. 40.

41. Lennart Erixon, 'What's Wrong With the Swedish Model?', Institute for Social Research, University of Stockholm, 1985.

42. Ibid. Among other things, Erixon notes that merger activity continued at a high level in the 1970s but did not yield the same kind of productivity gains as in the 1960s.

43. Pontusson, 'Unions, New Technology and Job Redesign at Volvo and British Leyland', in Golden and Pontusson, eds, *Bargaining for Change*.

44. On local wage bargaining and pay practices, see N. Elvander, *Lokal lönemarknad*, Stockholm 1992.

45. T. Nilsson, *Arbetare eller tjänstemän?*, Lund 1988. Cf. also Scott Lash, 'The End of Neo-Corporatism', *British Journal of Industrial Relations*, vol. 23, no. 2, 1985.

46. Cf. G. Brulin, *Från den 'svenska modellen' till företagskorporatism?*, Lund 1989, and G. Brulin and T. Nilsson, 'From Societal to Managerial Corporatism', *Economic and Industrial Democracy*, vol. 12, no. 3, 1991. On workplace industrial relations, see also Kjellberg, pp. 121–36.

47. The pervasiveness of the rhetoric of industrial renewal is itself noteworthy; see M. Elam and M. Börjeson, 'Workplace Reform and the Stabilization of Flexible Production in Sweden', in B. Jessop et al., eds, *The Politics of Flexibility*, Aldershot 1991.

48. Swedish Metal Workers' Union, *Solidarisk arbetspolitik för det goda arbetet*, Stockholm 1989, pp. 67–73.

49. See S. Svallfors, 'The Politics of Welfare Policy in Sweden', *British Journal of Sociology*, vol. 42, no. 4, 1991, and 'Policy Regimes and Attitudes to Inequality', in T. P. Boje and S. E. Olsson Hort, eds, *Scandinavia in a New Europe*, Oslo 1993.

50. In terms of parliamentary votes, the government could instead have struck a deal with New Democracy, a right-wing populist party that emerged in 1991, but such a move would not have inspired confidence in the exchange markets. In the end, the effort to defend the value of the currency failed anyway, and the government has since moved towards greater reliance on New Democracy for parliamentary support. See Olsson, pp. 358–72, for the crisis agreement of 1992 and the reforms introduced by the Bildt government. For the connection between unemployment insurance and union density, see B. Rothstein, 'Labor-Market Institutions and Working-Class Strength', in S. Steinmo, K. Thelen, and F. Longstreth, eds, *Structuring Politics*, New York 1992.

51. Cf. F. Castles, *The Social Democratic Image of Society*, London 1978, and G. Esping-Andersen, *Politics Against Markets*, Princeton 1985.

52. In a poll reported by *Dagens Nyheter* on 22 May 1993, 44.0 per cent of voters with a firm party preference favoured the bourgeois bloc, as compared to 52.9 per cent in the 1991 election; 19.5 percent favoured the Conservatives, as compared to 21.9 per cent in the election.

53. G. Therborn, 'A Unique Chapter in the History of Democracy', in Misgeld, Molin, and Åmark, eds, *Creating Social Democracy*.

54. Curiously, a comprehensive scholarly analysis of the internal politics of Swedish Social Democracy has yet to be undertaken. Some of the contributions to Misgeld, Molin and Åmark, eds address this gap; also, see J. Pierre, *Partikongresser och regeringspolitik*, Lund 1986, for an analysis of party congresses from 1948 to 1978.

55. For the historic relationship and organizational ties between the LO and the SAP, see Åmark, 'Social Democracy and the Trade Union Movement', in Misgeld, Molin, and Åmark, eds, and Martin, 'Wage Bargaining and Swedish Politics'.

2

Norway: Changing the Model

Lars Mjøset, Ådne Cappelen, Jan Fagerberg,
Bent Sofus Tranøy

Norway has been idealized, on more than one occasion, as the most successful single example of a society transformed by social democracy since the War. Grounds for the claim are not lacking. In strictly economic terms, the achievements of Norway under the rule of the Norwegian Labour Party (DNA) are even more striking than those of its larger and better known neighbour Sweden. Beginning the century on the poor agrarian fringe of Europe, Norway has become one of the richest societies in the world – while remaining one of the most egalitarian in its culture, and comprehensive in its social provision. How has this change come about? What are the specific problems it has failed to resolve, or actually generated? The foundations of the Norwegian welfare state were underlaid by a distinctive economic-policy model developed during the solstice of Labour rule, from 1945 to 1965. Foreign interest in Norway has typically focused on the social reforms introduced by Social Democracy. There is no question of the importance of these. But, as in Sweden, the condition of postwar social advance was historically high economic growth, and the way this was achieved is the central story of Norwegian Social Democracy – just as, today, it is the difficulties that have emerged with the passing of the original model that decisively affect the fortunes of Labour in Norway.[1]

Origins of the Model

From the late Middle Ages onwards, Norway was an outlying region of the Danish realm. In 1814 Denmark lost its colony to Sweden, and Norway gained home rule under Stockholm. Norway was at the time essentially a minifundia economy, with extensive peasant ownership

and no indigenous aristocracy. The groups in power – state bureaucrats, a small but growing bourgeoisie, a few rich farmers – were
politically divided, although the bureaucrats regarded the farmers as
their loyal clients and favoured enfranchisement of all freeholders and
leaseholders. The constitution of 1814 created a political system
particularly open to mobilization by peasants and other 'peripheral'
groups, who secured a high degree of local-government autonomy in
the 1830s. From the 1850s the ruling elites were also challenged at the
cultural level. Teetotal and lay Protestant movements were stronger
than elsewhere in Scandinavia. There was also a national movement of
linguistic revival, with the result that today Norway has two official
languages: standard Norwegian (akin to Danish) and new Norwegian
(constructed in the 1840s and 1850s as a combination of rural dialects).

In the second half of the nineteenth century, a cleavage between the
centre and periphery of the country defined the poles within parliament. The Liberals (Venstre) were the party of rural and 'counter-
cultural' groups, with important support among the urban intelligentsia, teachers in particular. The Conservatives (Høyre) united
high-level bureaucrats and certain business interests. The Liberals led
the struggle for a parliamentary system, conceded in 1884. The
Labour Party was founded in 1887, and initially collaborated with the
Liberals. In 1905 Norway won full independence from Sweden.
Manhood suffrage was general by 1900, and women received full
voting rights in 1915.

In the nineteenth century, the Norwegian economy was dominated
by a backward agriculture, offset by a few industries that were
resource- and infrastructure-based: forestry, mining, fisheries and
shipping. From 1850 the opening of the world economy under British
dominance spurred diversification into pulp and paper production,
whaling and canning, and by the 1880s Norway had developed the
world's third largest commercial fleet. By the turn of the century,
technologies to produce hydro-electricity were available, and Norway's
huge waterfalls became a major national asset, as they could be used to
produce electric power at a very low cost. Foreign capital now found
Norway an advantageous site for a variety of energy-intensive production processes: fertilizers, aluminium, zinc, chemicals. These heavy
industrial plants were located close to the waterfalls, often at the ends
of the Western fjords.

Soon after independence, nationalist business interests, farmers
sceptical of industrialization and a social reform movement – all
working mainly through the Liberal party – secured 'concession laws',
giving Norwegian authorities some control over the country's natural
resources, and requiring the creation of joint ventures between

national and foreign enterprises. Norway's economic structure today is still influenced by these historic foundations: timber, semi-finished metals and chemicals, and shipping. These sectors constituted the export enclave within a still predominantly agricultural society.

With the development of industry, the size of the working class grew, and conflict between Labour and the traditional parties began to dominate parliament. The anti-socialist front was very divided, however. The Liberals and Conservatives failed to fuse; farmers broke away from the Liberals to form an Agrarian Party in 1920; a Christian Party sprang up in the 1930s, from the teetotal and lay Protestant subcultures. The party structure descends from this matrix: a strong Labour Party with broad popular support, confronting a non-socialist camp fragmented into four parties, whose policies have always proved difficult to aggregate.

Originally quite radical, Norwegian labour turned towards a pragmatic reformism during the Depression. In Sweden in 1933, the Social Democrats had struck a deal with the Agrarian Party; and in Norway a severe rural debt crisis paved the way for a similar alliance. In 1935 the trade-union confederation (LO) and employers' association (NAF) reached a national pact for industrial peace, and a few days later the Labour Party took office with the support of the Agrarians. Pursuing a moderate course in office, Labour was able to manoeuvre successfully for the next four years between the Liberals and the Agrarians.

These events set the pattern for Norwegian reformism, whose formula was thereafter the same: a social compromise between labour and capital (administered by the respective federations), plus a political alliance with rural and liberal groups. Subsidies and market controls served to bolster the support of small farmers and agricultural workers, but also reflected a temporary convergence of interests between the labour movement and the wealthier farmers who would never vote for the DNA. The class compromise secured industrial peace, and strike activity declined as Labour came to power – while union and party grew steadily: the LO from 84,000 in 1922 to 357,000 on the eve of the Second World War, the DNA from 80,000 in 1930 to 170,000 in 1938. While private business still controlled investment decisions, workers expected Labour in government to resist unemployment and initiate welfare reforms.

The Postwar Golden Age

Five years of Nazi occupation created a strong sentiment of national unity and responsibility that found expression in an all-party programme for postwar recovery in 1945, of which the DNA was the chief architect. In the elections of that year, Labour won an absolute majority in the Storting. The Norwegian electoral system was not proportional at the time: this victory was secured with just 41 per cent of the vote. However, the Communist Party, sustained by its record of wartime resistance, polled another 12 per cent, leaving no doubt of the mood of the country. With the onset of the Cold War, Labour absorbed most of the Communist vote, steadily increasing its share of the poll in the next three elections, to reach a peak of over 48 per cent in 1957. The electoral system became more proportional in the fifties, but Labour continued to control an absolute parliamentary majority down to 1961, and to form the government until 1965. In twenty years of undivided power, it moulded Norwegian economy and society into a remarkably coherent system.

Labour's economic goals were fast and steady growth, balanced trade, full employment, stable prices and a more egalitarian distribution of income. These would lay the basis for expanded popular consumption and a comprehensive welfare state, which would in turn consolidate the social compromise and political alliances of the 1930s.[2] The first pillar of the structure now created by the DNA was a regulation of labour–capital relations, based on a constant long-run ratio of wages to profits. The institutional mechanisms for enforcing this model varied over time, from direct state crafting of an incomes policy, to devolved wage settlements inflected by subsidies and duties, to a 'contact committee' bringing together government, employers and unions. Common to all phases was the axiom that the parameters of responsible wage increases were set by world-market prices and productivity growth in the exposed sector of the economy. Economists formalized this as the 'Scandinavian inflation model'.

The second component of the model was an active *Strukturpolitik*. Norway's elongated geography has always created regional divisions, accentuated by the low productivity of much of its smallholder agriculture. The DNA sought to turn the traditional dualism of urban-industrial and rural-agrarian zones to advantage, by assuring a stable supply of labour-power from the agricultural sector into manufactures and services, without depopulating the countryside. Regional policies were designed to compensate for the disruptive effects of restructuring. One of the difficulties Labour faced was the very capital-intensive character of the enclave sector of the economy. Typically located in one-plant towns, these industries often formed just one link in the vertically integrated operation of international corporations. Bauxite or alumina, for example, would be shipped from Jamaica or Australia to Norway for melting in furnaces lit by cheap energy, and the semi-finished product re-exported for processing elsewhere in Western Europe. Even the shipping sector was quite isolated from the domestic economy – until the sixties, shipyards were small and Norwegian shipowners to a large extent contracted and financed their vessels abroad.

The macroeconomic impact of these import- and capital-intensive export sectors was unusual. Since few local resources other than energy were in play, fluctuations in Norwegian exports impinged only to a limited extent on the domestic economy. The main variations they determined were in inventories and imports. The result was to create a set of automatic stabilizers,[3] which relieved policy-makers – despite their enthusiastic Keynesianism – from major counter-cyclical tasks before the mid 1970s. In the immediate postwar years, when there were still many trade barriers, the function of the enclave sector was to generate most of Norway's export earnings. Employment was created by domestic manufacturing, which was much more labour-intensive. A number of small factories producing consumer durables had emerged by the late 1930s.[4] Spurred by the introduction of American technologies and Fordist production methods, this sector expanded under Labour's protective mantle. When trade was significantly liberalized in the sixties, with the creation of EFTA and the Kennedy Round, Norwegian small and medium enterprises proved quite competitive as producers of typically Fordist consumption goods.

The third and most original pillar of the Norwegian model was a system of fiscal and monetary policies that might be termed 'credit socialism'. In 1951 a Joint Committee (Samarbeidsnemnda) was set up between the ministry of finance, the central bank, the main organizations representing commercial and savings banks, and later insurance companies. Its function was to regulate the supply of credit to the private sector. Dominated by the authorities, this committee allowed Labour to enforce its view that low interest rates would help modest families and direct investment towards real capital rather than financial speculation or rentier activity. To achieve this end, credit had to be rationed. The committee determined both the volume of credit and the rate of interest. There were few worries about misallocation due to suppression of the price mechanism. The Norwegian breed of Keynesian economists – many of whom were important advisors and supporters of Labour – were confident that the state could engender dynamic effects by various control measures.[5]

There was also another lever to hand. In Norway, unlike most other Western countries, state banks had a long history. Created to provide credit for investment projects, state banks for farmers and fishermen – originating in the mid-nineteenth century – were consolidated in the early 1900s, and were followed in the postwar period by state banks for housing, education, and agriculture (1947–48), and later for regional industrial development (1960). The credit they supplied was financed partly by public-sector budget surpluses and partly by bonds. The state issued its own and guaranteed other bonds, whose purchase was negotiated in the Joint Committee. Since bond-issuing institutions were thus secured a market for their paper, the authorities had to regulate direct issue by legislation. In this system, as can be seen, private financial institutions played a subordinate role: one of their few remaining tasks was to take part in the rationing of credits for corporate investment. Norwegian Social Democracy had devised a kind of 'credit socialism'.

The state bank for housing (Husbanken) was of especial importance in the welfare design of the system. It financed residential construction according to specific standards at a very favourable rate of interest. Public or municipal housing was virtually non-existent in Norway. The goal of DNA policy – largely realized – was to ensure that as many families as possible had their own small house. In certain urban concentrations, however, there was substantial cooperative housing as well as privately owned flats; the larger cooperatives relied on Husbank financing, working closely with local authorities. The price of cooperative flats, unlike private houses, was controlled by the state.

The basic elements of the system of credit socialism were sustained until the early eighties, but the mechanisms to enforce it were revised in 1965, when the Joint Committee was replaced by an elaborate legislative framework for monetary and credit regulation. The new arrangements reflected a technocratic conviction within the Keynesian Oslo school that corporatist negotiations worked too slowly and imprecisely, preventing realization of the full potential of rational macroeconomic management. Henceforth the adjustment of banks' primary and secondary reserve requirements was intended to release the optimum volume of credit at any given time. In periods of exceptional demand, supplementary reserve requirements could function as more or less direct controls. The new legislation further enabled the authorities to regulate the lending of non-bank institutions. With this statute, the Norwegian model moved towards its culmination. The shares of national income accruing to labour and to capital were held more or less constant, while productivity-related wage growth assured rising popular living standards. The system of credit allocation directed investment towards industrial development, regional employment, construction of infrastructure, and sustained extension of the welfare state. Fiscal policy was held relatively tight, with budget surpluses to finance public credits, allowing for counter-cyclical fine tuning where necessary. For example, the state would fund inventories in the export enclave when prices slumped, or the housing bank would stimulate construction if demand slackened. Overall, this was a model quite distinct from that in any of the other Nordic countries.[6] It might best be called – with no evolutionary connotations – a form of state capitalism.

The construction of this model was a remarkable achievement by the DNA. But its hegemony was not indefinite. By the late sixties, the landscape had altered. Two developments were to undermine the stability of the model. The first was political. The DNA had a more authoritarian internal structure than its Swedish counterpart – inherited from its 'democratic centralism', complete with ban on factions, of the twenties. Long years in power led to a decline in its membership, which fell from a peak of 200,000 at the end of the forties to 130,000 by the end of the sixties. Power within the party became increasingly concentrated in a small leading nucleus, composed of its chairman and secretary, trusted cabinet ministers, the head of LO and the editor of its daily. Party culture placed overriding value on unity and discipline.

At the onset of the Cold War, Sweden had proposed a Nordic defence union to keep the region out of the force-field of the two military blocs. The DNA leadership opted instead for NATO. A substantial minority had supported the Swedish scheme, and an activist group continued to oppose Norwegian membership of NATO, gaining younger adherents once anti-nuclear mobilization grew, as in Britain, in the late fifties. In 1960 the DNA – whose secretary-general Haakon Lie was a hardened Cold Warrior – expelled it. The result was the creation of a Socialist People's Party (SF) to the left of Labour, on a platform of neutrality and disarmament, which cost the DNA its absolute majority in the Storting in 1961, when the new party won two seats. The SF was not a flash in the urn. More than a party of teachers and public employees, it won significant working-class support – its electoral geography corresponding closely to that of Labour itself: strong in the north and east, weak in the south and west. In 1965, it more than doubled its vote. The two parties together won over 50 per cent of the poll. Through the vagaries of the electoral system, however, the SF won no new seats and the DNA lost enough to give a majority in parliament to the four non-socialist parties. The continuity of Labour rule was broken.

The bourgeois coalition which now took office was dominated by the centre parties – Liberal, Agrarian and Christian – rather than the Conservatives, and for the most part adhered to established routines. It used the interventionist monetary instruments just enacted by Labour without hesitation, and introduced a social security scheme akin to the Swedish pension system, incarnating the principles of a universalist welfare state. Now, however, fault lines started to appear within the economic model built after the War. Traditionally, the export enclave had been assigned the role of wage leader, as most subject to the discipline of the world market. With trade liberalization, however, small and medium manufacturers were also exposed to international competition. The result was quite different from the logic of the Rehn–Meidner model in Sweden (a deliberate squeeze on the weakest manufacturing firms), for in Norway the leading exporters owed their position not to high productivity, but to cheap energy. To the extent that their profits continued to set the benchmark for wage growth, the rest of Norwegian industry was likely to be caught in a squeeze. This contradiction did not take full effect before the recession of the early seventies, but the Fordist sector was now heading towards potential difficulties.

At the same time, the new centralization of the instruments of 'credit socialism' was creating problems of management. For it discouraged corporatist collaboration, set more rigid limits to the volume of credit, and facilitated a political obsession with a fixed and very low nominal interest rate. The results were counter-productive, as financial institutions – especially the commercial banks – increasingly devoted their energy to devising ways to evade the regulations, which eventually played havoc with attempts to manage the supply of credit.

Social Democracy in the 1970s

These strains, however, were overshadowed by the crisis into which the Norwegian political system was suddenly plunged at the turn of the 1970s by the British decision to join the European Community. The defection of Norway's main non-Nordic trading partner from EFTA put the country's elites on the spot. The bourgeois coalition started to negotiate entry into the EC, but fell out over the terms, leaving a minority Labour administration to complete the process. The accord reached at Brussels was submitted to a referendum in September 1972, where it was narrowly defeated, after a vigorous popular mobilization against it. Labour's debacle was complete, as a third of its own voters turned against it. For the effect of the European issue had been to split the two halves of its historic formula for hegemony. The bloc that favoured entry into the EC comprised the two social partners: the peak associations of business and labour. The bloc that opposed entry drew its political force from farmers and fishermen, urban intellectuals and middle-strata employees. It also attracted a substantial number of workers, many of them swayed by the energetic No campaign of the SF.

A year later, the DNA's vote plummeted to 35 per cent of the electorate, its lowest level since 1930.

Ironically, however, Labour was able to form a minority government in 1973, despite the scale of its electoral defeat, because of the success of the left front formed by the SF and other anti-EC groups in denying the non-socialist parties a majority. After some seven years in opposition, it confronted a quite new international and national conjuncture: a deep and lasting crisis of the world economy, combined with a windfall for the national economy in the shape of North Sea oil. Between 1972 and 1980 the share of petroleum in total Norwegian exports leapt from 0.1 per cent to 35 per cent – assisted by the two oil shocks administered by OPEC in 1973–74 and 1979–80. There was a sense in which the Norwegian economy was not unprepared for this benefaction, for the oil sector in many ways prolonged its traditional dependence on an export enclave. There was the same capital-intensive production of raw materials or semi-finished products for dispatch abroad, import of advanced machinery, and financing by state or foreign capital. On the international money markets, banks competed with each other to lend for offshore drilling. Statoil – the public corporation sinking the derricks – became the new pinnacle of Norwegian state capitalism.

A very large petroleum rent would soon fall into the hands of the Norwegian state. What should be done with it was hotly debated in the country. Labour opted for a strategy of headlong expansion. Politically, it needed to regain votes after its disastrous showing in 1973; economically, it believed the recession required a strong counter-cyclical response. Furthermore, the minority government was not in full control of all budget decisions. The result was that wage growth in the economy as a whole came to depend on expectations of future oil rents. Generous incomes policies allowed the real disposable income of households to grow at a record average of 5 per cent a year between 1974 and 1977, while farmers' income doubled in the same period, as a result of a decision to equalize earnings in manufacturing and farming, broadly supported in parliament. Shorter working hours and earlier retirement were introduced. The public sector – particularly local government – expanded rapidly, with most of the new jobs being taken by women. Exposed parts of manufacturing industry benefited from generous financing of inventories and extensive crisis relief.

At the same time, mindful of the challenge on its left, Labour moved to introduce measures of industrial democracy it had traditionally ignored. The defeat of the party in the European referendum had undermined its rigid internal culture, anyway under notice as a new generation entered the leadership, imposing greater pluralism.[7] The DNA now harboured avowed factions of left and right, and as a compromise between them, the left – with strong ties to industrial unions – was allocated the chairmanship of the party in late 1975, while the right kept the office of prime minister, to be occupied by Nordli. An outcome of the new balance was legislation that came into effect in mid 1977, giving organized labour comprehensive rights of co-determination in issues of health, safety and work process.[8] The emphasis was on industrial rather than on economic democracy: as long as credit socialism operated in Norway, Swedish-type funds were not deemed necessary. Still, a revised law on joint-stock companies gave workers a third of the board of companies with more than fifty employees; while another required the councils of commercial banks to contain a majority of nominees elected from the work-force or appointed by parliament. These were years in which, it has been claimed, the 'social-democratic state' reached its high-water mark in Norway, and 'the power relationship between labour, the state and capital was definitely in capital's disfavour'.[9]

Labour's electoral calculation paid off. In 1977 the very rapid boom, rising real incomes, and bevy of social reforms allowed the DNA to recapture most of the voters who had strayed to its left four years earlier, and to return to power with just short of an absolute majority in the Storting. But now the bills had to be paid. What Labour had done was to administer the strongest dose of Keynesian pump-priming in postwar history. In doing so, it flouted central precepts of the Norwegian model. Wages had been allowed to rise much faster than productivity growth in the exposed sector and world prices, tightening cost pressures on industry outside the enclave: the share of manufacturing in total employment dropped from 27 per cent in 1970 to 21 per cent by 1980. Fiscal policy was loosened, but the rate of interest was kept low, so credit policy was also loose. The real rate of interest, indeed, turned negative – even more so after tax, since interest payments could be deducted from taxable income. The result of this combination of measures was a rapid consumption boom and the largest current account deficit in the OECD. By late 1978, net foreign debt had reached a record 47 per cent of GDP.

This was an unsustainable course. Once returned to office, Labour – already under heavy criticism from many economists and the Conservative party – switched towards austerity. The first step in a new direction was an adjustment of the credit market – most interest rates were untied. The nominal rates charged by banks promptly rose, and the real rate moved back above zero, albeit still negative after tax. Further increases were halted by the proclamation of a general wage and price freeze in September 1978. Official credit supply from banks and insurance companies was brought down, although this was partly offset by grey-market activity. Another effect of tighter monetary policy, leading to a decline in conventional private-sector lending, was to increase yet further the power of state banks, whose share of total outstanding loans increased from 27 per cent in 1970 to 35 per cent in 1980.[10] This growth, which was not the outcome of any conscious policy by Labour, provoked loud complaints of unfair competition from the private banks, backed by an increasingly neo-liberal consensus among Norwegian economists.

Two professional investigations initiated by the Labour government itself document this shift.[11] Suggesting that low interest rates were not necessarily to the advantage of low to middle-income families after all, these reports criticized the size of the state bank sector, the amount of subsidies channelled through them and the heavy regulation of the bond market. As a compromise they recommended a simulated market interest rate in the banking sector, to be estimated by the authorities. Confronted with these proposals, Labour acted slowly, and what it did was not enough. The real rate of interest increased, but Labour found it practically impossible to raise it significantly. It became ever more difficult to get the policy mix right, and regulated financial institutions were now channelling funds through 'brokers' subject to fewer controls, leading to over-shooting of credit supply.

To improve Norwegian competitiveness, the government devalued the currency by 16 per cent in 1977–78. To block claims for compensation against rising import prices, wages were frozen in 1978. For workers, the austerity course meant a decline in their real incomes until 1981. Recourse to direct state intervention was also pursued in the housing market. Public control and finance had kept the price of cooperative flats (allocated according to fixed rules of seniority) far below market prices, leaving members – unlike owners of private dwellings – unable to reap the wealth effects of inflation. A number of ingenious techniques were developed to evade the regulations, undermining Labour's goal of a low-price market for urban housing, and the government attempted to ban the irregular transactions. This allowed the Conservative Party to capitalize on popular pressure for the abolition of price controls. By late 1980, the two parties were level-pegging in the polls, each with a third of the electorate – a steep fall for Labour, and an unprecedented gain for the Conservatives.

In an effort to redress the situation, and resolve controversies within the party, Labour chose its first woman leader, Gro Harlem Bruntland, in early 1981 and shifted towards a more pragmatic programme, redefining socialism as a process rather than a goal and dropping demands for the socialization of financial institutions. The adjustment was of little avail. In September 1981, Labour was driven from office.

The clear-cut victor in the elections was the Conservative Party, which polled over three times the vote of its nearest non-socialist competitor. The blue wave sweeping the Western world had arrived in Norway. The Conservative leader, Kaare Willoch, became prime minister with the parliamentary backing of the Agrarians and Christians, who remained outside the government due to disagreement on the abortion question.

The Right in Power: 1981–86

As the new government took office, the world economy went into recession – average GDP growth in the OECD did not exceed 1 per cent in 1981–82. But the second oil shock that had contributed to the downswing benefited Norway. Exports of gas and petroleum rose sharply, increasing fiscal revenues and generating huge current-account surpluses. In these favourable conditions, the new regime set to work as Norway's first committed government of the right since the War.[12]

Taxes on higher income brackets and private business were promptly cut – reductions financed by the upswing in oil rent. The stock market, of marginal importance hitherto, was unleashed by fiscal incentives – transactions on the Oslo exchange quadrupled between 1981 and 1983, and the average share price climbed 70 per cent. The housing market was deregulated: the number of cooperative flats under price control was halved, the value of the remainder doubling overnight, and privatization was extended to the rented sector. The liquidity of the private banking system was increased by permission to borrow abroad. In four years the share of total lending by state banks tumbled from 35 to 28 per cent – by the end of the decade it was down to 18 per cent.[13]

The most fundamental change accomplished by the Willoch regime, however, was its burial of the model of credit socialism. Initially hesitant to tackle the established system, from 1983 onwards it moved with a series of increasingly decisive measures. Restraints on short borrowing from the central bank were abolished; supplementary reserve rules were repealed; mandatory purchase of Treasury bonds de facto cancelled; restrictions on new establishments lifted. Interest rates were let loose in September 1985 but the ministry of finance instructed the Central Bank to keep money market rates within a narrow band. This forced the Bank to supply the market with enormous amounts of liquidity, approximately 60 billion kroner in the year following this liberalization.

The immediate effect of these policies was to spur private banks into a lending spree. Overshooting – which had never been more than 20 per cent in the 1970s – rose from 50 per cent in 1984 to over 100 per cent of the credit budget in 1986. The international upturn after 1983 was amplified by the government's reckless domestic expansion. The result was a headlong boom, as private consumption exploded between 1984 and 1986, and unemployment disappeared. But the pattern of growth was not reassuring. Output in the manufacturing sector increased only slowly, and employment scarcely at all. Despite several further devaluations, Norwegian firms had only become marginally more cost-competitive, and the share of manufacturing in GNP continued to decline. On the other hand, in the financial sector and business services – traditionally a small number of jobs – employment jumped by more than 40 per cent. The stock exchange flourished, but new shares contributed no more than an annual 12 per cent of total investment in industry. The household savings rate turned negative in 1985–86, and a large current-account deficit appeared after the oil price plummeted in late 1985 and early 1986. The major trend of these years was the rise of a speculative economy in which it became much more profitable to strip assets, or change homes, than to create new investment in the industrial sector.

The consumer boom gave a fair wind to Willoch's coalition in the 1985 elections. But it did not last long thereafter. The business cycle in Norway was now more influenced by the world price of oil and the exchange rate with the dollar than by West European developments. When these two parameters suddenly slumped, the government was forced to jam on the brakes, at a time when the EC was continuing an upturn. In the midst of the crisis, the Conservatives threw their support behind a nationwide lock-out in the engineering industry in the spring of 1986, which was a disastrous failure. International confidence in the Willoch regime ebbed, with a wave of speculation against the Norwegian krone, and when the government lost a parliamentary vote over a minor tax issue, it resigned – to all appearances with relief. A minority Labour government took office in early May.

Recession and Financial Crisis: 1986–93

By the late eighties, the DNA had altered. The election of Brundtland as party leader in 1981 marked a social and generational change. The LO-based left responsible for the shift towards industrial democracy in the mid seventies was outmanoeuvred by Brundtland, who stressed the need to modernize the party and internationalize its outlook. The new Labour leadership, unlike the cohort of Gerhardsen and Bratteli after the War, had few close links with traditional working-class constituencies. It was less ideological and more flexible, willing to vary its policy approaches, and to cater to consumer as well as producer interests. After the 1985 election, it had launched what it described as a Freedom Campaign, whose aim was to recapture the idea of liberty from the Conservatives, by exploring a range of problems confronting Norwegians. Economic democracy, however, was not among them – Brundtland had already deflected proposals to increase wage-earner representation on the boards of public companies. The emphasis of the campaign was on individual choice, served where necessary by market solutions. But it also drew attention to the increasing number of households in which both parents worked, and urged that social policy on schools, working hours, pensions and other areas be adapted to the new patterns.

This was the political mixture now put into practice. The Brundtland government was in a minority in the Storting, where – unlike the situation in the seventies – there were no longer enough SV votes to save it from parliamentary defeats. (SV was an election alliance of SF, various communists, and social democrats, and later became a party.) There was, however, broad parliamentary support for what was called a 'turning operation' into a new period of austerity. After an immediate further devaluation of 12 per cent in May 1986, the government committed the country to a fixed exchange rate, and free movement of capital. Fiscal policy was tightened, and tax reform made credit more expensive for higher income groups. A restrictive monetary policy – intended to bolster the krone – further increased the real rate of interest. Finally, in the spring of 1988, the LO was induced to accept a very moderate two-year wage settlement, which was then generalized by law to block any possibility of the non-LO federations (YS and AF) reaching better terms. The cumulative effect of these measures spread through the economic system, and by 1988 Norway was in full recession.

Labour's austerity cure for the country was a shock therapy, which had many consequences the DNA leadership had not foreseen. The first of these was the emergence of major unemployment. Some job loss in sheltered sectors and the construction trade was perhaps expected, but the Labour elites were taken aback when the 'turning operation' led to general layoffs, and business leaders started to view unemployment as a necessary catharsis.[14] By 1989 the jobless rate had reached 5 per cent, still low by international standards, but very high by Norwegian. There was, however, a second and more dramatic knock-on effect to come: a classic cascade of asset deflation.

Falling real incomes, rising rates of interest, and tax changes made many households retrench, to reduce their debts. The real-estate market was immediately hit. Demand for housing declined, and so did prices. The fall in values in turn reduced the wealth of households, leaving them even more exposed, and prone to cut expenditure – putting many firms into difficulties, and thereby depressing (among other things) the market in commercial property. This then led to the collapse of many investors in real estate, who had borrowed to finance their purchases – transferring ultimate losses to the banks. During 1988 the first banks had to be rescued by a safety fund set up by the banking sector. But more failures followed, and the funds ran out. Deregulation of the credit market had not led to higher efficiency, but to a more unstable economy. By late 1990, the most important banks were losing their equity capital, bringing the whole financial sector to the verge of collapse. Ironically, the successful assault on Norwegian credit socialism ended with the state bailing out the largest banks. Facing the danger of a complete breakdown of payments and credits, the government had no choice but to rescue the banks by means of large cash injections. The cumulative instabilities triggered by the drive for deregulation forced the authorities into re-regulation, leading to more extensive public ownership in the economy than ever before. By 1993, the state had become the majority shareholder in the three largest commercial banks, and spent the astounding total of twenty billion kroner – more than 3 per cent of GDP – to stabilize the financial system.

What were the positive pay-offs of the 'turning operation'? While the Norwegian economy moved into recession in 1986, international demand was growing. Oil prices also picked up after 1986. The result was to bring the current account back into balance by 1989, enabling the government to risk a looser fiscal stance, in the hope of stemming the rise in unemployment. In the spring of 1990, LO and NHO (the reorganized employers' federation) agreed on a small increase in real wages, and private consumption revived somewhat. Exports continued to grow rapidly, while monetary policy remained tight.

The early nineties have thus seen a modest recovery, but not one to be compared with the booms of 1974–77 or 1983–86. Unemployment has stabilized at a postwar record of around 6 per cent, and investment has not recovered. But otherwise growth has been respectable by current international standards, at 2 per cent a year; inflation has been kept low, at 2½ per cent; and an external surplus sustained. When the European currency crisis broke in the wake of the uncertainties over Maastricht, Norway was eventually forced to devalue in December 1992 – but whereas the Swedish and Finnish currencies, caught up earlier in the turmoil, have floated downwards since their devaluation, the Norwegian has held relatively firm. Nominal interest rates have fallen to a low level, stimulating substantial increases in house prices and private consumption. Norway is today the only country (except for

Luxembourg) that meets the conditions of convergence laid down at Maastricht for a common European currency.

The long-term problems, however, remain: in particular, a vicious circle of declining investment and declining employment. Labour has tried to respond with a number of supply-side measures. These have so far included an energy law to increase competition among hydro-electric producers; a nominal reduction in agricultural subsidies; a tax reduction and closing of loopholes, favouring industrial investment; and targeting of advanced sectors – information, off-shore materials and equipment, ocean farming, biotechnology – for research support. Norway has joined its West European counterparts in the race for in-dustrial restructuring.[15] But the results remain very uncertain. Nor-wegian R&D has been falling as a proportion of GDP since the late eighties, and the concentration of public funding on the small high-tech sector of the Norwegian economy looks misguided, since by inter-national standards R&D in the branches that matter for output and employment – food, textiles, wood and pulp – remains low.[16]

Labour macroeconomic management since 1986 has given priority to external balance and price stability over full employment. In its own terms, it has been effective. Norwegian social democracy has avoided the fate of its Swedish counterpart. But if Labour still holds power in Oslo, when the SAP has lost it in Stockholm, fortunate contingencies have a good deal to do with the difference. Labour inherited a major crisis, for which Conservative rule bore clear responsibility, at a time of world boom – allowing it to adjust away from its postwar model with a plausible degree of legitimacy, and recoup with the resource assets of petroleum. In Sweden, the Social Democrats – pursuing policies not entirely unlike those of the Norwegian Conservatives – were them-selves the authors of a crisis, coinciding with the world recession of 1989, in which Swedish manufacturers were more vulnerable. The DNA has exhibited much adaptive skill. But it has not yet found a real substitute for its traditional model. The system of credit socialism has been largely dismantled. Today, the Norwegian state influences the allocation of investments by its own expenditures, and its intimacy with large firms. So far, Labour has eschewed use of the banks that it had rescued as instruments of active policy – the state remains a passive owner. But it has worked hard to establish an informal entente with top managers of both public (Statoil, Hydro) and private (Uni-Storebrand) corporations, trying to find reliable partners, willing to take risks and stick to serious business. These efforts have not always been successful, as the recent scandal engulfing Uni-Storebrand – the insurance com-pany that tried to take over a Swedish counterpart, with official compli-city, and miserably failed – testifies. Possibly, more formal arrangements may emerge in future. In early 1992, the employers' federation (NHO) indicated that it was contemplating withdrawal from most public committees, as the Swedish employers have done. Very soon, however, its mood changed, and it yielded to yet another grand corporatist vision, a 'Forum for the Creation of Values' (in more mundane language: industrial innovation), led by the prime minister, and composed of business elites, two ministries, the NHO and LO. Whether this sort of concertation will replace more informal contacts remains to be seen. But some version of 'Norway, Inc.', state activism in disguise, seems for the moment to be Labour's main approach.

Meanwhile, the Brundtland governments have by no means just been the steward of the Norwegian economy. From the outset of the Freedom Campaign, the new DNA leadership advocated a new social strategy for Norwegian welfare. If the postwar model of development has passed away, the values it was intended to serve have not. The Nordic 'passion for equality' still runs strong in Norway. Its principal focus, however, has altered. Gender rather than class now took front stage. The Labour government of 1986 captured the imagination of the world with a cabinet not only headed by Brundtland, but containing eight female ministers out of eighteen. This *Feminat* was not a chance occurrence, but the outcome of a deliberate quota policy fought through by the women's movement within the DNA.[17] Its impact on Norwegian politics was such that within a few years most of the bourgeois parties have followed suit – today, both the Conservative (until 1993) and the Agrarian Party have also been led by women. In the high political sphere, Norway can claim to be the country of the most advanced sexual equality in the world.

In the social sphere, matters are not so straightforward. In Norway as elsewhere, the focus of the social-security system that had emerged by the sixties was the male breadwinner in a single-income family, with the woman as mother and housewife. Wage workers and informal carers did not have equal standing in the welfare state. Care of children or the elderly did not entitle women to compensation for sickness or unemployment benefits (in the case of mothers wanting to return to jobs when children were grown-up). All citizens were entitled to a basic minimum pension, but the supplementary pension that was earnings-related presupposed formal employment. From the seventies onwards, however, female employment rates began to grow rapidly in Norway, in a pattern visible a decade earlier in Sweden or Denmark. In this Nordic configuration, the welfare state takes over caring functions – staffed by women – which in continental Europe are largely performed by women at home, and in Anglo-American societies increasingly by low-paid

female workers in the private sector.[18] In Norway, as throughout
Scandinavia, female employment growth was virtually all concentrated
in public services – above all, health and education. But the late start of
this process made a difference. Norwegian working mothers have not
been supported by publicly funded day-care to anything like the extent
as Swedish; to a larger extent they must resort to private and informal
solutions.[19]

The Brundtland governments have sought to address these new
conditions with an active family policy. A series of reforms have brought
Norway close to Sweden in public acceptance of parents both as workers
and carers, with generous schemes for maternity, paternity and
parental leave – although day-care still lags behind Swedish provision.
In 1992, the work of unpaid carers responsible for children below the
age of seven, or for elderly, sick, or handicapped persons,
was accepted as equivalent to employed labour in the national insurance
system, securing supplementary pensions for many women who may
never take part in the formal labour market. One consequence of this
reform could be to encourage more women to stay home, in a break with
the general ethos of the blessings of employment outside the household.

The position of Norwegian women has no more been completely
transformed than that of Norwegian workers. As in Sweden and
Denmark, the concentration of female employment in the welfare state
has led to sexual segregation of job markets – mirrored even at elite
levels, where the salience of women in public office has no counterpart
in private institutions. The radical criticism of a social-democratic
mixed economy, that capital still dominates the organization of work
and the direction of investment, has its parallel in the feminist critique
of the present limits to gender equality: the dual-earner family is not
typically a dual-carer family.[20] Real gains for women have been made.
But the social context in which they have been achieved is in some ways
more precarious. The economic pressure on the welfare state is now
greater. For it was originally connected to an economic model which
helped ensure full employment: it was not designed to finance mass
unemployment. While many dimensions of equality have been preserved or strengthened in Norway, financial instability and unemployment may still have increased inequalities in life chances and incomes.

Prospects for the Nineties

There was one other thrust of the new Labour leadership. From the
outset, it aimed at a more active international profile for Norway. Here
it has undoubtedly achieved success – but at the same time incurred
risks that are still not played out. The temporary eclipse of Swedish

Social Democracy has allowed Brundtland's government to step into the position that Palme once occupied, brokering the Israeli–Palestinian truce in the Middle East, mediating the conflict in Bosnia, and championing environmental causes round the world. This is a record appreciated at home. But the Labour leadership has also committed itself to European integration, and here dangers await it.

After the referendum of 1972, the question of the country's relationship to the EC was banished from Norwegian politics for the better part of two decades. But in May 1989, as the Single Market loomed, the EFTA countries – spurred by Brundtland – agreed at a meeting in Oslo to start negotiations for a European Economic Area (EEA) with the EC. In September, punished by younger LO members for its austerity programme, Labour lost votes heavily at the elections, dropping to its lowest share of seats in the Storting since 1933. A three-party bourgeois coalition took office, under a Conservative premier. Soon the Conservatives were pressing for full membership of the EC – and as in 1971, the Agrarians rebelled. The government broke down in October 1990, letting Labour back into office by default.

The Brundtland leadership was itself, however, by now convinced of the need for Norway to join the EC. It calculated that the end of the Cold War, and the sudden shift of Sweden, Austria and Finland in favour of membership, would create greater popular support for Europeanism. Party speakers explained that nagging unemployment and sluggish investment could only be solved by coordinated international action, and that the entry of the Nordic bloc into the EC would lend powerful support to Delors' vision of a social Europe. In November 1992, the DNA congress voted by a majority to approve an application for full Norwegian membership of the Community. A significant minority, mainly from the north of the country, was not persuaded.

Negotiations started in Brussels in June 1993. The principal issues of contention are familiar – in fact, they are as old as Norway's concession laws. Disposition of petroleum is one: Labour wants to maintain Statoil as a privileged partner, at variance with the 'oil directive' which is likely to pass the European Council of Ministers in the next few months. Oslo also insists on control of a wide band of fisheries – Brundtland going so far as to declare that the fisheries minister, a Euro-sceptic, will have a veto over the final result of the negotiations. This proviso is intended to allay hostility to Labour's course in the northern regions of Norway. It has been clear for some time, however, that Labour's arguments for entry into the EC have encountered widespread resistance in Norway. A broad 'No to EC' movement currently has more members than any political party in the country.

The European issue has thus become a serious hazard for the DNA.

Its long-term goal is an ambitious one: a continuation of the social-democratic project at the level of the Community. But short-term costs of integrating Norway into EC will inevitably be large. The Norwegian welfare state is in advance of EC standards, not just in social provision, but in regional equality as well, with high transfers to poorer areas, and subsidies to small farmers. The campaign against the EC has had no difficulty in pointing out the likely victims of integration. To counter its arguments, the Labour leadership has been forced into a strongly ideological stance that does not suit its pragmatic style,[21] and has little resonance in the country. The party's traditional appeal has been to solidarity within Norway. Its new call does not find the same listeners – as in most other countries, there is no strong feeling of European identity in Norway.

Realizing that if it stuck to its principles too firmly, it risked serious electoral consequences, the Labour leadership drew back as elections approached in September 1993. Its campaign sought to finesse the European issue, by arguing that it was not on the agenda till negotiations were concluded, when it would be decided by a national referendum. The result of the poll was satisfactory. The DNA reaped the benefits of the economic upturn and interest-rate fall, recovering working-class voters lost in 1989, without incurring the potential costs of its European option. But there was an upheaval over the EC nonetheless, in the non-socialist camp. Mounting a vigorous campaign against Brussels, under the spirited leadership of Anne Enger Lahnstein, the Agrarian Party trebled its mandate, displacing the Conservatives – still vehemently pro-EC – as the second largest party in the Storting.

In the short run, this division of the opposition makes life easier for Labour. Still a minority government, it can muster two different majorities across the middle of parliament: with the Conservatives on economic, and the Agrarians on social and regional policies. But in the longer term, the prospects of its European strategy look bleaker. The Norwegian constitution requires a two-thirds majority for its amendment, as signature of the Maastricht Treaty would demand. Over a third of the MPs elected in 1993 are against membership of the EC. So even a positive vote in a referendum – against precedent – would not necessarily guarantee entry.

Labour's political position is not so strong that it can afford to ignore these warning signs. Its ties with the LO have loosened, as the party looks for support in the academic and craft federations (AF and YC), that have gained ground since the seventies. The LO itself, now down to some 60 per cent of organized wage-earners, is frustrated with the DNA's lack of solutions for unemployment. Collective affiliation of union members to the party is being phased out. The two sides need each other too much for a real divorce, but the synergy has gone out of the relationship. Within the party, a small left opposition to the leadership has emerged, now middle-class rather than trade-union in background, that rejects the EC option. Its most prominent figure is the mayor of Oslo, Rune Gerhardsen, son of Norway's most famous postwar premier, who runs a city administration in which the DNA and SV collaborate. This is the formula that might seem to offer the hope of a real broadening of the base of Norwegian Social Democracy. For the security issue that originally divided the two parties has lost significance with the end of the Cold War, and the gap between them on social questions has narrowed, as the SV has moved rightwards in tandem with Labour. But here too, the European issue is the barrier. The SV remains the leading force on the left against entry into the Community. The successful conclusion of Labour's negotiations in Brussels has now inevitably driven them apart. In November 1994, Norway will face its second referendum on EU membership. In the calculus of the Brundtland government, prior approval of entry by Finnish and Swedish voters should smooth the path for a reversal of the Norwegian electorate's verdict of 1973. If this *mise en scène* succeeds, it will mark a turning-point in the history of the country. But Brundtland is an agile politician. Even were it to fail, Labour's advantage – over an opposition deeply divided by the issue of entry into the EU – would doubtless continue, at least for the interim.

Notes

1. For a survey of our work on Norway and the Nordic countries, see Lars Mjøset, 'On the Influence of Regulation Theories on Nordic Studies of Economic Policies and Economic Development', *La Lettre de la Régulation*, no. 6, February 1993.

2. G. Esping-Andersen and W. Korpi, 'From Poor Relief to Institutional Welfare States: The Development of Scandinavian Social Policy', in R. Erikson et al., *The Scandinavian Model*, Armonk 1897.

3. See P. Schelde Andersen and J. Åkerholm, 'Scandinavia', in A. Boltho, ed., *The European Economy: Growth and Crisis*, Oxford 1982.

4. T. J. Hanisch and E. Lange, 'Vekst og Krise', *Tidsskrift for Arbeiderbevegelsens Historie*, no. 2, 1979.

5. Bent Sofus Tranøy, *Styring, selvregulering oq selvsosialisering. Staten, bankene og kredittpolitikken 1950–1988*, unpublished thesis, Dept of Political Science, University of Oslo 1993.

6. For a comparison, see Lars Mjøset, 'Nordic Economic Policies in the 1970s and 1980s', *International Organization*, vol. 21, no. 3, 1987.

7. Knut Heidar, 'Towards Party Irrelevance? The Decline of Both Conflict and Cohesion in the Norwegian Labour Party', in D. Bell and E. Shaw, eds, *Conflict and Cohesion in West European Social-Democratic Parties*, London 1994.

8. Bjørn Gustavsen and Gerry Hunnius, *New Patterns of Work Reform: The Case of Norway*, Oslo 1981.

9. William M. Lafferty, 'The Political Transformation of a Social-Democratic State', paper presented to the seminar on Professional Governance and Social Democratic Policies, Oslo, 21 June 1990, pp. 8–9. While Lafferty counts a number of policies concerning public employment and control of the financial sector as expressions of strategies to strengthen the social-democratic state, we argue that some of these policies were rather adjustments to more difficult problems of economic management, and that they led to incoherent economic policies.

10. Hege Imset Matre, *Norske Kredittinstitusjoner 1850–1950*, Research on Banking, Capital and Society, Report 42, NORAS, Oslo 1992, Table 2E.

11. *Rentepolitikk*, NOU [Norwegian Public Investigations], 1980, 4; *Struktur og styringsproblemer på kredittmarkedet*, Bank of Norway, Publication Series, no. 7, Oslo 1979.

12. For an extensive account of the economic policies of the two non-socialist governments, see Fagerberg et al., 'The Decline of Social-Democratic State Capitalism in Norway', *New Left Review* 181,May–June 1990, and 'Structural Change and Economic Policy: The Norwegian Model Under Pressure', *Norwegian Journal of Geography*, vol. 46, 1992.

13. The share further declined to 18 per cent in 1988/89. Matre, *Norske kredittinstitusjoner 1850–1950*, Table 2E.

14. Hege Torp, 'Arbeidsløshetens struktur 1989 og noen sammenlikninger med 1983', *Søkelys på arbeidsmarkedet*, 1989, p. 26.

15. Gerd Junne, 'Der strukturpolitische Wettlauf zwischen den kapitalistischen Ländern', *Politische Vierteljahreshrift*, vol. 25, no. 2, 1984.

16. Tore Sandven and Keith Smith, 'R&D and Industrial Structure in a Comparative Perspective', Norwegian Computing Centre, Fremtek-notat no.5, Oslo 1993.

17. Hege Skjeie, 'The Uneven Advance of Norwegian Women', *New Left Review* 187, May/June 1991.

18. Gøsta Esping Andersen, *The Three Worlds of Welfare Capitalism*, Cambridge 1991.

19. Arnlaug Leira, 'The "Woman-Friendly" Welfare States? – The Case of Norway and Sweden', in J. Lewis, ed., *Women, Work and the Family in Europe*, London 1993, p. 61, p. 64ff.

20. Leira, 'The "Woman-Friendly" Welfare States?', p. 68.

21. Robert Geyer, 'The Contradictions of Integration and Community: British and Norwegian Social Democrats in an Integrating Europe', paper to the 1992 meeting of the American Political Science Association, Chicago.

3

Denmark: End of an Idyll?

Niels Finn Christiansen

In the middle of August 1982 the Danes were informed that they lived in the best country in the world. Denmark was ranked number one among 107 countries in an American report which characterized quality of life by a broad spectrum of geographical, economic, social, political and cultural variables.[1] In an almost simultaneous opinion survey of the EC countries, the Danes declared that they were content with their lives and their country. In glaring contrast to these happy tidings all politicians, economists, newspaper editors, and many foreign observers – on the right as well as on the left – claimed that Denmark was in the throes of the most severe crisis since the 1930s, on the verge of national bankruptcy, and that, within a very short time, it would be deprived of its economic self-determination by the tycoons of international finance. Or as a Norwegian daily more poetically put it: the Danes are heading for hell, but they are still travelling first class.

Behind these divergent assessments, there was in fact – as sub-sequent developments were to show – a watershed. The crisis of 1982 had an economic and social as well as a politico-ideological dimension. Throughout the 1970s, the welfare state and the extension of the public sector were increasingly financed through borrowing on the international capital market. By the early 1980s Denmark had a huge public debt, and an increasing proportion of GNP and of the budget was devoted to interest and repayment. During the same period unemployment increased tenfold, so that 300,000 (about 12 per cent of the aggregate labour force) were temporarily or permanently out of work. In building and construction, in agriculture and manufacturing industry, enterprises – large and small alike – were daily closing down. Still, the basic elements of the social-security system were as yet successfully defended against massive attacks from the bourgeoisie and sections of the petty bourgeoisie, particularly from the traditional non-socialist parties and the aggressively neo-liberal Progressive Party led by Mogens Glistrup. Ever since this party appeared on the parliamentary arena in 1973, the Danish political system had experienced severe shocks. Between 1972 and 1982 there were seven changes of government in Copenhagen. All but two of these, nevertheless, had resulted in governments led by the Social Democratic Party (SDP), under Anker Jørgensen as prime minister. But in September 1982, the Social Democrats were replaced by a four-party Liberal–Conservative coalition under Poul Schlüter, which was to last more than a decade. A turning-point in Danish postwar politics had arrived. How should the long exile of the Danish labour movement from office be interpreted?

A Farmers' Democracy

The political crisis of the early 1970s was not directly caused by the international macroeconomic crisis, though this accentuated and deepened the political problem. It would be more correct to say that the political crisis stemmed from the disintegration of a class structure that had remained relatively stable between the turn of the century and the 1950s.

Capitalism came to Denmark in the latter half of the nineteenth century, in a mainly agrarian social formation. From the end of the eighteenth century, and particularly from the 1840s, the country found its place in the international division of labour, becoming an agrarian exporter to the large European industrial nations, especially Britain. At first the main export was grain, but in the 1860s and in the international crisis of the mid 1870s this was gradually replaced by processed animal products. About 1900 manufacturing industry still only contributed 10 per cent or so to GNP. Agriculture, though in decline as a proportion of national output, accounted for almost 75 per cent of Denmark's total exports against the 20–25 per cent recorded by manufacturing industry – a share which remained largely unchanged until after the Second World War. The service sector composed 44 per cent of GNP, and Denmark always seems to have been above the international average as far as this sector is concerned.[2]

The general laws of capitalism and tight dependence on the world market were obviously crucial determinants in the shaping of the Danish economy. At the same time, the national class structure, social relations and political life left very specific marks on the course of class struggle in the country. The century following the comprehensive agrarian reforms of the late eighteenth century witnessed the development of a small class of agrarian capitalists running their estates by means of wage labour. Indeed, until the First World War agricultural workers – a good many of whom owned a house and possibly a small plot – were clearly the largest and most oppressed section of the Danish working class. Moreover, they remained unorganized throughout the whole period.[3]

A class of small farmers, whose medium-sized farms were relatively homogeneous in form and output, grew up alongside the agrarian capitalists. Supplemented by a few farmhands and maids, and the occasional use of wage labour, this agrarian petty bourgeoisie owned some 75 per cent of the land and became of increasing importance to the national economy in the nineteenth century. When production was reorganized in the 1880s and processed animal produce became of major importance, this class was integrated into the international division of labour.

Unlike the petty bourgeoisie in almost all other countries, the Danish farmer class developed an independent identity based on economic, political and cultural self-organization. From the 1840s farmers participated actively in an alliance with a small – mainly intellectual – urban bourgeoisie and constituted the necessary mass basis for the establishment of a bourgeois democracy, as presaged in the extremely liberal constitution of 1849. The 1850s and 1860s, however, were marked by a conservative constitutional and political offensive; and, particularly after the Danish defeat at the hands of Prussia and Austria in the 1864 war (when Denmark lost the duchies of Holstein and Schleswig), an alliance was formed between the landowners and the bourgeoisie. From about 1870 to 1901 this alliance retained executive power in spite of an overwhelming majority in the Folketing (the lower house) for the farmers' party Venstre (the Liberal Democratic Party). During this period an intensive class struggle was fought for the parliamentary-democratic principle that executive power should originate from a majority in the lower house. To a certain extent the landed interest in Denmark may be compared with the German junker class: its leader, Estrup, was certainly a character of Bismarckian stamp, if not of the same calibre.

The affairs of the whole farmer class, meanwhile, were being intensively organized. From the 1840s onwards Danish farmers created their own insurance institutions and credit banks, and later merchant and savings banks. From the 1880s this economic breakthrough manifested itself in the organization of cooperative dairies, slaughterhouses and food-processing plants, so that the farmer class became totally independent of the major landowners and able to withstand attempts by commercial capital to take over the agrarian industries. To some extent it also proved possible to manage exports on a cooperative basis.

The farmers also organized politically, both at local level – where partial self-government was introduced in 1841 – and through the political party Bondevennerne ('friends of the farmers', later Venstre or 'Left'), which embraced various ideological fractions of the agrarian petty bourgeoisie. This was an anti-hierarchical political formation in which local branches, functioning as election committees, enjoyed extensive autonomy and the parliamentary party was relatively independent in its actual formulation of policies.[4]

The farmers' struggle for an independent class culture originated in a widespread religious revival movement directed against the rationalism of the state church and its clergy-dominated structures. This lay movement, which crossed class barriers between farmers and agricultural workers, served a dual purpose. It both provided schooling in capitalist norms, and built up a grassroots organization that fostered a combination of individual responsibility and collective solidarity – which, in a different context, could become a mainspring of political struggle. Institutionally the religious movement stayed within the framework of the 'people's church', which had been established in accordance with the amendment to the constitution in 1849 as a replacement for the absolutist state church. The major effect of this cultural class consciousness was on the educational structure of the country. The farmer class built up an alternative to the state system, introducing free schools and people's high schools for young men and women from its ranks. Between 1860 and the First World War a very large percentage attended these schools, which constructed a remarkable socio-cultural identity for the farmers by reviving the teaching of religion and Danish history combined with various practical subjects.

At all levels of society, then, the Danish farmers made a massive effort to disprove Marx's view that peasants were incapable of establishing themselves as an independent, self-conscious and politically dynamic class. Through its ideology and practice, the class formed a model of liberal democracy which had consequences stretching well into the twentieth century – one which exercised a deep influence on the political outlook and practice of the working class itself. As early as the 1880s, an alliance was formed between the Democratic Liberals and the Social Democratic Party in which the farmers played the dominant role. The function of the pact for them was to muster the votes of workers to break the bourgeois and petty-bourgeois monopoly of power in the towns. Success followed rapidly. For the working class, the result was an early integration into bourgeois democracy and a deeply rooted view that the transformation of society could be achieved by no other means.

It is a significant element of the Danish democratic tradition that the state itself financially supported the alternative cultural practices of the farmer class through the provision of education grants and payment of religious ministers directly elected by their local congregation. Throughout the twentieth century, even in critical periods of class conflict, religious, educational and political organizations – many of them left-wing – have continued to have most of their expenses covered by the state, without being subject to any kind of ideological control. It scarcely needs to be said that the liberality of the state has often been dictated, not by love for the movements in question, but by a desire to integrate or domesticate them.

The breakthrough of capitalism into an agrarian social formation, in which there was no large or dynamic industrial sector, had two consequences. First, a strong industrial bourgeoisie never developed. Until the later decades of the nineteenth century manufacturers remained a small fraction within the Danish bourgeoisie as a whole – inferior in number to the agrarian, commercial and financial fractions. It was not until the First World War that certain independent politico-economic objectives were formulated by industrialists. Second, the nucleus of the emergent working class – if the agricultural workers mentioned above are disregarded – consisted not of industrial workers but of post-feudal craftsmen. The industrial structure was dominated by small units in trade as well as in industry. Apart from a few bigger enterprises (shipyards, engineering works, textile mills and tobacco factories) employing over a hundred workers, the typical size of the Danish work-force was between five and twenty. Consequently, in liberal capitalist conditions before the First World War, powerful paternalist features persisted in the close relations between owners and workers.

The formative period of the working class was characterized by large-scale migration of agrarian workers and rural craftsmen to the towns, particularly Copenhagen. In 1901 more than half of the workers in the capital had been born in the country – to this day, large sections of the working class have direct family ties to the agrarian strata. Coming from the land, these workers had naturally often been under the cultural and political sway of the farmers. One of the aims of the SDP and the trade-union movement thus became to transform elements of a petty-bourgeois outlook into a working-class consciousness, which would transcend the individualist, property-centred strands of agrarian ideology, and yet preserve its democratic potential to strengthen the reformist position of the party.

Within a few decades from the beginning of the 1870s, the labour movement proved able to organize the majority of skilled workers, a large number of the unskilled, and a significant proportion of women workers. During the 1880s and 1890s a national union network took shape in all trades. This organizational drive was closely linked to an intensive class struggle that reached its climax in the great 1899 lock-out – one of the longest and most comprehensive labour disputes in the history of the Second International. The agreement which ended the dispute – 'the September accord of 1899' – laid the foundations for the dialectic of class conflict and class cooperation that has persisted in Denmark to the present day. A special judicial system was established to regulate the relationships between employer and employees, trade unions and employers' associations. The new courts, composed of appointees of the organizations in question plus a 'neutral' presiding judge, had their own rules of procedure and sanctions. The patterns they sought to enforce included an obligation to maintain industrial peace during an agreed period (usually two years) and a responsibility of the main organizations for the actions of leaders or members of sub-organizations. The early emergence of this legal system, with its semi-official character and its extensive range, was a quite exceptional development in a comparative perspective. It laid the basis for centralized bureaucratic organizations of labour and of capital, while at the same time facilitating smooth cooperation between them, and between the state and class associations. The trend it set has grown steadily throughout the twentieth century.

Once the principle of cabinet responsibility to the lower house was finally achieved in 1901, the Democratic Liberals became the natural party of government and created an unambiguously anti-socialist image for themselves. Breaking their earlier alliance with the SDP, they now increasingly acted as representatives of large freeholders, and of sections of financial and commercial capital, entrenched in the conservative Landstinget or upper house. During the same period the SDP developed its own strategy for re-organizing society into a socialist democracy by means of gradual reforms. Aware that the working class was not yet strong enough to pursue a fully independent policy, the SDP leaders looked for cooperation with other classes and strata, and found an ally in the Radical Liberals, who had split off from the Democratic Liberals in 1905. The social basis of this party ranged from smallholders to a progressive liberal intelligentsia, particularly school-teachers, in both town and country. Social reform, anti-militarism and cultural liberalism were the principal components of its platform.

The alliance between the Radical Liberals and the SDP became the pivot of Danish politics until the middle of the 1960s. From 1929 to

1966 they were the natural parties of government – only to be interrupted by the Second World War and two short periods of Liberal–Conservative rule: 1945–47 and 1950–53. The Danish party system was effectively completed by the formation of the Conservative People's Party in 1915, representing traditional landowners, the industrial bourgeoisie, sections of the urban petty bourgeoisie, and conservative intellectuals. From the time of the First World War onwards, the SDP was always the largest party: its electoral support reached a peak of 46 per cent in 1935. Unlike its Swedish counterpart, however, it has never enjoyed an absolute majority. The relative strength of the other parties has varied, although the fluctuations between them have been limited. In local politics, always of major importance in Denmark, the Democratic Liberals usually predominated in rural constituencies while the SDP's strongholds were in the towns. Throughout this period – 1905 to 1966 – the class and party structures were largely in harmony with each other. The petty bourgeoisie was represented in all parties, and functioned as a catalyst for the kind of class cooperation which lay at the root of almost all political and social reform. In 1915 the constitution was amended to give women the franchise and modify the first-past-the-post system by a number of supplementary seats to assure proportionate representation from all parties. The upper house was preserved, in spite of opposition from the SDP, until a root-and-branch reform introduced a unicameral system in 1953. Today the Folketing has 175 Danish members, plus two from Greenland and two from the Faroe Islands. The combination of proportional representation and a low electoral threshold (2 per cent for entry into parliament) has been decisive for shaping the political system.

As in most other European countries, the last phase of the First World War set the scene for deepening social antagonisms and open confrontation between the major classes, and indeed within the working class itself. But although sizeable revolutionary-syndicalist currents appeared, social-democratic reformism maintained its grip on the Danish working class. When various revolutionary tendencies combined in the Danish Communist Party in 1919–20, they were unable to win the kind of support achieved by their Norwegian counterparts. The DCP only secured parliamentary representation for the first time in 1932. The political struggles of the twenties were dominated by a bourgeois and petty-bourgeois offensive against the working class. A brief SDP minority government (1924–26) was unable to accomplish anything in its term of office.[5]

In 1929 a majority government was formed by the SDP and the Radical Liberals, which ruled unchallenged until the German occupation in April 1940. The policy responses of this coalition to the recession were supported by the Democratic Liberals. The rationale of this broad alliance between farmers and workers was a common wish to secure the position of Danish agricultural produce in the world market and to establish a modest security of existence for the working class. The outcome was reflationary public support for the crisis-ridden agricultural sector, extension of social reform legislation, and moderate attempts to boost industry and trade. In the eyes of the SDP, this experience was a departure from its traditional goals, representing a 'people's policy' crossing class lines – an attempt to balance social interests in which active state power was to be the driving force. A high price would be demanded of the working class, which of course increased during the Second World War, when an all-party coalition (excluding only the DCP) ran the administration under German occupation. Through most of the thirties strikes were more or less illegal, as the SDP and its unions kept the class in a tight grip which left little scope for opposition from the left.

Danish Social Democracy thus developed a dual pattern. On the one hand, there was a steady reform orientation, and concern for the material welfare of the working class; on the other, the exercise of a strict discipline over the class, and repression of left-wing critics or revolutionary currents. Crucial to this duality has been a high level of membership of the work-force in centralized industrial unions, together with the system of industrial courts, which was further tightened during the thirties.

The social structure of Denmark was such that some form of class cooperation was, in fact, necessary to achieve welfare reforms. For no classes or fractions were powerful enough to secure their interests on their own. In Sweden a decades-long alliance between the working class and a dynamic industrial bourgeoisie laid the foundation for the modern welfare state. In Denmark, however, where such a bourgeois layer hardly existed, the alliance of the SDP with an agrarian petty bourgeoisie set narrower limits to social-democratic strategy. After the Second World War the party attempted to introduce dynamic trade-cycle and industrial policies, based on trade-union acceptance of the need for economic rationalization. Yet it was not possible to implement this programme until the late 1950s. At the same time, challenges to official moderation rarely emerged from radical sections of the working class. Immediately after the Second World War, the DCP registered a significant increase in strength. But this was readily contained with the onset of the Cold War, as a long neutralist tradition was abandoned for integration into NATO, in an atmosphere of general anti-communism.

In 1957–58, however, in the wake of the Twentieth Congress of the

CPSU and the Hungarian revolt, the DCP itself split from top to bottom. The majority formed a new Socialist People's Party under the former chairman of the DCP, Aksel Larsen. In some ways its outlook anticipated that of Eurocommunism. But it was in favour of anti-militarism and neutralism, and owed much of its electoral success – 9 per cent of the ballot in 1960 – to its close links with the Campaign for Nuclear Disarmament and other anti-imperialist movements in Denmark. The party sought to bring pressure to bear on the SDP to break from its collaborationist mould and pursue policies that could make Denmark a socialist democracy. In 1966 the SPP polled 11 per cent of the vote, and the for the next twenty years political forces to the left of Social Democracy maintained a comparable level of parliamentary strength.[6]

Classes and Parties

The emergence of the Socialist People's Party was the first indicator of the break-up of the traditional Danish party structure. It coincided with the onset of fundamental changes in Denmark's economy and class composition. Traditionally Denmark has of necessity been among the most open economies in the world, a huge portion of its GNP being traded in the international exchange of goods and services with the leading capitalist countries. In spite of close integration with the world market, however, it was not until 1958 that the Danish economy began to enjoy the fruits of the postwar Atlantic boom.

But the arrival of the boom, coinciding with the reflationary course of an SDP-headed three-party government, transformed the balance between agriculture and industry in Denmark. As early as 1960 industrial exports exceeded agricultural, and by 1970, nearly 70 per cent of the one-third of GNP that was exported came from manufactures (compared with 27 per cent in 1950), as against about 25 per cent from the agricultural sector. The export drive focused on standardized foodstuffs and enclave manufactures, ships and subcontracts for Swedish and other international corporations. In this phase, the level of technology was high in both agriculture and manufacturing industry. Investment was promoted by tax reliefs and direct grants; regional development policies scattered industry to virtually all parts of the country. Both newer sectors (electronics and chemicals) and older mass-production lines (textiles and furniture) tended to go where labour was cheap and abundant. Small and medium-sized industrial units still predominated, with only a few really large enterprises. The result has been a very heterogeneous capital structure, with a highly differentiated articulation of business interests.

National class structure and economic geography thus underwent drastic changes over the next twenty-five years. Between 1960 and 1980 the aggregate labour force increased by about a third, and approximately three-quarters of the growth occurred in local and national public-sector employment, mostly located in towns. Today, one out of every three Danish workers is employed by the state. This is naturally a shift of major political significance. Behind the crude statistics lie broader changes within and between classes.[7] The most conspicuous of these has been the massive reduction in the agricultural share of the labour force. The class of rural workers has been totally eliminated, and the number of independent farmers and smallholders has dwindled to the point where those working on the land comprise no more than 4 per cent of the employed population. Farming remains, of course, an important sector of the Danish economy – mechanization has ensured no substantial fall in the volume or value of agricultural output. Danish farming families are still the hardest-working section of the population, clinging to the ideal of freehold ownership, although hard pressed by rising mortgage repayments incurred when property values increased tremendously after Danish entry into the EC. Young families find themselves in an almost inescapable squeeze between hard labour and creditors.

The fall in the size of the agrarian labour force and in the number of petty-bourgeois units of production has been accompanied by major changes in manufacturing. Whereas Copenhagen and a few provincial cities used to concentrate nearly all output, today there is a 'multicentred industrial structure' with many plants in small or medium-sized towns of Jutland and Zealand – or out in the countryside. In some areas, wholly new industrial centres have grown up, based on a combination of advanced technology and cheap, unskilled labour. Here former agricultural workers and smallholders, and a high proportion of women, are the typical components of the labour force. Sometimes, farms will be maintained – the husband working in a plant, the wife running the farm, with the help of an external machine pool and the husband's weekend labour.

On the other hand, former key industries based on skilled labour have declined – for example shipyards, traditionally a vanguard of class struggle. While middle strata poured into the big cities, and new industrial workers emerged in outlying regions, the traditional core proletariat moved to new detached houses or concrete blocks of flats on the outskirts of the major towns. This extensive shift led to an explosive development within the building and construction sector, where traditional petty-bourgeois craftsmen had difficulty in coping with competition from industrial firms increasingly based upon unskilled labour.

In almost all sectors of the Danish economy, productivity has been high.[8] Ever since the 1950s trade unions and employers have cooperated in managerial rationalization and technological innovation, with productivity-linked wage systems. During the boom, workers readily accepted these, since a technically increased rate of exploitation was accompanied by the almost total elimination of unemployment, a general increase in material well-being, and an extension of the public sector in social reproduction. In keeping with the SDP strategy of welfare through growth, a vast edifice of public provision met capitalist needs for a robust and well-educated labour force, while the trade unions and courts ensured orderly discipline in the workplace. The Danish trade-union movement, the fulcrum of this system, is perhaps the most centralized in the Western world (its only rival is the Norwegian). Its hold is reinforced by a work ethic that still bears traces of its origin in agrarian society – a habit of hard and steady effort, cautious towards any disruption,[9] that has been reproduced by the latest recruits to industry. A large number of women work for low pay in unorganized sweatshops, or on a part-time basis in shops and offices. Former agricultural labourers or smallholders perform repetitive, fragmented labour without any collective influence over the work-process. These new workers tend to be sceptical about industrial struggle, and get on badly with trade-union hierarchies. They respond more easily to the classical liberal vision of the autonomy of the individual and of the common interests between labour and capital.

With the world recession of the 1970s, the re-emergence of unemployment – which would have been much higher without the expansion of the public sector – acted as a further discipline on the working class. Unemployment benefit is relatively high in Denmark, being set in principle at 90 per cent of former pay. However, a maximum limit ensures that better-paid workers and middle strata receive only about 60 per cent of their previous earnings. The drawing of benefits is subject to strict control and stiff incentives to find low-paid employment; while in Liberal–Conservative propaganda the jobless are exposed to a social stigma that fits with the prevailing work ethic. The most severely affected group, as in many other Western countries, has been young people. In the past fifteen years or so, a post-school stratum has been created who have never had the chance of a job, developing into a sub-proletariat whose political identity falls outside the norms of the labour movement.

The result of these changes has been a drastic differentiation of attitudes and ideas among the popular classes. Conflicts have centred on the roles of the public sector and of the trade unions. The first clashes, which occurred in the middle of the 1960s, took the form of a cultural battle over public subsidy of the arts. A storm of protests and petitions against the funding of modern art descended on parliament from the newly industrialized regions, particularly Jutland. The signatories, ranging from recently proletarianized workers to residual petty bourgeois and new entrepreneurs, refused to have their taxes spent on paintings or sculptures they did not understand and which – they declared – scorned their arduous labour and cultural values. There was a deep feeling that the state was a hostile alliance between the SDP and a new intellectual elite which, far from catering to the interests of ordinary people, ground them down.[10]

These tensions were accentuated by the emergence of a new left in the late sixties. The events of 1968 exhibited much the same pattern in Denmark as they did in Germany and France. Ferment had been prepared by anti-imperialist actions in earlier years, and the nucleus of the 'revolt' came from a student population that had grown precipitously during the 1960s. However, the destruction of traditional norms and assumptions had consequences stretching far beyond university student circles. The most important result was an extensive and open politicization of almost all spheres of public and private life – a development which has characterized the country ever since. In this process the women's movement was undoubtedly the leading force. The most significant short-term effect of the upheaval was a complete reorganization of university government, giving large sections of students, all lecturers, and eventually non-academic staff decision-making rights that made this statute one of the most democratic in the world.[11] In the longer run processes of democratization spread beyond the campus, as grassroots movements demanded a say in the everyday affairs of many spheres.

Within the party system, the impact of the new left came in a split within the SPP, and the foundation of a new party: the Left Socialists. For several years this brought together almost all left radicals – from hippies to Marxist-Leninists – within a single organizational framework. The party always had a rather limited base in the working class, but it did play a role in the numerous wildcat disputes of 1969–70, leaving its stamp on their form and content. This wave of strikes revealed the tensions that had developed since the 1950s in the system of cooperation between the state, employers and trade-union leaderships. The number of stoppages increased five-fold in the second half of the 1960s, many of them in areas where there was no tradition of industrial struggle and where women formed a high proportion of the workforce. Usually the strikers found themselves under triple pressure from the employers, the state and the unions, and so had to build independent action committees and fund-raising machinery. Attempts were also made to develop a national alternative to the trade-union bureaucracies.[12]

The unrest showed that the hegemony of the SDP within the labour movement had weakened. The extent of the decline, however, only became clear when the party leadership under its long-standing premier, Jens Otto Krag, took the decision to negotiate Danish entry into the EC, and submitted the terms it had secured to a national referendum in 1972. The result was the most explosive political debate in Denmark since the Second World War. All classes and strata divided, but none more dramatically than labour. The working class broke in two, as half of the SDP's electorate rejected entry – many of its own cadres rebelling against it.

A year later, general elections saw an earthquake in the traditional party system. Since the war, the four so-called 'old parties' – Social Democrats, Radical Liberals, Democratic Liberals and Conservatives – had traditionally polled between 80 and 90 per cent of the vote, and the SDP between 35 and 42 per cent; four to six parties had been represented in the lower house. In 1973, the share of the vote won by the old parties collapsed to 58 per cent. The SDP lost nearly a third of its vote and ended with a mere 25 per cent. The Conservative People's Party saw its support drop from 16 to 9 per cent; while the Democratic Liberals suffered a less punishing decline from 15 to 12 per cent. The losses did not benefit the left. Although the Communists won 3 per cent of the electorate and regained parliamentary representation, the Socialist People's Party lost a comparable number of voters. The victors were two parties representing new versions of the right: the Centre Democrats (7 per cent) and the Progress Party (16 per cent). A small Christian People's Party, and a Justice Party influenced by the teachings of Henry George, also gained representation. There were now ten parties in the Folketing.[13]

In retrospect, the Danish elections of 1973 – the year of the first oil shock, when the world economy plunged into its long downswing – can be seen as the first harbinger of the tide of reaction that swept Western politics in the eighties. The two parties that upset the status quo in Denmark pioneered the themes that became the standard agenda of the new right a decade later. The Centre Democrats, under their charismatic leader Erhard Jacobsen – a right-wing fugitive from the SDP – took up cudgels for owner-occupied housing and individual forms of transport, a stronger police and tougher line against strikes.

But the keynote of this party's campaign was cultural: a ferocious attack on the 'politicization' of the educational system – from kindergartens to universities – and denunciation of left 'infiltration' in the mass media. The core of its electoral support were petty-bourgeois and middle-strata voters, warming to the party's crusade on housing, education and culture.

The Progress Party was a more flamboyant affair. Its founder and leader, Mogens Glistrup, built up a successful lawyer's practice in the 1960s specializing in the formation of limited companies for the sole purpose of avoiding income tax. He became famous during a short appearance on television, when he boasted of paying no tax on his earnings of more than a million kroner a year. Income tax, he proclaimed, was both damaging to the national economy and unjust even to the workers – tax avoidance was the modern equivalent to resistance in the Second World War. Soon afterwards, Glistrup formed the Progress Party, which in 1973 became the second-largest force in the Folketing. The party's call to arms was a rabidly populist onslaught on the whole edifice of the social-democratic state – represented as a murrain of public bureaucracy, petty officials, mandarins and highly paid university graduates, issuing an endless flow of circulars, directives and laws in a language that no ordinary person could understand, to a tax-burdened citizenry. Glistrup unleashed an all-out attack on the social welfare system, as a trough for social workers and their idle dependents; on avant-garde artists who could not earn a honest day's living on the market; on indoctrination in the schools that undermined the values of the family and of work. What the country needed was a a massive reduction in the public sector, and dispatch of its employees into productive labour. Taxes could then be brought down, and real incomes would rise, as incentives to work and save came into play again – regenerating the national economy after decades of Social Democratic and, to a certain extent, Liberal–Conservative misrule. The ingredients of this ideological concoction were quite new to Denmark, and many of them in the West more generally. Here was the beginning of the anti-tax revolt that led to the insurgency of Proposition 13 and the victories of Thatcher and Reagan.

The affinities between the Centre Democrats and the Progress Party were clear enough. They were both parties of law and order, and champions of private property. Their cultural and educational policies were all but identical. Both revolved around their leaders, each of whom displayed gifts of demagogic communication, especially on television, unrivalled in Danish political life – Glistrup, a florid speaker, continually coining new phrases which quickly passed into common usage. However, unlike the Progress Party, the Centre Democrats were not hostile towards the state as such – in fact, they advocated tight public control of the schools and the media. (Jacobsen's most important base was a society called 'Active Listeners and Viewers' that monitored 'reds' on radio and television.)

Glistrup's more libertarian version of reaction had a wider popular appeal. The Progress Party brought together a heterogeneous bloc of small shopkeepers, wholesalers, farmers, fishermen, estate agents, lorry and cab owners, minor industrialists, some privately employed salaried workers, and – importantly – a section of the working class. It is not difficult to understand why many petty bourgeois should have been attracted to it. This was a stratum that had been squeezed between capitalist monopolistic trends in production and distribution (nearly a quarter of small businessmen had been eliminated between 1960 and 1972),[14] and increasing pressures from the state for new services, VAT returns, social welfare payments. In its self-image, both husband and wife work all day long, then in the evening have to do villein service to the national or local authorities. Many of them were completely alienated from the welfare state. Ironically, the immediate background of the movement was a Liberal–Conservative government which, fearing Social Democratic accusations that it wanted to dismantle the welfare state, embarked on a major expansion of the public sector – in just three years (1968–71) raising the proportion of taxes from 35 to 43 per cent of GNP.

But why did workers join or support a party bent on demolishing virtually every gain made by the labour movement since the War? Well over a fifth of Glistrup's electoral support was proletarian, about 10 per cent of all workers voting for the Progress Party in 1973, when it became the second biggest working-class party in the country. Most of its electors were young, unskilled and poorly paid, often working alongside their bosses in small enterprises. Mainly first generation, taking a pride in 'making their own way', they had generally voted earlier for the Liberal or Conservative parties. But Social Democratic legacies – the size and unevenness of the tax burden on Danish workers, and the individualizing effect of wage systems resting on internal competition – affected their outlook too.

The other side of the new fragmentation of the political scene in the 1970s was the growth of parties appealing to the middle strata employed in the public sector, among them the SPP and a regenerated DCP on the left. This is now the most numerous class of Danish society, not only staffing central and local bureaucracies and educational institutions, but also positions in semi-state financial agencies such as banks, credit houses and insurance companies. Public-sector employment expanded faster in Denmark in this period than in any other country, attaining dimensions equalled only perhaps in Sweden.[15]

This new stratum is typically recruited from almost all traditional classes: bourgeoisie, petty bourgeoisie and working class. Most of its members have lost their class roots. In a sense they have no history: they cannot identify with the cultural or political struggles fought by their ancestors or currently fought between other classes. They are highly differentiated internally, in a spectrum running from permanent undersecretaries, judges, policemen or professors to the lowest-grade clerical workers and attendants in day nurseries and kindergartens. Their pay, working conditions and social status vary tremendously. But they have one thing in common: they are dependent on the public sector and have an interest in its preservation and expansion.

Politically, they therefore tend to support those parties which make defence or extension of the public sector a principal objective. Historically, the SDP was the natural bastion of this layer, since it always considered the state as the pivot of its political strategy. Social redistribution, educational equality, economic growth, and counter-cyclical steering were all tasks for the state – which at the same time served as an instrument of social control, to discipline the labour force and population at large.

In theory these middle strata can be seen as a contingent within the army of wage-earners. In practice, however, the growth of groups performing what classical political economy regarded as unproductive labour, absorbing surplus value, has predictably led to tensions with the traditional surplus-producing sectors of the working class (not to speak of the bourgeoisie). Many workers in Denmark have tended to view public-sector employees as parasites living on taxes extracted from hard-working producers in industry, farming, fishing, retailing, and so on – without seeing the extent to which the growth of this kind of state is a consequence of capitalist development, which often subjects its employees to low pay and hard work too. The result has been that labour militancy by these groups – often considerable and directed at other objects than pay – is readily perceived as the greed of a pampered group trying to extort still more cash from producers. A further source of misunderstanding lies in the cultural norms of this stratum, which tend to politicize the private sphere more comprehensively than the traditional labour movement in Denmark ever did. In this sense too, it poses a challenge to older working-class or petty-bourgeois values, and the way these were reflected in the SDP.

The tremendous shock of the 1973 elections was a warning signal. Its immediate upshot, however, was not to displace the centre of gravity of the parliamentary system to the right, so much as to introduce a new volatility into Danish politics. The impetus of the late sixties is by no means yet exhausted on the left. The three socialist parties – SPP, DCP and Left Socialists – on the outside flank of Social Democracy continued to attract some 10–15 per cent of the electorate. Their success – like that of the new forces of the right – reflected the growing crisis of the postwar model of Danish development. But it also expressed the very advanced form that capitalist democracy has taken in Denmark. Liberal traditions are deeply rooted in all social classes, in a small nation of no more than five million people. Equal access to radio and TV is guaranteed to all parties seeking parliamentary representation – even those without MPs can gain it, on mustering a petition of about 20,000 voters, which is not difficult. The fact that small parties get as much screen-time as the major ones enables outsiders to present ideological platforms which, under standard Western conditions, would never reach the whole nation. In these conditions, leaders or candidates of hitherto marginal groups can become famous public figures quite quickly. The space this system opens up for initiatives from below allowed anti-capitalist pressures from parties or movements of the outside left to have a real influence on political debate. One sign of their impact across the spectrum is the absence of a Green Party in Denmark, which might have been thought ideal ground for one.

When the Venstre-led government of 1973 fell after two ineffectual years of office, the SDP returned to power on the crest of the greatest upsurge of electoral support for the combined left since 1945. Since the late sixties, it had tried to pursue a post-Keynesian programme designed as a substitute for its traditional welfare-growth policies. This envisaged a combination of incomes policy, 'economic democracy' and extension of the public sector. Vulnerable to criticisms from both right and left that its effect would be to increase bureaucratic hypertrophy and confer exorbitant power on the huge trade-union apparatuses, this package failed to arouse much enthusiasm in the working class and was never implemented. The resistance of the centre parties saw to this. The prime minister for most of the 1970s was Anker Jørgenson, the leader of the unskilled workers' union who had become chairman of the SDP in 1972. His solid working-class background and evident moral integrity gave him a national popularity that crossed all social barriers. But the postwar welfare tradition he personified was now in increasing crisis, as inflation took off, foreign debt escalated, and budgetary deficts widened. The room for Social Democratic manoeuvre had greatly narrowed. Since the First World War, no party has ever had an absolute parliamentary majority in Denmark – all governments have been coalitions or minority cabinets. With the multiplication of parties in the 1970s, parliamentary arithmetic became finer than ever. For most of the time Jørgensen headed a minority government, but there were constant pressures for an SDP–Venstre coalition. These stemmed in part from the situation in municipal government, a traditional power base and training ground in Danish politics, where the two parties enjoyed a virtual monopoly of office, in contrast with the position at national level. The Democratic Liberals – who then rarely polled more than 10 per cent in parliamentary elections – provided nearly half the country's mayors, a tribute to the resilience of century-old agrarian traditions in the localities. The Social Democrats controlled another third of the town halls. This division of power gave rise for long periods to a tacit understanding that important political, social or cultural reforms had to command the support of both parties. As the economic situation worsened in the late seventies, an SDP–Venstre coalition was formed in 1978 to find a stable political situation to the crisis of the country's finances. It was short-lived. The remedies of the partners for the recession were still too divergent, and the trade unions opposed the government so strongly that the risk of a split between party and unions that would have broken the backbone of Danish Social Democracy appeared imminent. The coalition, however, disintegrated in 1979. For a couple of years, the SDP then tried to manage the crisis more or less on its own. By now its resistance to neo-liberal solutions had greatly weakened, and it was the least advantaged groups in society that bore the brunt of its belt-tightening course. But this was still quite insufficient to lift the enormous burden of external debt or win the confidence of international financial markets. In 1982, this dispirited administration came to an end, without a general election. A Liberal-Conservative coalition headed by Poul Schlüter came in. The Danish political scene was about to be transformed.

The Decade of Reaction and its Aftermath

For the Conservative–Liberal alliance now reaped where the Progress Party had sowed. In the early seventies the breakthrough of a new Danish right had been spectacular, but too isolated from international trends and too identified with the exotic personality of Glistrup to set its stamp on government. But it prepared the ground for a lasting shift of attitudes in civil society, which could now finally find expression at the level of the state. By the time Schlüter came to power, the external environment was far more favourable. Thatcher and Reagan had set the dominant agenda in the Atlantic world. If few initially expected the new regime in Copenhagen to last long, least of all the SDP, Schlüter soon confounded predictions. Immediately after its installation in 1982 the Conservative–Liberal government announced a wage freeze and cuts in unemployment benefit, and launched a massive pro-gramme of deflation, deregulation and privatization. Confronted with this unvarnished offensive against wage-earners, Social Democracy did not know how to react. Incredulous that any other political force could really rule the country, the SDP adopted a waiting policy, in the belief that matters would soon to revert to normal.

The Danish working class and union movement was less passive. A wave of official and unofficial stoppages swept the country, and some of the biggest political demonstrations since the War protested against government intervention in traditionally free collective bargaining. Public employees and their unions, singled out for harsh treatment by the new administration, were at the forefront of the movement, which culminated in a general strike in 1985 aimed at toppling the govern-ment. The Schlüter regime, however, held firm. Its victory in this test of strength can be compared to Thatcher's defeat of the miners' strike in Britain. Unlike its counterpart in London, however, the government did not go over to a legislative counter-attack against the trade unions. After the crisis of spring 1985, labour militancy faded away as unemployment grew and disputes broke out among the unions themselves.

Once the public sector was tamed and capital given a freer hand, the government was able to claim a series of economic successes. Inflation was reduced to one of the lowest rates in Europe. The huge foreign trade deficit was eliminated. The Danish krone, pegged to the deutschmark, became one of the most stable currencies in the world. Modest, but steady, growth resumed. The cost of this neo-liberal achievement was high. Unemployment climbed remorselessly to some 12 per cent of the work-force – a level well above the EC average – without counting early retirement or other camouflages. Women have been the worst hit, but social cleavages have generally deepened, with the emergence of large groups of neo-paupers, especially among youth and single-parent families. Many of these drop out of the traditional welfare net, into a subculture where the miseries of unemployment are compounded by moral destitution – often drug abuse or alcoholism.

The welfare state itself was too deeply entrenched in Danish consensus to be dismantled by the Schlüter regime. Limited reductions of benefits were achieved, but more radical measures were blocked by the smaller centre parties on which the coalition depended. The Conservative–Liberal partnership never enjoyed an outright majority in the Folketing, always depending on support from other forces. Schlüter displayed considerable tactical skills in holding his series of anti-socialist governments together. At their core was a division of labour between the Conservatives and Liberals, whose differing outlooks in many ways resembled the two wings of Tory party under Thatcher. The Conservatives stood for a traditional right-wing pragmatism that had long been the mark of the party in Denmark. Schlüter's own best-known dictum was: 'Ideology is rubbish'. The Venstre, on the other hand, became the champion of a doctrinaire neo-liberalism of international stamp. The one-time party of the farmers' democratic movement and cultural pluralism was captured by aggressive ultra-capitalistic ideologues headed by the outspoken foreign minister Uffe Ellemann-Jensen. The Venstre now led an unprecedented combination of independent farmers, industrial capital, and big finance, mustering a new generation of economists and columnists dedicated to the struggle against Keynesianism.

If the Liberals took the lead in attacking the welfare state – especially the high rate of unemployment benefits and constantly real or imagined abuses of them – and setting an ideological agenda in which individualism, inequality and acquisitive drive became much more widely legitimate, it was the Conservatives who garnered the major electoral fruits of the regime, receiving an inrush of former Glistrup supporters and picking up voters from the other coalition parties.

The confident anti-socialist offensive of the Schlüter regime left the SDP in disarray, and successfully portrayed it as the real conservative force in Danish politics, clinging to outdated ideas of solidarity and statism. Accused of responsibility for all the ills of the country, Social Democracy was put on the ideological defensive, and showed itself at a loss for new directions. Much of the neo-liberal course it silently accepted, as dictated by Denmark's vulnerable position in the global economy. The trade unions kept their membership largely intact, and could still claim perhaps the highest rate of blue- and white-collar unionization in the world. But after the defeat of 1985, the leadership was very reluctant to exercise its potential power, partly because it realized that the size of its organizations was not matched by any militancy, let alone socialism. Its inaction also reflected the absence of any political sense of direction coming from the SDP.

Anker Jørgensen remained leader of the party for five years after his resignation as prime minister in 1982. But for all the respect he enjoyed, he was too anchored in the past to be able to initiate a rethinking of social-democratic strategy in the drastically altered conditions of the eighties. In 1987 the party elected Svend Auken to succeed him. The choice proved a controversial one. From a well-known academic family, the 44-year-old Auken had himself held a university position, and brought a quite new style to Danish Social Democracy. Possessed of a sharp analytical intelligence, and outstanding skill as a political debater, his caustic wit made him many enemies among the other parties and, indeed, not a few among his own members. Outside the SPD, he was soon intensely unpopular, and from about 1990 it became clear that no other group would accept him as a future prime minister, except perhaps the Socialist People's Party. But for all his shortcomings, Auken was a man of socialist conviction and under his leadership the SDP began to reconsider its position. The one area of movement under Jørgensen had been foreign policy, where the Social Democrats made cautious approaches to the peace movement – galvanized in Denmark, as elsewhere, by the new arms race between NATO and the Warsaw Pact of the eighties. Auken launched a more general programmatic debate, to equip the SDP to confront the problems of the nineties. In the elections of 1990, he led the party to a major recovery at the polls – bringing its vote back to 37 per cent.

Soon afterwards, the neo-liberal economic revival lost its shine, as the speculative wave unleashed by financial deregulation broke, leaving a swathe of insolvencies in the real-estate, banking and insurance sectors. The bursting of the bubble undermined the credit of the Liberal–Conservative regime. An SDP-led coalition seemed possible once again. To secure its chances, the party for the first time in its history dethroned its chairman. In the spring of 1992, Auken was replaced by Poul Nyrop Rasmussen – an academic from a working-class background, with a reputation for problem-solving, a man of compromise rather than division. In the autumn, the party congress adopted its new programme. When discussion of it had started, there was high optimism that the breakdown of the Communist regimes in Eastern Europe would lead to a spread of social democracy in the region – what could be more natural, it was widely felt, than for the liberated peoples to opt for a democratic welfare state along Scandinavian lines, as a way out of their misery? It came as a painful surprise to realize that 'socialism' was so compromised in Eastern Europe that even moderate social-democratic solutions were out of the question, and that monetarism or nationalism were stepping in instead. The repercussions of this shock were visible in the document now accepted as the party's charter. The new programme embodies a complete acceptance of the market economy – 'humanized' by the social and political rights of the individual. The internal rationality of markets finds its complement in welfare rationality outside it. The document strives to achieve a balance between the individualism of the eighties and older ideas of community and solidarity, but it is noticeable that the word 'socialism' is entirely absent from it. The classical optimism of the labour movement has been replaced by a cool analysis of future options, which not include socialism in any meaning of the term.

A few months later, in January 1993, the Schlüter government collapsed in disgrace. The issue that brought it down was symptomatic of its record – immigration. Like other regimes of the European right in the eighties, it had played the xenophobic card, but in the liberal Danish context acted more surreptitiously than elsewhere. When the report of a Supreme Court judge made it clear that Schlüter's former justice minister, Erik Ninn Hansen, had sought to break the law in order to limit the number of (political) refugees from Sri Lanka, and that Schlüter himself had covered up the scandal, the government had to resign. Ninn Hansen will now be impeached by the Folketing, and Schlüter and several other prominent figures in the Conservative Party have lost all political influence. Three small centre parties switched sides, for an SDP-led coalition in which Poul Nyrup Rasmussen became prime minister.

The end of the decade-long dominance of the right came as Denmark, for the first time since the seventeenth century, found itself at the centre of the European political scene. The Treaty of Maastricht, negotiated by the Conservative–Liberal government, and requiring the consent of all its signatories to come into force, had been rejected by popular referendum in June 1992 – the Danish sword over European Union. Attitudes towards the EC had, in fact, for more than twenty years divided the whole nation in two almost equal halves. Only a very small minority of Danes are keen enthusiasts for the Community; about half of the electorate have been persuaded that it is a necessity without which the country cannot survive. But right from the first referendum on EC entry in 1972 most Danes have regarded it as a construction totally out of tune with Danish and Scandinavian political and cultural traditions. It is striking, however, how constantly the state of feeling in the working class has been misread by the SDP and the unions. In 1972 they recommended a 'yes', but a majority of their members voted 'no' and entry was only secured by massive affirmative votes from other social classes. In 1986 the SDP urged rejection of the Single Market, the trade unions were divided and the outcome was a resounding approval, supported by the working class. In 1992 all the major parties in Denmark, except for the SPP, called for ratification of the Maastricht Treaty. It went down to defeat when more than 60 per cent of the labour movement voted against it.

With the European diplomatic scene in turmoil, the Social Democrats and the Radical Liberals (by now a very small party) moved to reach an agreement with the most prominent force opposing the

Treaty, the Socialist People's Party – which was thought to hold the key to a solution of the national deadlock. The result was a so-called 'national compromise' which was then endorsed by the government. At the Edinburgh summit of the EC in December 1992, a unilateral Danish declaration was accepted that exempted Denmark from the final phase of Economic and Monetary Union, the common European currency, European defence policy, and rules for a European citizenship. A month later Schlüter and Ellemann-Jensen were out of office, and it fell to Rasmussen to organize a referendum on the revised terms.

Thus in May 1993 the Danes went to their fourth referendum about the EC. The outcome was a majority of 56 per cent for ratification. Considering that every party in the Folketing save one (the Progress Party) called for acceptance, the level of opposition was still remarkably high. On European issues, Danes do not follow party leaders. If the verdict had nevertheless altered, it was two factors that had made the difference. The first was the return of the Social Democrats to office. For many rank-and-file SDP voters, especially older people, to reject the Treaty this time seemed tantamount to a vote of no-confidence in the Rasmussen government, which they were not willing to risk so soon after the relief of the change. Even so, over 45 per cent of the party's electorate still voted against. If the number was not higher, this was also due to the SPP's recommendation of acceptance, which was vital for the overall result because it legitimized a yes vote in the eyes of many hesitant Social Democrats. Paradoxically, for the Socialist People's Party itself, the results of the referendum were a disaster. Its leadership totally miscalculated the attitudes of its voters, more than 80 per cent of whom rejected the revised terms. For more than twenty years the SPP had formed the core of parliamentary opposition to the Community. A few paragraphs issued by a summit in Edinburgh were not going to change the minds of the party's voters.

For many years the EC question has been the overarching problem in Danish politics and it will probably remain so in spite of the ratification of Maastricht. It is striking that Danes on the whole regard the issue as one which transcends party divisions, and the various referenda have till now had little effect upon the party system. The campaigns engage the nation enormously, divide families, trade unions, and almost all economic and cultural associations, but after the ballot most people return to their traditional parties. This time, however, the 'national compromise' has altered the parameters of Danish politics in one important respect. It has, for all practical purposes, eliminated any parliamentary opposition to the Social Democrats from the left. By its participation in the compromise the SPP disarmed itself politically. Repudiated by its voters, it has lost few members, but is no longer the independent force it was in the past. Denmark today has what are in reality two social-democratic parties, representing generally moderate and somewhat more radical tendencies which, in other countries, coexist within the same formation. The persistence of two separate parties in Denmark is now more an effect of the electoral system, and a question of style and history, than of essential political difference. Outside parliament, the left is no stronger. Most of the small Marxist or leftist circles, once active, are languishing: new recruitment among young people is minimal. Some of these groups try to rally around independent socialist journals and a handful have joined forces in a small 'United Socialist Party' based on a red–green minimum platform. Such eddies are far from the mainstream of Danish politics. There, Social Democracy tries to rehabilitate a measure of social intervention, very cautiously, speaking more of unemployment than the outgoing regime, and offering a better welcome to refugees from the Balkans – but still without much vision of the future. In Denmark, both the old and the new left have vanished. It will be a formidable task to create another one.

Notes

1. *Spokesman Review*, August 1982, and *Politken*, 19 August 1982. The analysis was conducted by Ricard Estes at Pennsylvania State University.

2. Svend Aage Hansen, *Early Industrialization in Denmark*, Copenhagen 1970, p. 11.

3. Hans-Norbert Lahme, *Sozialdemokratie und Landarbeiter in Dänemark: 1870–1900*, Odense 1983; and Henning Grelle, *Socialdemokratiet i det danske landbrugssamfund: 1871–1903*, Copenhagen 1978.

4. The relationship between agrarian structure and politics is discussed in Oyvind Osterud, *Agrarian Structure and Peasant Politics in Scandinavia*, Oslo 1978.

5. W.M. Lafferty, *Economic Development and the Response of Labour in Scandinavia*, Oslo 1971, discusses the different developments of the Scandinavian social democracies.

6. Ursula Schmiederer, *Die Sozialistische Volkspartei Dänemarks – eine Partei der neuen Linken*, Frankfurt 1969.

7. Data about changes in class structure are taken from *Lavindkomstkommissionens Betaenkning 1982* (report of the Low Income Commission), pp. 70, 71 and 336, and Jorgen Goul Andersen, *Mellemlagene i Danmark*, Arhus 1979, pp. 98ff.

8. Hans Erik Avlund Frandsen, *Klassekamp og klassesamarbejde: Danmark 1840–1978*, Copenhagen 1980, pp. 173 ff.

9. Throughout the 1960s there were virtually no serious industrial disputes: Henrik Morkenberg and Anders Rosdahl, eds, *Arbeydsloshedsundersogelserne 3*, Copenhagen 1982, pp. 288 ff. and Frandsen, op. cit., p. 425.

10. A. M. Kastrup and I. Laerkesen, *Rindalismen. En studi i kulturmonstre, social forandring og kultursammenstod*, Copenhagen 1979.

11. In 1992 the university statute was drastically revised by the Liberal–Conservative government, greatly limiting the influence of students.

12. Frandsen, pp. 316 ff.; and Karen Jespersen, 'Strejkebevaegelsen i Danmark: 1969–1970', *Socialistik Politik 5*, December 1976, pp. 3–41.

13. Gunnar Rasmussen, *Det smalborgerlige opror*, Copenhagen 1977; and Johannes Andersen, *Fremdskridtsbevaegelsen, arbejderklassen og venstreflojen*, Copenhagen 1977.
14. Frandsen, p. 345.
15. Goul Andersen, pp. 157 ff.

4

Germany: Stagnation of the Left

Stephen Padgett and William Paterson

Over the past decade, left politics in the Federal Republic of Germany –
the largest and most powerful state of the European Union – have
stagnated. The Social Democratic Party, after sixteen years in government (1966–82), has now been out of power for over a decade. From
1980 to 1990 its national vote fell from 42.9 per cent to 33.5 per cent;
and electoral decomposition has penetrated deep into its core constituency, the manual working class. Ideologically, the guiding principles of
its postwar programme, adopted at Bad Godesberg in 1959, are now
largely obsolete. But the SPD's attempt to 'redefine social democracy' in
the eighties has proved abortive, merely highlighting the social and
cultural divisions between old and new contingents within the party.
Fragmentation has led to loss of internal cohesion. Policy conflict,
exacerbated by the acute political tensions of national reunification and
its aftermath, pervades all levels of the party, including its once
compact leadership elite. The SPD of Lafontaine, Engholm and
Scharping often appears a shadow of its former self under Brandt,
Wehner and Schmidt.

The Social-Democratic Volkspartei

The achievement of that trio looks all the more remarkable in
retrospect. Fighting its way out the electoral ghetto in which Adenauer's regime had confined it in the first decade after the war, the SPD
became the role model of a progressive *Volkspartei*, based on a strong
alliance between manual workers and new middle strata. Its electoral
success reflected the clarity and coherence of its basic project. The
SPD's course in this period was set by the need to adapt to the
socio-economic and political landscape of the early years of the Federal

Republic. In West Germany, the decline of class politics noticeable elsewhere in the fifties was especially marked. For this was a society with a double 'ideological trauma', from the experience of the Third Reich on the one hand, and the installation of a repressive Communist regime in East Germany on the other. The result was a recoil from radical ideas that accentuated the effects of increasing affluence and social homogeneity which weakened class identities in most Western countries. The early postwar years, moreover, had witnessed an unprecedented influx of refugees from the East – some twelve million by 1947. A demographic upheaval on this scale inevitably disrupted social traditions and class ties, 'an important precondition for the development of catch-all parties in West Germany'.[1] Another central determinant of SPD strategy was the success of Adenauer's CDU and its Bavarian CSU partner in re-establishing the cross-class tradition of political Catholicism, from Wilhelmine and Weimar days, and extending it to a cross-confessional alliance with Protestant forces, which created an exceptionally powerful apparatus of electoral catchment, with roots in labour as well as capital. The Christian Union parties became the prototype of Otto Kirchheimer's description of the *Volkspartei*, in which class politics and overt ideology were de-emphasized.[2] The logic of this model was such that Christian Democrat electoral success would force opposition parties to emulate their style.

In the first years after the War the SPD, although it had long ceased to be a Marxist party of the working class, remained bound by the socialist traditions of the pre-1933 era. After 1952, however, the Social Democrats undertook a rapid and clear-cut reorientation – conceived explicitly as the transition from a 'workers' party' to a 'people's party'. The transformation had three dimensions: programmatic, organizational and electoral. The Bad Godesberg programme of 1959 explicitly disavowed the party's Marxist heritage, emphasizing instead an eclectic array of sources for democratic socialism in the Christian ethic, classical philosophy, and humanist tradition. It endorsed the liberal pluralism of the Federal Republic and its uncompromising Western orientation. Adapting to the success of the slogan of the social market, a formula of the bourgeois parties, the programme unconditionally embraced the axioms of arm's-length Keynesianism for the management of economic growth.

In organizational terms, the party streamlined and centralized its structure, narrowing the scope for internal democracy, in the interests of gearing its machinery for electoral mobilization. The residual elements of what had once been the culture of – in Lösche's term – a 'solidarity community'[3] were phased out, and recruitment deliberately broadened to the professional and white-collar strata of the *neue Mitte*.

Table 4.1 New SPD Party Members by Occupation 1958–82 (%)

Social Group	1958	1966	1972	1982
White-collar employees/civil				
servants	21.0	27.5	34.0	33.1
Manual workers	55.0	49.4	27.6	21.1
Housewives	11.2	9.0	9.0	13.7
Pensioners	5.4	4.1	3.7	9.2
Students	–	–	15.9	12.8

Sources: Susanne Miller, *Die SPD vor und nach Godesberg*, Bonn–Bad Godesberg 1974: Sozialdemokratische Partei Deutschlands, *Jahrbuch 1981–83*, Bonn 1984.

The social composition of the party began to change very rapidly (see Table 4.1).

This transformation, designed to widen the SPD's electoral appeal, had the intended result. The party's vote increased steadily in four successive elections after Bad Godesberg, rising from just under 32 per cent in 1957 to over 39 per cent in 1965 and nearly 46 per cent by 1972. This political growth was largely due to the party's ability to ride with the changing composition of the electorate, as the manual working class declined in size and the *neue Mitte* multiplied. While the SPD's proletarian constituency remained stable during this period, its relative weight in the Social Democratic electorate fell as the party increased its share of the burgeoning new middle straa of West German society, leading to a significant change in the class balance of SPD support. The *neue Mitte* was always ambivalent in its identifications: the party's most reliable support came from sectors of it that were both secular (free from clerical influence) and unionized – the most volatile sectors were secular but non-unionized, which were a source of SPD strength in the 1965–72 period.[4]

In late 1966, the Free Democrats – the junior partners in the Christian Democratic regime – walked out of Erhard's government, leaving the CDU–CSU without a majority in the Bundestag. Seizing the opportunity, the SPD leadership negotiated – over much initial opposition within the party – entry into a Grand Coalition in Bonn with its historic antagonist. Gaining credibility in office over the next three years, in which it controlled the ministries of economics and foreign affairs, the SPD switched alliances after the 1969 elections, forming a government with the FDP in which Brandt became Chancellor. An attempt by the CDU to overthrow it by a parliamentary coup in 1972 boomeranged, in an electoral backlash that for the first – and so far – only time in the history of the Federal Republic gave the SPD a higher total vote than the Union parties. For the next decade, the Social–Liberal coalition governed West Germany.

In the period of high Cold War, the SPD had always been at a political disadvantage in the area of foreign policy, since it could not hope to compete – however much it sometimes tried – with the CDU–CSU in militant anti-communism and pro-American alignment. The advent of a measure of détente in Europe created a more favourable climate for it. Brandt used the international opening with great skill, in three years of dynamic *Ostpolitik* that brought treaties with the USSR and Poland, settling postwar frontiers, and diplomatic relations with East Germany. The creative initiatives of this period gave the government prestige abroad and popularity at home, assuring the coalition a long run. But they absorbed the best energies of the SPD. Domestic reform, to which Brandt was personally committed, was put into a siding. After a few initial welfare measures, all significant proposals for change – social, fiscal, educational, or industrial – were blocked by the FDP, or threat of veto by the Union majority in the Bundesrat.

In 1973, the economic conjuncture worsened sharply, as the Atlantic world slid into recession. Stabilization now became the overriding priority of the government. Under Helmut Schmidt, who became Chancellor in 1974, the SPD-led regime concentrated on crisis-management. The growth of public expenditure was curbed, and monetary supply held tight. There was an occasional limited stimulus for employment – and electoral – purposes, but the general direction of policy was orthodox. The results were, in their own terms, quite successful. The strength of the West German economy withstood the downswing well. Export performance remained buoyant, and growth – though modest – was above the EC average. Schmidt's authority as a firm leader in a time of trouble, guiding a Germany that set an example to the rest of the world, was high throughout the seventies. The SPD projected the image of *Modell Deutschland* to voters, as the proof of its competence.

But with the second twist of recession in the early eighties, harsher choices had to be confronted. By now there was a large budgetary deficit; inflation was rising; unemployment was over a million, and growing. In the summer of 1981, the government decided to cut social spending and reduce taxes on business, under pressure from the FDP – emboldened by its increased poll in the 1980 elections, and now moving confidently to the right. Presenting the budget, Finance Minister Hans Matthöfer announced that the state could no longer underwrite full employment. Schmidt approved the package, but he was now isolated between rising discontent within his own party, and increasing hostility from his Liberal partners. When the FDP signalled it wanted more draconian measures, and was manoeuvring to switch alliances to the CDU, Schmidt dissolved the coalition. In October 1982, Helmut Kohl became Chancellor with FDP support. Six months later, the Christian–Liberal alliance won a comfortable majority at the polls, consummating the *Wende*.

The fall of the SPD from office was, of course, not an isolated German episode. It belonged to the general pattern of North European politics in the eighties, as a tide from the right swept away one social democracy after another. But in the Federal Republic, the predicament of the left now acquired a quite specific cast. The problem confronting the SPD in its search for a new direction was not just the need to recover ground lost to its traditional foe, the local version of conservatism, but to come to terms with a novel version of radicalism on its other flank. For during its years in power, the political landscape in Germany had changed. In opposition, it was to discover how much.

The New Left Challenge

The origins of the new force that erupted into national politics in the eighties lay in the course taken by the SPD itself, while in power. In the early sixties, the party had expelled its student association for criticism of the moderation of its official policies. The SDS, now an independent organization, became the nucleus of a widespread generational revolt against the established order of the Federal Republic by the late sixties, mobilizing large numbers of rebellious youth against the American war in Vietnam, and the authoritarian stamp of official culture and politics in West Germany. The collaboration of the two leading parties of the country in a Grand Coalition, one of whose principal pieces of legislation was an Emergency Powers Act (for which the CDU had demanded SPD support, as a condition of joint government), precipitated the emergence of an Extra-Parliamentary Opposition (APO). This movement, part of an international new left ferment, attracted sympathy in the rank and file of the SPD, and a following within the Young Socialists (Jusos).

Although the movement itself soon disintegrated, its impact on the SPD was not insignificant. The party was still growing in size, and influx of radical youth was altering its composition. Values advocated by the APO, above all direct political participation, took hold in the Jusos, whose activity at the grassroots of the SPD – the party's *Basis* – helped revitalize often torpid local structures. The SPD leadership under Brandt, wary of an electoral challenge to the party from the left, and demarcating itself from any extra-parliamentary mobilization as such, tried to integrate the new generation as far as it could. But a lively radical subculture, caustic or hostile to the party, now had an independent existence in the big cities.

In 1972, the Social–Liberal coalition passed legislation restricting the entry of leftists into public employment. This decree, by any standards an over-reaction, alienated new left milieux yet further. Anti-terrorist measures aroused protests against the erosion of civil rights. In the short run the SPD did not suffer from its repressive profile in these years. The mass student revolt of the late sixties passed away, and the tiny groups that went over to violence against the state were easily defeated. Inside the party itself, the Jusos failed to make any contact with the labour wing, falling into sectarian postures that weakened the organization and allowed the SPD hierarchy to expel their more militant leaders.

With the growth in size of the SPD parliamentary delegation in 1969 and 1972, there was a significant left presence in the *Fraktion* for the first time. Organized initially in the Group of the Sixteenth Floor (their location in the Bundestag building) and later in the Leverküsener Circle, it numbered around thirty to forty deputies, with occasional support from about twenty others – offering solidarity when members defied the party whip, or sought posts in the *Fraktion*, and seeking to win over deputies of centre-left persuasion.[5] Factions of this kind, however, have tended to perform a stabilizing function in the SPD, structuring the careers of their members and integrating them into the party mainstream.[6] The emergence of a left in the Bundestag never seriously challenged the domination of the right during the era of Social–Liberal coalition.

Nor was dissent any stronger outside it. Power in the SPD is formally concentrated in the executive and the presidium. But since the inception of the presidium in 1958, it is this smaller body, meeting weekly, which directs policy and takes decisions.[7] During the Social–Liberal decade, the presidium identified closely with the government, endorsing policy which had usually originated with the Chancellor or in government ministries. The executive reflected the political composition of the party more accurately, and the left was usually able to secure between a quarter and a third of the seats on it. Occasionally, the executive would adopt a position at variance with the government – for example, when it urged a moratorium on the development of nuclear energy in 1977; but its typical role was to mediate between government and party, attempting to reconcile state policy with social-democratic principles. Theoretically, of course, the party congress is the sovereign policy-making body of the SPD. But the reality is quite different. The executive largely controls its agenda and secures approval for decisions emanating from the party leadership, which in these years had no difficulty in manipulating congresses: both Brandt and Schmidt repeatedly invoked their electoral mandate and national responsibilities to free themselves from accountability, although Schmidt faced increasing opposition in the later years of his rule.

In the mid seventies, factional tensions within the party receded, and dissent outside it seemed to have subsided. But the gulf between the SPD and the legacy of sixties insurgency remained. By the end of the decade, two new causes had revived the spirit of protest against established politics, precipitating movements that then flowed together into a more serious challenge to German Social Democracy from the left than anything it had experienced since the War. The first of these issues was the Schmidt administration's decision – motivated by the oil shock – to expand the production of nuclear energy in Germany. Opposition to this programme was widespread inside the SPD itself. However, at successive party congresses it was consistently, if narrowly, defeated. The result was to disillusion activists on the left, especially the young – many of whom found a more congenial home in the fast-growing *Bürgerinitiativen* (citizens' initiatives) outside the party.

The second explosive decision of the ruling coalition was Schmidt's request to the USA for the stationing of Cruise and Pershing missiles in West Germany, which became official NATO policy in 1978, in the event of Soviet refusal to withdraw SS20s behind the Urals. Here too there was widespread misgiving inside the SPD about the wisdom of the government's course, when Reagan came to power soon afterwards and embarked on a massive military build-up around the world. But so long as Schmidt remained Chancellor, grassroots revolt against the decision was – with increasing difficulty – contained. Within West German society as a whole, however, a peace movement of formidable dimensions arose to resist the arrival of the missiles.

It was from the confluence of these concerns, with the environment and with peace, that there surged a new political force – the Greens. Ecological issues were, of course, arousing increased public attention throughout the West by this time. But the emergence of a significant political party around them was specific to the Federal Republic. Green parties contesting elections have, a decade later, become fairly common in Western Europe. The German movement, however, was not only the pioneer phenomenon: it still remains the most important in domestic politics. In size and function, the Green Party which took root in the eighties might be compared to the Left Socialist parties that have long been a feature of the Scandinavian scene, skirmishing along the flank of Social Democracy. In the Federal Republic, however, the generational revolt of the late sixties was a much more intense process than in the Nordic countries, leaving deeper counter-cultural effects; while West Germany is a more heavily industrialized and militarized society, in which ecological and security issues loom far larger – and also, arguably, traditions of cultural romanticism run deeper. The distinctive cast of the Greens arose out of this matrix.

Against the background of ecological protest and peace mobilization, scattered Green groupings already existed when the first direct elections to the European Parliament in June 1979 supplied an immediate incentive to create a national organization. Participation held out the promise of enough financial support to maintain a permanent infrastructure, since any party competing would receive DM 3.50 in state subsidies for every vote gained. A federal congress was held in Frankfurt in March, at which it was agreed to launch a proto-party, the Sonstige Politische Vereinigung: Die Grünen (SPV). To conform with West German regulations, the party elected an executive committee, but no agreement was reached on an electoral programme or organizational framework.

The SPV achieved 3.2 per cent of the vote in the European election, and at a conference in Karlsruhe in January 1980 a decision to form a Green Party was taken by over 90 per cent of the delegates, though it took a further gathering at Saarbrücken in March to agree its formula. During these discussions, the conservative wing of the movement was marginalized, and the final programme clearly placed the Greens to the left of the SPD. In the federal elections of 1980, the CDU–CSU's choice of Franz Josef Strauss as candidate for Chancellor squeezed the Green vote as many potential supporters switched to the SPD to prevent a victory for Strauss. But by 1983 the Greens had secured representation in a number of *Länder*; and in the national elections following the SPD's ouster from office, they polled 5.6 per cent of the vote, entering the Bundestag with twenty-seven seats. Four years later, in the elections of 1987, the party increased its vote to 8.3 per cent and its parliamentary delegation to forty-two.

The Green electorate was young (mostly under thirty-five in the early eighties) and highly educated. Located mainly in large towns, where sixties radicalism had been strong, it was somewhat detached from the rest of society, with its own generational culture. The most committed members of the Green Party, however, had typically been activists in the SPD, which they had attempted to move towards the agenda of '1968', only to be checked by the institutional sclerosis of the Social–Liberal period. Determined to replace the top-down, Bonn-centred model of the established parties, their aim was to create a structure ensuring 'the permanent control of all office and mandate holders and institutions by the grassroots (openness, time limits on mandates and party offices) and the permanent possibility of recall in order to make organization and politics transparent for all, and to counteract the estrangement of individuals from their grassroots'.[8] They were also concerned to assert the legitimacy and importance of extra-parliamentary activity, since they did not accept the the assumption that the Bundestag was the dominant locus of legitimate authority.

The rules adopted by the Greens were designed to realize these aims. Office-holding in the party was to be unpaid beneath the federal level. Parliamentary representatives were expected only to draw the salary of a skilled worker, with the considerable residue to be paid into party funds during their tenure of office. They were also expected to 'rotate' and make way for a designated successor at the midway point in a legislative session. Participation was to be encouraged by very loose membership structures. All meetings were in principle open and all members could participate in conferences. The holding of multiple offices, widespread in other parties, was expressly forbidden. Imperative mandates, a favourite idea of the SPD left in the seventies, bound MPs to the instructions of the local party that had sent them to the legislature.

The Greens' organizational principles represent a very optimistic reading of human nature, and putting them into practice has proved difficult. Rotation proved extremely problematic, and was eventually dropped at the federal level, although an expectation remained that members should not serve more than one term without a break. At the local level, in some areas like Frankfurt rotation is still encouraged; in others it is ignored. It also proved difficult for the unpaid executive to control Green deputies who enjoyed the advantages of fully paid support staff. At the Münster conference in March 1989, it was therefore decided to pay all eleven members of the federal executive, though the level fixed, in conformity with the anti-elitist stance of the party, was below that of parliamentary assistants.[9]

Paradoxically, because the loose structures of the Greens place little premium on joining, the ratio of members to voters is actually the lowest of the parties in the Bundestag. Nor is the proportion of the membership that is active any greater. In 1982, the *Land* congress in Hesse, convoked to determine the party's election programme, was attended by only eighty of 2,500 members – ten of whom were members of the *Land* executive.[10] Where Green members do participate in greater numbers, their energy is often directed at a single issue and direct action. In these conditions, the hope of reducing the autonomy of the parliamentary delegation was of little effect. The imperative mandate was soon ignored, when it became clear that the heterogeneity of the party meant that local instructions would conflict and the *Fraktion* could not act coherently if deputies respected them. In any case, loose conditions for party membership create a fluctuating base of activists that militates against any consistent enforcement of accountability. The federal executive, often in conflict with the *Fraktion*, was no more successful in curbing an autonomy that increased as Green deputies became more experienced in the Bundestag. This was to be expected in a party where resources and paid jobs are concentrated at the parliamentary level; but it also reflected the decline of the new social movements, especially the peace campaign, which lost momentum from the mid eighties, no longer putting continuous pressure on the *Fraktion*.[11]

The Greens have had some success in maintaining a dispersion of power in the party by banning multiple office-holding. Their experiment with collective leadership has not, however, been especially happy. The party has never had a single leader, but rather three chairpersons with equal rights. This practice has served to encourage rather than inhibit factionalism: internal elections show a marked tendency to select individuals who give their primary loyalty to faction rather than to party. For the development of the Greens was soon dogged by a running battle between the 'Realos', the pragmatic wing, and the 'Fundis' or fundamentalist wing. The realists, according higher importance to parliamentary work, were interested in cooperating – where possible – with the SPD to achieve common political goals, and willing to envisage coalitions with it, initially at *Land* and ultimately at a federal level. The fundamentalists were unimpressed by parliamentary politics, arguing that the real centres of power in the Federal Republic lay outside the Bundestag and the *Land* assemblies, in business circles and the bureaucracy. Accordingly, compromises to achieve parliamentary victories should be avoided since they rest on the illusion that parliament itself is the site of the decisive encounters in an advanced industrial society. This faction was opposed to any arrangement with the SPD, arguing that since the latter's long-term strategy must be to absorb the Greens ('drain the marshes'), the party should not help Social Democracy to achieve this aim.

The boundary between these positions was not fixed or absolute, and individuals could move from one to another without difficulty. The open nature of Green decision-making bodies meant that their composition frequently altered, shifting the balance between the two from one conference to another. The majority of party members have in fact been Realos, who were also strong in the parliamentary delegation. The Fundis predominated in some *Länder*, such as Hamburg, and on the executive. If the conflict between the two has often threatened the Greens with inconsistency and immobilism, the underlying vitality of the party has so far saved it from disastrous division. Although it has not developed much of a press of its own, Green ideas are diffused by a wide variety of counter-cultural publications, local listings magazines and – very importantly – *Tageszeitung*, a daily newspaper based in Berlin with a circulation of 100,000. The SPD lacks any equivalent, and has had a dismal record with its weekly *Vorwärts* (although it does publish a good discussion journal, *Die Neue Gesellschaft*, edited by Peter Glotz, and receives support from trade-union sheets with a nominal distribution of 1.5 million). For much of the eighties, cultural initiative was Green rather than Social Democrat.

Perhaps the most striking example has been in the field of gender politics. In 1986 the Greens officially adopted the zip principle for candidates to party and public office – that is, alternating female and male candidates. Women subsequently increased from 36 per cent of the Green parliamentary delegation to 57 per cent after the 1987 elections – the highest level of any party in the EC. In the Hamburg elections of 1986, all the Green candidates were women. There is less difference at the level of the membership itself, of whom about a third are female, as compared with a quarter in the other parties; while the Green electorate – like the Social Democratic – was actually more male than that of the FDP or CDU–CSU at this time. Indeed, the most remarkable feature of the Green commitment to women's emancipation is its inversion of the normal rule of West German politics that female participation decreases as one ascends the party pyramid towards Bonn. Not only has the Green delegation in the Bundestag been more female than the party. Between 1985 and 1987 women held all the leadership positions in the *Fraktion*, and between 1988 and 1990 two-thirds of them. This record is all the more striking since the general absence of paid posts, apart from in parliament itself, makes Green engagement a very costly activity – which would normally affect women more adversely, since those who are mothers must pay child-care costs while involved in political work.

The Dilemmas of the SPD

The sudden emergence of the Greens posed a set of quite new problems to the SPD. Firstly, a rival on the left obliged the party to re-examine its own first principles, impelling it into 'a debate about its own aims and position in German society'.[12] Secondly, the party had to formulate an electoral strategy to recover the voters it had lost. Thirdly, since the political landscape of the Federal Republic exerts an ineluctable pull towards coalition government, the SPD now had to define its relations with the enlarged array of parties confronting it, in particular to decide to seek a renewed opening to the centre or to court the Greens.

The immediate problem for the party managers was the electoral crisis of the SPD. In the federal election of 1983, the SPD suffered a haemorrhage of 1.6 million votes to the CDU–CSU on its right and 750,000 to the Greens on its left. The party's share of the poll, at 38 per cent, was its lowest since 1961. Four years later, it fell again – as, despite a slight reversal of losses to the CDU–CSU, a further 600,000 votes went to the Greens.[13] Behind these setbacks lay longer-term social changes in the West German electorate. The decline in the relative size and cohesion of the manual working class has whittled away the party's core electorate. Accounting for 79 per cent of all wage-earners in 1950, this class had dropped to 58 per cent in 1969 and to 42 per cent by 1986 – by which time a significant proportion of those who remained were *Gastarbeiter* with no vote in federal elections. Increased social mobility had, on the other hand, not only enlarged the size of the middle strata, but accentuated its political differentiation and electoral volatility. Side by side with the salaried or professional layers that had emerged in the fifties, there were now new cohorts accustomed to the unprecedented affluence of the sixties and seventies, whose outlook was much more 'post-materialist'.

The SPD's dilemma was twofold. It had been clear since the mid seventies that the party's electorate straddled a span from the most traditional bulwarks of the old industrial working class, to the newly emergent outposts of a post-materialist middle class.[14] Now, it faced both a seductive competitor for the latter, in the shape of the Greens – and a shift of the former (together with much of the salariat) towards values of individual achievement rather than social solidarity, favourable to gains by the Union parties. Electoral strategy in the eighties revolved around attempts to reconcile the increasingly disparate aspirations and interests of these different constituencies. The result, as abortive attempts were made to regain the youth vote whilst simultaneously consolidating the manual working class and attracting the upwardly mobile, was much confusion. The contradictions of the SPD's efforts to adjust in all directions reached their apogee in its campaign for the 1987 federal elections, when a candidate for Chancellor identified with the party's traditional working-class base was obliged to stand on an incongruous new left platform, nevertheless rejecting any possibility of cooperation with the Greens.[15]

This disorientation also had an organizational dimension. In the seventies bureaucratic controls had maintained stability in the seventies by suppressing or neutralizing left opposition, but at the cost of sterility and passivity at the party base. The result was a weakening of the SPD's

Table 4.2 SPD Voting Behaviour in State Elections 1988–93

State	SPD Share of Vote	Change Since Last Election
Berlin (January 1989)	37.3	+5.0
Saarland (January 1990)	54.4	+5.2
Lower Saxony (May 1990)	44.2	+2.1
North-Rhine-Westphalia (May 1990)	50.0	−2.0
Bavaria (October 1990)	26.0	−1.5
Hessen (January 1991)	40.8	+0.6
Rhineland-Palatinate (April 1991)	44.8	+6.0
Bremen (September 1991)	38.8	−11.7
Schleswig-Holstein (April 1992)	46.2	−8.6
Baden-Württemberg (April 1992)	29.4	−2.6
Hamburg (September 1993)	40.4	−7.5

Table 4.3 Breakdown of Party Support by Social Class (%)

Party	Old Middle Class		New Middle Class		Working Class	
	1980	1987	1980	1987	1980	1987
CDU–CSU	64	63	39	46	35	36
SPD	28	13	47	31	58	54
FDP	7	18	13	14	6	4.5
Greens	1	5	1	9	1	6

Source: Karl Cerny, *Germany at the Polls*, Durham, North Carolina 1990, p. 284.

capacity for electoral mobilization or diffusion of social-democratic values at large. An exodus of left activists to the Greens prevented a sharp swing against the leadership in the wake of defeat, of the kind experienced by the British Labour Party after 1979. But there was still sufficient reaction for Schmidt to go into opposition in 1982, while Brandt was nearing the end of his office as chairman. A new leadership was clearly needed for the SPD, but here too uncertainty prevailed. Although there was a shift towards the left in the mood of the party at large, there was more continuity than change in its top bodies, where 'old guard' figures like Hans-Jochen Vogel and Johannes Rau – successive candidates for Chancellor in 1983 and 1987 – retained their authority.

Throughout this period, the problem of coalition strategy remained. Nationally, the response of the SPD leadership to the Green challenge unfolded in three phases. During the period 1980–84, Willy Brandt as party chairman advocated the reintegration of the SPD's 'lost children' through a greening of policy and a degree of cooperation with the new

Table 4.4 Breakdown of the West German Electorate 1950–85 (%)

	1950	1961	1970	1979	1981	1985
Working Class	51	48	46	42	42	40
New Middle Class	21	30	38	45	46	48
Old Middle Class	28	22	16	13	12	12

Source: Karl Cerny, *Germany at the Polls*, Durham, North Carolina 1990, p. 274.

Note: The categories used here are based on standard occupational definitions. The 'working class' refers to manual workers and their families; the 'old middle class' to proprietors, professionals and self-employed; the 'new middle class' to white-collar workers and their families.

party – a strategy geared to the establishment of 'a majority left of the Union parties'. This prospect was resisted by the right, which aggressively reasserted the historic roots of the party in industrial society, and attacked the Greens as irresponsible utopians. After 1984 the SPD distanced itself from the Greens, rejecting any suggestion of cooperation with them – a strategy taken to its limits in Rau's election campaign of 1987. The new objective – 'a majority of our own' – was, however, an illusion: encouraged by mid-term *Länder* successes, its bankruptcy was exposed in the federal polls.

After this fiasco, there was a reorientation of the party towards the centre. Tacitly, the SPD now appeared to envisage an electoral division of labour conceding the post-materialist left to the Greens. Less competitive with the new party, coalition strategy was now geared to winning a 'structural majority' – that is, an electoral position that would make the SPD indispensable for the formation of a government. In its choice of partner, the party sought to maintain the maximum possible flexibility. Sitting on the fence in relation to the Greens, formerly indicative of futility, now acquired a semblance of strategic relevance.

Relations between the Social Democrats and the Greens at state and municipal level, conducted independently of the federal leadership, were rather more complex. Coalition choices have been heavily dependent on both the local electoral landscape and the local composition of the party. Ad hoc arrangements of an opportunist type with the Greens when the balance of seats allows or even dictates such a course are one thing. A commitment to establishing a stable working relationship with the Greens, capable of bridging the programmatic and organizational gulf between the two parties, is another. The experience of municipal coalitions suggests this is only possible where the new left is securely dominant in the SPD, and as a consequence there exists a clear-cut preference for a red-green coalition over other options.[16]

Underlying all the ambiguities and zig-zags of attitude towards the Greens was the continuing inability of the SPD leadership to decide how to read the logic of electoral change. On the one hand, there were signs of a two-bloc system, with a gulf between the camp of the left and the 'bourgeois parties'. On the other, there clearly remained common ground between the traditional parties, suggesting that a centre-left or even grand coalition might once again be formed. Decisive here was the fact that the electoral arithmetic of the eighties never added to a left majority. In the Bundestag election of 1983 the combined vote of the SPD and the Greens was 43.8 per cent, increasing to 45.3 per cent in 1987. Although the entry into the Bundestag of the far-right Republikaner (politically ineligible as coalition partners for the bourgeois parties) might redress the balance, the SPD leadership was unlikely to commit itself to a red-green alliance while these ratios held. On the other hand, there was no sign of the FDP repenting of its now close compact with the CDU–CSU.

It was against the background of these uncertainties that the SPD sought to find a new programme to redefine the party's identity. The SPD embarked on this quest in 1984. It took two years to generate a first draft. This document, on which the left had visible impact, advocated a path of 'qualitative growth' capable of reconciling economic advance and environmental protection. Ecological modernization, it argued, required R&D into clean and sustainable technologies, which would create a dynamic growth fostering exports and employment. The credibility of this concept depended upon support from the labour wing of the SPD, important sectors of which had been hostile to the 'greening' of party policy. Here endorsement by the crusty Chemical Workers' Union was perceived as a significant breakthrough. Qualitative growth was hailed as 'the centrepiece of a social-democratic reform programme for the rest of the century'.[17] However, while it may have been tailored to the concerns of the new left, it met with little resonance in the broader electorate.

Further concessions to the left could be found in the draft's sections on defence and security, which followed the decisions of the Cologne and Essen congresses of 1983–84, condemning (to Schmidt's indignation) the deployment of Cruise and Pershing missiles and calling for a reform of NATO strategy. The strategy of 'forward defence' was rejected in favour of a nuclear-free zone in Central Europe, and hope expressed of an ultimate dissolution of the two armed blocs. If these visions were uncongenial to the right, they were not as unacceptable as some of the economic sentiments that found their way into the draft. For the document declared that: 'Democratic socialism aims not only to improve capitalism but also to replace it with a new social and economic order . . . the economy must have clear framework conditions set for it.'[18] These formulations drew fire from the party's chief economics spokesmen, who intervened late in the drafting process. Dismissing 'woolly conceptions and outdated formulas which no longer bear any resemblance to reality',[19] they dissociated themselves from the draft's hostility to the market and idealistic trust in the state, stressing the need for a greater measure of 'economic realism'. Their objections were incorporated unconditionally into the programme, whose ambivalence towards market capitalism and dirigiste overtones were expunged. The Godesberg credo, 'as much competition as possible; as much planning as necessary', was explicitly reiterated. Despite the elaborate search for new values, in these respects the programme ended up echoing familiar phrases.

The most radical intervention in the programmatic review, however, came with an unprecedented attack on SPD orthodoxy from the group known as Brandt's *Enkel* (grandchildren) around Oskar Lafontaine. Designed to attract 'target groups' in the 'affluent majority' identified by electoral analysis, this initiative called for a new industrial order, combining a reduction in the working week with deregulation of the labour market. 'The European left has at its disposal, if only it can grasp the opportunity, a concrete utopia which can move millions; a shortening of work time, not only as a technocratic instrument but as a human idea capable of integrating and binding together different strata in society . . . bringing work and leisure into a new balance.'[20] There was cunning in this choice of issue. For on the one hand, a shorter working week appealed to post-materialist and home-centred concerns – while on the other, it connected with a classic labour demand. The mid eighties had in fact seen a trade-union campaign, including strikes waged by the metal workers, in favour of a statutory 35-hour week. But Lafontaine's plan provoked a sharp clash with the DGB, which opposed advocacy of flexible hours with no overtime rates. Cutting across left and right – it was criticized from both ends of the party spectrum – the initiative was a calculated attack on trade-union orthodoxies, and a deliberate attempt to distance the party from the labour movement. The SPD, another *Enkel* explained, had to be responsive to the whole of society, and that means entrepreneurs, professionals and higher-grade civil servants as well as trade unions.[21]

In the end, some of Lafontaine's proposals were included in the programme finally agreed at the Berlin congress in December 1989, although they were hedged around with qualifications and concessions to the trade unions. Advertised as a redefinition of Social Democracy, the new document in fact did little more than graft onto the central formulations of the Godesberg Programme a series of new commitments

– to the environment, 'humanization of the workplace', gender equality, and 'critical dialogue between elected representatives and citizens'. What the prolonged exercise essentially underlined was the social and cultural fragmentation of the SPD, as its various party groupings mobilized to leave their mark on the new programme. Incorporating something from all of them, the eventual upshot has been compared to 'a department store catalogue . . . contradictory in style and argumentation . . . more of an internal scorecard than a statement of policy'.[22] Launched in December 1989 just as the GDR was collapsing, its impact was almost entirely eclipsed by larger events.

The Bombshell of Unification

The Berlin congress of the SPD confirmed Oskar Lafontaine, the 47-year-old premier of the Saar, as the party's candidate for Chancellor in 1990. With the nomination of this lively and aggressive politician, the generational torch appeared to have passed within the party. But its predicament had not substantially altered. In the summer of 1989, it was already clear that the most likely outcome of the next federal elections was a continuation in power of the ruling CDU–CSU–FDP coalition, even if it was uncertain to what extent the Republicans would take votes from the bourgeois parties. Despite Chancellor Kohl's low personal standing in the opinion polls, the left seemed unlikely to make great advances given the steady upturn in the West German economy and the anticipated benefits of the tax reform, timed to bear fruit towards the end of the electoral cycle.

This scenario suddenly appeared called into question by the disintegration of the East German state. As the drama unfolded, it seemed possible that the 'wild card' of all-German upheaval could lead to real gains by the SPD, or push the FDP to break with its coalition partner. But as it turned out, virtually every section of the SPD and the West German left felt profoundly ambivalent about the prospect of reunification – a sentiment shared, interestingly enough, by trade-union organizers and intellectuals, reds and greens, functionaries and activists, Realos and Fundis. There were a number of reasons for this reaction. The continuing potential of nationalism as an agent of collective identity had been underestimated by the postwar left, in its recoil from the experience of the Third Reich – particularist or naturalistic forms of identification being anyway alien to its vocabulary.[23] The SPD's own approach to the national question, as it had developed in the seventies, concentrated on efforts to persuade the East German regime to improve human rights and freedom of movement for its people, in exchange for recognition – a line extended into the eighties with a second *Ostpolitik*, of active engagement in pursuit of détente. In its time, this stance had been innovative and popular in both parts of the country. But having led the way out of the impasse of the high Cold War, the SPD was slow to adjust to the pace of the demise of Communism in Eastern Europe, and the collapse of the GDR, whose acceptance it had pioneered.[24] Outside the party, some also felt misgivings about the imposition of the constitution of the Federal Republic on the East, under Article 23, as the blunt instrument of unification. Critics like Habermas argued that a new constitution, drafted by a convention of representatives from both German states and ratified by referendum, would be a more democratic and egalitarian procedure.

In September 1989, as events gathered pace, the SPD leadership cancelled at short notice a routine exchange visit with its SED counterparts. Within the Federal Republic Lafontaine put himself at the head of opinion critical of pan-German aspirations. He had at various times suggested a revision of the German nationality law, which in effect operated as a 'law of return' on the Israeli model, in favour of an emphasis on the separate citizenship of the GDR and the FRG. Lafontaine was also constantly critical of the social costs imposed on the Federal Republic by the inflow of 'ethnic Germans' from Eastern Europe encouraged by the federal government.

In the early phase of the break-up of the Honecker regime, the running in East Germany was made by intellectuals and dissidents loosely grouped in the New Forum, whose aim was to reform the GDR rather than to demand unity with the Federal Republic. The West German left sympathized with this approach. But the momentum of popular opposition in the East soon revealed a widespread aspiration to join up with the West. The opening of the Hungarian and Czech borders, and the enthusiasm for unity expressed in growing mass demonstrations in Leipzig and other cities, created inexorable pressures for unification.

Historically, the SPD had been suppressed in East Germany when the Communist regime was set up after the War, by forcible 'fusion' into the ruling party itself. The party therefore had to be refounded, as the Honecker regime disintegrated. The SPD in East Germany began to form itself only in October 1989, but it soon attracted a body of support. However, from the beginning there existed a mismatch between the aspirations of the new members of the East German SPD, who were keen to press ahead to unity, and the West German SPD, which was still uncertain of its response – a strong current of opinion suggesting it would be better to stabilize a democratic state in East Germany, since immediate unity would be tantamount to annexation by the Federal Republic. At the Berlin congress in December 1989 Willy Brandt pleaded with the party to accept a wholehearted commitment to German unity. The principle was endorsed; but Lafontaine continued to stress the practical difficulties. The Greens, meanwhile, often taxed with German nationalism by conservative opponents for their advocacy of neutrality, found it even harder to develop a coherent policy. Their relations were close with many of the dissidents in New Forum, whose outlook Green statements dwelling on the difficulties of unity tended to reflect. The ramshackle decision-making structures of the Greens also made it more difficult for them to effect a rapid strategic turn than for the SPD.

Against expectations, however, the national issue initially looked as if it might work out well for the SPD. In the West, Lafontaine did not appear to be suffering from his lack of enthusiasm for German unity: it seemed that his warnings of its social costs, echoing those of the trade unions, might strike a chord with the electorate. In the East, there was a founding congress of the party in February 1990, and most early polls put it in a very strong position for the election of 18 March, with some predicting it would win an outright majority. There were good historical reasons, in fact, for thinking that East Germany would prove natural electoral terrain for the SPD – Brandt's enthusiasm for German unity had a rational as well as emotional basis. Prussia and Saxony had been strongholds of the labour movement in the Weimar period. The overwhelming majority of the East German population was Protestant – and in West Germany, SPD regional strength had always been very strongly correlated with the predominance of Reformed religion (hence its strength in the north, and relative weakness in the south). Last but not least, the social structure of the GDR was much more heavily dominated by the industrial working class than that of the Federal Republic. Political, social and confessional factors all seemed to point to Social Democratic hegemony beyond the Elbe.

The election of March 1990, however, confounded every such expectation. The result was a resounding success for the Allianz für Deutschland – a bloc of the CDU in East Germany, Demokratischer Aufbruch (Democratic Awakening), and the Deutsche Soziale Union (German Social Union), which together polled 48.1 per cent of the vote. The Alliance was in effect the arm of the West German conservative parties and of Chancellor Kohl in the East. Unlike the SPD, the CDU had always formally existed in the GDR, as a tame junior ornament of the regime, but still with the material apparatus – offices, finances, and members – of a political party, which now proved a substantial advantage. With the democratized successor to the Communist party, the Partei des Demokratischen Sozialismus, polling an unexpectedly high 16.3 per cent, the SPD was confined to 21.8 per cent. The electoral tide for the Alliance was essentially a vote for immediate reunification on the terms laid down out by the West German government (including a virtual promise of currency union at a highly favourable exchange rate of 1:1). Manual workers rallied in particularly large numbers on this basis: no less than 55 per cent of the total Alliance vote was from the industrial working class.

The Bonn government, with complete freedom of manoeuvre, in effect commanded the situation. As mass civic opposition surfaced in the East, the historic Christian Democrat commitment to eventual reunification had returned to the field of practical politics. Just as Kohl could move decisively to do a deal with Gorbachev, he could also oblige the Bundesbank to comply with a form of currency union designed to consolidate CDU support in the East. The SPD was left appearing to carp at and criticize a unification policy that could be presented as simultaneously generous and responsible, acceptable to the 'international community', and legitimately satisfying to the long-divided German nation. While the left inclined to suspicion of nationalist sentiment, for many voters unification was, quite simply, a family matter. In these conditions, the SPD's ambivalence could easily be perceived as an unworthy opportunism.

Matters came to a head in June 1990 over the issue of whether the SPD should support the inter-German State Treaty, that was to be the instrument of monetary, economic, social and environmental integration. To oppose currency union at a 1:1 exchange rate as an economic adventure might have popular resonance in the West, since polls showed fears about the outcome to be widespread. On the other hand, opposition to the Treaty could be presented as obstructing national purposes of historic moment, and would sow doubt in the East about the SPD's intentions. At one point the party argued that elections in the West should precede unification. In the event, the State Treaty publicly divided the SPD. Lafontaine advocated opposition to the Treaty in its existing form, but party chairman Vogel and economic spokesman Wolfgang Roth argued this would be wrong. The outcome of the conflict was a defeat for Lafontaine, underlined by the subsequent designation of Vogel as chairman of the 'new' all-German party. The episode inevitably undermined Lafontaine, and weakened the party, in the run-up to the December poll.

The Greens found themelves in an even worse position. The quintessential postmodern party of the Federal Republic, few of whose members had any experience of a united Germany – unlike the SPD, where the older generation rallied round Brandt – the Greens had never taken part in the official commemorations of 17 June in the

Bundestag. Most of their deputies were committed to a two-state view of Germany, on the grounds that acceptance of existing borders was a condition of ending hostilities between East and West. The only support for unification came from a small minority around Alfred Mechtesheimer, who adopted a national neutralist position.[25] The party therefore opposed both German Economic and Monetary Union and the *Staatsvertrag*, on the basis of the right of the East Germans to self-determination – a stance fatally undermined by the massive endorsement of the pro-unity parties in the GDR election of March 1990. The weaknesses inherent in Green decision-making processes were cruelly exposed by the fast-moving unification process: as Hesse leader Joschka Fischer put it, 'we simply pulled the bedclothes over our heads'. When the election campaign got under way in the autumn, unification drove environmental issues – where Lafontaine's appeals were now often indistinguishable from theirs – right down the political agenda.

For the left, the first all-German election after the War was thus an all-German disaster. The SPD vote fell to 33.5 per cent (35.9 per cent in the West; 23.6 per cent in the East). Its poor showing in the industrial areas of the five new *Länder*, and subsidence in its erstwhile strongholds of the Ruhr, were particularly disturbing. The Greens in the West polled 4.7 per cent, falling short of the 5 per cent required to qualify for representation in the enlarged Bundestag – slight recompense came from the pact between Bündnis 90 and the Greens in the East; 5.9 per cent of the eastern vote gave them eight deputies. (Though had the Greens in the West not rejected the option of merging with their Eastern counterparts they would have qualified for entry on the basis of a joint list.) The PDS, although polling only 2.4 per cent of the overall electorate, won seventeen Bundestag seats by virtue of its 9.9 per cent support in the East, where the party succeeded in attracting some support from younger voters under an able new leader, Gregor Gysi, a lawyer who had defended dissidents against the Honecker regime. For its part, the SPD remains very hostile to the PDS because of its roots in the SED – Social Democrats in the East remember their persecution, and in the West the political dangers of any confusion between social democracy and Stalinism. The presence of the PDS in the newly elected Bundestag thus adds a new fissure to the fragmentation of the German left. By contrast the Free Democrats and Christian Democrats have so far been able to take over, without public embarrassment, large numbers of party members and much valuable property from the former Christian Democrat and Free Democrat parties of the East, once loyal allies of Honecker. Indeed East German members now comprise a majority in the FDP.

Post-Unification Conflicts

The electoral debacle of December 1990 inevitably led to the search for a new leader in the SPD. At the Bremen party congress the next year, Bjorn Engholm became chairman. This was a choice from the same generation and background as his predecessor – the *Enkel*, protégés of Brandt whose leading figures had made their names as up-and-coming politicians in the *Länder*: Lafontaine (Saarland), Engholm (Schleswig-Holstein), Schröder (Lower Saxony), Scharping (Rhineland-Palatinate). Formed in the sixties, a number had been prominent in the Jusos of the seventies. The affinities of these leaders with a newer left were tempered by a strong streak of pragmatic flexibility. Engholm himself, cooler in style than the charismatic and mercurial Lafontaine, was more inclined to the centre of the spectrum. It was often said that the older generation of Brandt, Schmidt, Wehner were made of sterner stuff – the *Enkel* being, by contrast, 'of less robust material; more spontaneous and independent; confessing their doubts more readily in public; bon viveurs, who enjoy cultural events, preferring an evening at the opera to laborious reports and debates at a regional party congress'.[26] Their rise reflected changes lower down in the party apparatus, where the *mittlere Basis* of intermediate functionaries had been most thoroughly permeated by attitudes akin to the new left.

Among these was criticism of the closed character of party organization and *unter uns gesagt* (between ourselves) style of decision-making. Under Engholm's leadership, proposals were now made for the introduction of primary elections to choose candidates for elected offices, and the creation of a lattice of working groups and cultural associations to strengthen links between the party apparatus and its members and voters. The role of *Arbeitsgemeinschaften* ('working groups') had, in fact, been increasing dramatically in the party, where they were steadily acquiring an institutional identity of their own. Prominent amongst them are the Arbeitsgemeinschaft für Arbeitnehmerfragen (AfA – Working Group for Labour Affairs), formed as a defensive response of the labour wing of the SPD to the rise of the new left, and the Arbeitsgemeinschaft Sozialdemokratischer Frauen (ASF – Working Group for Social Democratic Women), which has achieved a quota system in the party – by 1994 women should constitute 40 per cent of the SPD's office holders and elected representatives. Another, less formally organized, grouping is the Sozialdemokratische Wählerinitiative (SWI – Social Democratic Voter Initiative), originally formed to muster campaign support from leading figures in intellectual and cultural life, which has since become a forum for the left intelligentsia in the party, running cultural events and participating energetically in programmatic debate. Working groups have even recently been permitted to accept members from outside the party, and there are proposals to formalize their status further by granting them the right to submit congress resolutions.

However commendable the intention to let air into the party, the progressive institutionalization of different social and cultural milieux within the SPD threatens to lead to its Balkanization. The internal life of the party in recent years has been termed a 'loosely coupled anarchy', in which a disparate variety of cliques, factions, patronage groups and interest organizations form temporary and unstable alliances.[27] In themselves, tendencies towards social heterogeneity and organizational pluralism are not new to German Social Democracy. Previously, however, they were contained within a tightly disciplined and centralized apparatus, under the control of a relatively cohesive party elite. The new generation of SPD leaders lacks the collective sense of its predecessors: individualist by temperament, it has been unable to contain personal or political conflicts in the same way.

These weaknesses have taken a sharp toll on the performance of the SPD since its electoral humiliation in 1990. The calamitous aftermath of unification should have favoured it. Kohl's demagogic promises of rapid and universal improvements in living conditions in the East, without any substantial increase in taxes in the West, were exposed within a little over a year. Wide-scale dislocation and misery was visited on the population of the former GDR, as its industry was scythed down, while after a brief spasm of hectic growth, the economy of the West plunged into its worst recession since the War, interest rates soared and emergency taxes were imposed. Amidst all this, the coalition in Bonn was rent by internal tensions and scandals, disputes between its parties, resignations of successive ministers. By 1993, unemployment had risen to 3.3 million (7.1 per cent in the West, 14.7 per cent in the East), the economy was contracting by around 2 per cent a year, and the budget deficit was spiralling out of control. There was a growing perception that the downturn was neither just a temporary effect of unification, nor of the international business cycle, but reflected deep structural problems in the new German economy. Pessimism over economic prospects was compounded by alarm at social disorders in the country, and sense of a power vacuum at the centre of government. Yet German Social Democracy was still unable to breach the hegemony of the right. Far from being able to capitalize on these uniquely favourable circumstances, the SPD was itself tainted by the syndrome of *Parteiverdrossenheit* – a profound disaffection towards the entire 'political class'.

Politically, the party might at least have been expected to extract advantage from its structural majority in the Bundesrat, the upper house of the Federal Republic, composed of representatives of *Land* governments (the SPD is currently in power in eleven out of sixteen regional capitals). For the Bundesrat plays a key role in constitutional amendments and financial legislation. Yet Kohl has been able to neutralize the SPD's leverage in the Bundesrat by inducements to Social Democratic *Länder* to break ranks and vote with the government. Thus in 1992 Brandenburg secured additional revenues by voting for government measures to increase VAT, thereby undermining the party's campaign to pin the label of *Steuerlüge* (tax-lie) on the Chancellor. Unable to mount an effective assault on the ruling coalition, the SPD found itself increasingly obliged to share responsibility with it for the medicine administered to the country – agreeing a 'Solidarity Pact' for financial stabilization as negotiated between the governing parties, federal SPD, and state governments in spring 1993. Here, for some Social Democrats, lay an attractive rehearsal for a future grand coalition, requiring a *Schmusekurs* (soft-soap approach) towards Kohl, rather than vigorous opposition. Thus, for all his own unpopularity, Kohl was consistently able to outmanoeuvre the SPD.

In this he was much assisted by the internal schisms that have rent the SPD over the contentious issues arising out of Germany's post-unification traumas. The Chancellor has repeatedly managed to turn his dependence on opposition consent for controversial measures to his own advantage, by deflecting attention away from the divisions in the government and towards the disunity and indiscipline in the SPD.[28] The response of the party to the emotionally charged issue of stricter rules for political asylum, after the explosion of racial violence against refugees in a number of German cities, is a graphic example. The constitutional amendment required by the change triggered a bitter and debilitating internal conflict at all levels of the party. Opposition to it was strongest in the *mittlere Basis*. The parliamentary delegation and party executive were both divided on the issue. The strongest advocates of changing the rules were SPD state and city officials with responsibility for the reception and accommodation of asylum seekers.

This convoluted spectrum of conflict put the party chairman in an unenviable position. Initially Engholm remained somewhat detached from the debate, reluctant to commit himself to measures for which he was uncertain of winning majority support. With his leadership coming under critical scrutiny, and the SPD driven into an untenable corner, he then reversed his position, urging the party to accept the need for more restrictive rules. Eventually, at a special congress in November 1992, the SPD endorsed the principle of constitutional change, with qualifications – but in a resolution of such obscurity that the continuing ambivalence and disunity of the party were only underlined. The same disarray was exposed by Kohl's demand for a constitutional amendment to enable German armed forces to operate outside the NATO area. The SPD proved unable to put up any effective opposition to the reckless initiatives of the Bonn government in the Balkans, widely criticized in other European capitals, and floundered over definitions of Germany's new security role.

The fallout was not long in coming. Decisions once reached by informal understanding within a like-minded party elite are now subject to acrimonious public discussion, compounded by personal rivalries and conflicts.[29] The hard-fought election of Hans-Ulrich Klose as chairman of the parliamentary delegation early in 1992 was symptomatic of this atmosphere. The party is even more riven in the East, where the SPD's cult of participatory democracy, pursuit of ethical issues, and proclivity for infighting, bear a strong resemblance to the Greens.[30] Relations between the Eastern and Western wings of the SPD remained strained, and the party's organization in the new *Länder* weak. It was in this context, of a pervasive disunity in the party, that Engholm suddenly resigned as chairman of the SPD in May 1993, after a relatively trivial impropriety in his conduct came to light, in a parliamentary commission of inquiry into the scandal surrounding his opponent in the Schleswig-Holstein election of 1987. Frustrated in his efforts to lead the SPD towards the political centre, and undermined by the fractiousness of the party, Engholm lacked the will to withstand the affair, and bowed out.

In the contest for his succession, the two principal candidates for the succession tacitly represented conflicting strategic objectives. Whilst Gerhard Schröder, state premier of Lower Saxony, stood for a strategy of coalition with the Greens, Rudolf Scharping, his counterpart in Rhineland-Palatinate, indicated greater readiness for coalition with the centre-right parties. The choice between the two was for the first time put to the membership of the SPD as a whole. The result of the poll was a convincing win for Scharping, whose low-key style and moderate outlook seemed the safer option to a rattled party. The leaders of Christian Democracy and Social Democracy now both come from the same state in the far west of the country – hardly a good augury for the re-centring of a united Germany.

The SPD remains a powerful force in the enlarged Federal Republic. A membership that still numbers some 900,000 is the envy of Social Democratic parties in other European countries. Its loyal voters may have dropped to around a third of the electorate, but not many of its counterparts now do significantly better. The Federal Constitution ensures that it is not reduced to the impotence of the Labour Party in Britain. The party currently holds office in two-thirds of the *Länder*, and commands a majority in the Bundesrat. Control of regional government provides it with a steady supply of leaders who have earned administrative experience – indeed, perhaps to the point of weakening the continuity of federal leadership: Scharping is now the fifth successive candidate in ten years to be put up against Kohl. In the past, the SPD has resourcefully adapted to seemingly adverse new conditions, establishing its own variant of the *Volkspartei,* pioneering *Ostpolitik,* and succeeding at least partially in incorporating the Green agenda. After more than a decade in opposition, however, the party is no nearer to finding a formula for returning to federal government.

The impasse of the SPD is emblematic of a wider malaise of the European left in the 1990s. The electoral decomposition of the party is an outcome of the break-up of customary social formations in an increasingly post-industrial society, that creates new opportunities for some strata, while marginalizing and disorienting others, and divides traditional from postmodern milieux along generational and cultural lines. These cross-cutting cleavages dissect the SPD electorate, confronting the party with two virtually impossible tasks – to reconcile the aspirations of the upwardly mobile with the insecurities of the socially vulnerable, and to synthesize customary values with the cultural currents of postmodernism.

The values of social solidarity (howevever ill-defined) are the legacy of the SPD's origins in the class politics of industrial society, expressive of the party's bond with the labour movement. Their centrality to its traditional identity has inhibited their adaptation to the realities of mass affluence and an ethos of individual achievement. The dilemma of party is encapsulated in the career of Oskar Lafontaine. As a political spokesman, he was the most prominent advocate of deregulating labour markets and embracing individual competition; as a practical premier in the Saarland, however, he was adept at continuing to secure large federal subsidies for the loss-making mines and steelworks of his region. His inconsistency exemplified the contrary pulls of social democracy today.

Which are likely to predominate in Germany? In 1990 the SPD party suffered very heavy losses to the CDU amongst manual workers, especially in its traditional industrial stronghold of the Ruhr, and was far outdistanced by the CDU in the proletarian bastions of Saxony in the East. *Länder* elections since 1990 indicate that the party's working-class electorate is now vulnerable at the edges to the Republicans. On the other hand, the SPD has progressively adjusted to newer constituencies of the left – in its programmatic appeal, its choice of leaders, and its electorate. In 1990, it regained some of the ground it had ceded to the Greens. They have since recovered, after an initial period of recriminations that saw the departure of several leading Fundis like Jutta Dittfurth. The party has scored a series of regional successes, and now governs together with the SPD in five *Länder* (Bremen, Brandenburg, Hessen, Lower Saxony and Saxony-Anhalt). In spring 1993, the Western Greens merged with the Eastern Greens/Bündnis 90 to form a unified party, whose prospects of returning to the Bundestag in 1994 look good.

The recuperation of the Greens and the reorientation of the Social Democrats has made local alliances between them easier. But at the federal level, the electoral arithmetic leaves a red-green coalition far short of a majority. By the summer of 1994, economic recovery – carefully tended by the Bundesbank with lower interest rates, under its new chairman Hans Tietmeyer, formerly one of Kohl's closest aides – had boosted the CDU's standing in the polls again. With the PDS gaining ground on its left flank in the East, Scharping's leadership of the SPD has thus continued to look for openings on the centre-right. If the FDP were to fail to cross the electoral threshold in October 1994, a Grand Coalition with the CDU would no doubt take shape. This is a prospect that some of the SPD's managers, resigned to failure once more at the national polls, would welcome. The bill, however, will sooner or later fall due, if tactical dexterity gains priority over electoral realignment, programmatic definition and organizational reconstruction. In the long term, these are the tasks the SPD must acquit if it is to reassert itself as a potential party of government.

Notes

1. Eva Kolinsky, *Parties, Opposition and Society in West Germany*, London 1984, p. 20.
2. Otto Kirchheimer, 'The Transformation of the Western European Party Systems', in J. La Palombara and M. Wiener, eds, *Political Parties and Political Development*, Princeton 1966.
3. Peter Lösche, 'Ende der sozialdemokratischen Arbeiterbewegung?', *Die neue Gesellschaft/Frankfurter Heft*, no. 5, 1988, pp. 453–63.
4. Hans-Dieter Klingemann, 'West Germany' in I. Crewe and D. Denver, eds, *Electoral Change in Western Democracies*, London 1985, p. 252.
5. Gerard Braunthal, *The West German Social Democrats 1969–82: Profile of a Party in Power*, Boulder 1983, p. 209.
6. Ferdinand Müller Rommel, *Innerparteiliche Gruppierungen in der SPD*, Opladen 1982, p. 267.
7. Stephen Padgett and Tony Burkett, *Political Parties and Elections in West Germany: The Search for a New Stability*, London 1986, pp. 71–4.
8. Die Grünen, *Federal Programme 1980*.
9. *Grune Blätter*, vol. 4, 1981, p. 18.
10. Kolinsky, *Parties, Opposition and Society*, p. 310.
11. For particulars, see W. Paterson, 'The Greens from Yesterday to Tomorrow', in P. Merkl, ed., *The Federal Republic at Forty*, New York 1989, pp. 340–66.

12. Gordon Smith, 'The Changing West German Party System: Consequences of the 1987 Election', *Government and Opposition*, no. 22, 1987, p. 137.

13. INFAS, *Report für die Presse*, 26 January 1987.

14. Wolfgang Gibowski and Max Kaase, 'Die Ausgangslage für die Bundestagswahl am 25 Januar 1987', *Aus Politik und Zeitgeschichte*, Bd. 48, 1986, p. 5.

15. See Stephen Padgett, 'The West German Social Democrats in Opposition 1982–1986, *West European Politics*, no. 10, 1987, pp. 351–2.

16. Ibid., pp. 165–6.

17. SPD Partevorstand, *Politik*, no. 7, July 1985.

18. SPD Parteivorstand, *Entwurf für ein neues Grundsatzprogramm*, Bonn 1986, pp. 7, 25.

19. *Frankfurter Rundschau*, 6 January 1989.

20. Peter Glotz, *Wirtschaftswoche*, 29 April 1988.

21. Gerhard Schröder, *Wirtschaftswoche*, 29 April 1988.

22. Peter Lösche, 'Zur Metamorphose der politischen Parteien in Deutschland', *Gewerkschaftliche Monatshefte*, no. 9, September 1992, p. 535; Stephen Silvia, 'Loosely Coupled Anarchy: the Fragmentation of the Left', in Stephen Padgett, ed., *Parties and Party System in the New Germany*, Dartmouth 1993, p. 175.

23. For arguments to this effect, see Andrei Markovits, 'The West German 68-ers Encounter the Events of 1989', *German Politics* 1, April 1992, pp. 14–17; and Herbert Kitschelt, 'The 1990 German Federal Election and National Unification', *West European Politics*, October 1991, p. 131.

24. W. Paterson, 'Foreign Policy and Security', in Smith, Paterson and Merkl, pp. 192–210.

25. Hubert Kleinert, *Aufstieg und Fall der Grünen*, Bonn 1992.

26. See Peter Lösche and Franz Walter, *Die SPD – Klassenpartei, Volkspartei, Quotenpartei: zur Entwicklung der Sozialdemokratie von Weimar bis zur Vereinigung*, Darmstadt 1992, p. 38.

27. Lösche and Walter, op. cit., pp. 380–6.

28. Werner Perger, 'Ein Winter der Ohnmacht', *Die Zeit*, 5 February 1993, p. 6.

29. W. Weege, 'Zwei Generationen im SPD-Parteivorstand', in T. Leif, H-J. Legrand and A. Klein, eds, *Die politische Klasse in Deutschland: Eliten auf dem Prüfstand*, Bonn 1992, pp. 211–13.

30. Silvia, 'Loosely Coupled Anarchy', in Padgett, ed., *Parties and Party System*, p. 183.

5

Britain: Labour and Electoral Reform

Peter Mair

Representative government in the United Kingdom has a very special character, compared with the pattern elsewhere in Western Europe. Firstly, and most obviously, the House of Commons is the only parliament in Western Europe which has never been elected under a system of proportional representation. The closest parallel to the British experience in this regard is France, which has maintained a majority two-ballot voting system for most of the period since the advent of the Fifth Republic in 1958, when a more proportional system was abolished. Proportionality was reintroduced, however, for the elections to the Assemblée Nationale in 1986, with the majoritarian formula being restored once again in 1988. Second, the House of Commons is now also the only parliament in Western Europe whose membership has been consistently and exclusively elected in single-member constituencies. Here too France is the closest parallel, but when proportional representation was temporarily adopted in 1986 it also necessitated the use of multi-member constituencies. Single-member constituencies also exist in Germany, but in this case they fill only half of the seats in the Bundestag, the remainder being allocated on the basis of regional party lists; and now also in Italy, where they fill 75 per cent of the seats.

   Third, the United Kingdom government is currently one of only two governments in Western Europe which command a majority of parliamentary seats while at the same time representing only a minority of popular votes. While minority governments are far from exceptional in many Western European countries, these are administrations which not only represent fewer than half the popular votes, but also – by definition – command only a minority of parliamentary seats. Today, Spain and the United Kingdom alone possess governments able to translate minority electoral support into a parliamentary majority. The British case is much more striking, for here many of the individual members of parliament who sustain that majority do not command one even within their own constituencies. In the 1992 election, for example, some 40 per cent of the seats were won without an overall local electoral majority, the winning threshold falling as low as 26 per cent of the vote (and just 19 per cent of the electorate) in the constituency of Inverness, Nairn and Lochabar.

Fourth, and perhaps most importantly, the British principle of parliamentary sovereignty, when coupled with the practice of executive dominance, allows for the creation of a government which, despite its relatively weak representative base, enjoys more effective and more centralized power than almost any other in Western Europe. This is a government which is free from the constraints that might be imposed by a written constitution or a bill of rights; which has never had to face the challenge of an independently elected upper chamber of parliament; and which, due to the virtual absence of strong local or regional government, rarely has to confront opposition from alternative centres of political power.[1] Finally, and more circumstantially, the United Kingdom is now also the only political system in Western Europe in which there has not been even a minimal degree of alternation in the party composition of government since the beginning of the 1980s.

From a Two-Party to a Three-Party System

Although it is this sheer cumulation of political and institutional peculiarities which has prompted a renewal of the debate on constitutional reform in the United Kingdom since the late 1980s, it is the working of the electoral system in particular, and its translation of minority electoral support into governing parliamentary majorities, which has tended to provoke the most widespread comment and criticism in recent years. In one sense this new wave of criticism is surprising, in that the electoral inequities which are evident today are not necessarily very different from those which existed in earlier periods. For the fact is that *no* postwar government has ever enjoyed majority electoral support: the last occasion on which a single party won an overall electoral majority was in 1931. It is also worth recalling that the average electoral support won by the Conservatives over the past four elections (42.6 per cent) was substantially higher than the average vote which brought Labour to power in the mid 1970s (38.3 per cent). But what is very different now, and has spotlighted the inequities of the system in a very striking manner, is the sheer strength of the third-party vote and its extraordinary degree of under-representation in parliament.

132   MAPPING THE WEST EUROPEAN LEFT

Table 5.1 Combined average share of the vote won by the two largest parties in various Western European party systems, 1950s to 1980s

	1950s	1960s	1970s	1980s
Austria	87.1	90.2	93.1	87.6
Belgium	81.0	63.3	47.3	34.4
Denmark	63.1	59.1	50.2	50.4
Finland	48.8	46.7	43.5	48.0
France	43.4	56.4	46.5	57.2
Germany	78.0	85.8	91.0	85.2
Iceland	63.9	66.4	61.3	51.6
Ireland	74.1	79.1	81.2	79.1
Italy	63.9	64.7	69.2	58.4
Luxembourg	75.0	70.1	57.9	63.5
Netherlands	61.4	55.0	52.4	63.5
Norway	65.1	64.9	59.7	65.5
Sweden	68.2	65.1	66.1	65.5
Switzerland	50.2	48.6	46.7	43.8
United Kingdom	93.9	88.7	80.1	71.6

For all its inadequacies, the British electoral and governmental system did seem to work reasonably evenly in the 1950s, 1960s, and – albeit to a lesser extent – in the 1970s, at a time when electoral preferences remained relatively concentrated around the two major parties. For although neither of the two ever managed to win an overall electoral majority, their combined support effectively dwarfed that of any alternative party. Thus while the constitutional structure of the British state always marked it as an oddity in Western Europe, its peculiarities seemed suited to what was also a relatively exceptional party system, for in almost no other West European polity did just two parties together account for such an enormous share of the vote. This is no longer the case, however. In the 1950s, for example, Labour and the Conservatives together polled an average of 94 per cent of the vote, well above the figure polled by the two largest parties in any other West European system (see Table 5.1). In the 1960s, they polled almost 89 per cent, a figure which was second only to that in Austria. By the 1970s, however, the combined share of the two parties had fallen to just 80 per cent, less than that in Austria, Germany, or Ireland, and by the 1980s it had fallen further to just 72 per cent, a figure which was not substantially higher than that received by the two biggest parties in multi-party systems such as the Netherlands, Norway, and Sweden.[2]

Nor was it the case that this very marked decline in the two-party vote in the 1980s was the result of a simple fragmentation of political support, in which the residual 30 per cent or so was dispersed among a wide variety of small alternative alignments. On the contrary, this aggregate electoral shift resulted from the effective transformation of a two-party system into a three-party system, in which Liberal (and Alliance) support had increased from an average of 5 per cent in the 1950s and 10 per cent in the 1960s, to 15 per cent in the 1970s and to a striking 24 per cent in the 1980s. Indeed, by the 1980s, Liberal–Alliance support in the United Kingdom had grown to exceed that of Liberal parties in almost every other West European system, even though the strength of its parliamentary representation remained well below that of most of these parties.[3] In practice, and as a result of the workings of the British electoral system, what has recently become a three-party system at the electoral level has therefore remained a solidly two-party system at the parliamentary level, with the Conservatives and Labour together winning an average of almost 95 per cent of Westminster seats in the 1970s, and just over 93 per cent in the 1980s – a combined parliamentary representation which continued to reflect their once secure, but now clearly bygone electoral predominance.

This imbalance is most graphically illustrated by looking at the average number of votes for each party in relation to its number of seats (see Table 5.2). Over the past three elections, for example, each Conservative seat has cost an average of 37,244 votes, while each Labour seat has cost an average of 42,379 votes. Each Liberal or Alliance seat, on the other hand, has cost an average of 325,399 votes, almost nine times as much as the comparable Conservative figure, and almost eight times that of Labour.

Proportional Representation and Political Fragmentation

In the 1950s there was a generalized debate on the merits and drawbacks of proportional electoral systems in Europe and the United States, which focused principally on the extent to which the proportional system in Weimar Germany had facilitated the rise of fascism. Its upshot was a widespread assumption that the use of proportional formulae led to the development of multi-party systems, whereas the use of majority or (as in the UK) plurality voting systems generated two-party systems. At the time, this causal connection between the type of electoral system and the degree of political fragmentation was thought to have been clearly established – and likewise its direction: the electoral system was the cause, the type of party system was the consequence. In historical reality, however, the relationship is by no means obvious. Indeed, if anything, multipartism was less the consequence of proportionality than its cause. For the typical pattern was that those countries which opted for proportional

Table 5.2 Votes and Seats in British Elections, 1983–92

	Total Votes	Total Seats	Number of Votes Per Seat
Conservative			
1983	13,012,316	397	32,777
1987	13,760,583	376	36,597
1992	14,231,884	336	42,357
Labour			
1983	8,456,934	209	40,464
1987	10,029,807	229	43,798
1992	11,619,306	271	42,876
Liberal/Alliance			
1983	7,780,949	23	338,302
1987	7,341,633	22	333,711
1992	6,083,661	20	304,183

voting systems did so precisely because their political alignments were already fragmented.

The abandonment of what had been the more or less universal practice of majoritarianism in elections in Western Europe generally accompanied the introduction of universal male suffrage, and came about in two distinct stages.[4] In the first of these, proportional systems came to be adopted by those countries in which there existed a significant minority – whether ethnic, linguistic, or religious – the continued allegiance of which was required if these polities were to be assured of long-term political stability. Had these minority groups been excluded from the public decision-making system, and denied full representation within the newly democratized legislatures, it was felt that they would sooner or later pose a threat to the legitimacy of the regime itself. It was for this reason, for example, that both Belgium and Switzerland, each of which was characterized by a high degree of religious and linguistic fragmentation, were among the earliest countries to adopt proportional representation, even though they were later to prove among the last to extend full voting rights to women.

The second wave of proportionalism came in those countries in which, as in contemporary South Africa, existing factions within the established elite felt threatened by an emerging alternative majority. More specifically, proportional electoral systems were introduced in those countries where a bourgeois bloc which had previously governed on the basis of a restricted franchise was obliged to grant the vote to the newly-mobilizing working class and the propertyless, that is, to that section of society which was then considered to constitute a 'natural' electoral majority.[5] This fear of the new majority was particularly acute in those countries in which the bourgeois bloc was internally divided into distinct parties, reflecting conflicts based on region, religion, or economic sector. In these circumstances, it was felt that the evident bias of majoritarian voting systems could easily give a relatively unified mass working-class movement a dominant political position. There were then only two options. Either the granting of the vote to the working class could be accompanied by an attempt to subordinate internal divisions, so creating a unified anti-working-class party; or the separate minority identities could be preserved, and the existing bourgeois parties could persist, but only through the adoption of a system of proportional representation which would not bias representation against smaller parties. In general, it was the latter course which was taken. In the Netherlands, Norway or Sweden, for example, acceptance of proportional representation was the price exacted for extension of the franchise.

In both sets of circumstances, therefore, fragmentation actually preceded the adoption of proportional voting systems. Neither, however, was of much relevance during the period in which the franchise was extended within the United Kingdom. So far as ethnic, linguistic, or religious minorities were concerned, for example, the only group of any real importance in the late nineteenth century were the Catholic Irish, who, because of their regional concentration, were at no disadvantage in a majority voting system.[6] Nor were there serious divisions within the bourgeois bloc which might have opened up the possibility of its displacement by a natural working-class majority in the wake of enfranchisement. Indeed, what is most striking about the British case is that the first major extension of the suffrage to the working class in 1867 occurred at a time in which no separately-organized mass working-class party had been established, and in which no mass political threat therefore seemed apparent.[7] Hence the fact that the United Kingdom proved unique in Western Europe in *not* accompanying universal male suffrage by the adoption of some form of proportional representation was hardly surprising. For Britain was also exceptional in its sheer lack of political fragmentation, and hence the absence of pressure to introduce the sort of 'electoral compromise' which had accompanied democratization elsewhere.

Albeit somewhat belatedly, however, this historical tendency for political fragmentation to give rise to demands for proportional electoral formulae is now also apparent in the British case, with the pressure for a change in the electoral system coming hard on the heels of the decline in the two-party vote. Moreover, it is increasingly evident that this pressure is coming not only from the massively under-represented Liberal constituency, where calls for a more equitable voting system have long been advanced, but also from within the Labour Party, and the left more generally.[8] There are two reasons for this. The first is a sense of democratic principle reluctant to see even erstwhile political opponents such as the Liberal Party discriminated against so badly, and sceptical about the legitimacy of those exclusive claims to govern (whether voiced by the Conservatives or Labour) which are sustained only by minority electoral positions. Such a standpoint suggests that the adoption of a more proportional voting system is a democratic imperative, even if makes the prospect of an overall Labour majority in parliament highly unlikely and so points to coalition government.

The Weakness of Labour

The second reason for contemplating a change in the electoral system is one of practice more than principle. It stems from the need of the left to find some way in which to prevent the persistent re-election of Conservative governments and the equally persistent exclusion from office of the Labour Party. For given the growth both of support for the Liberal Party and regional bias in the distribution of the Conservative and Labour vote, even many socialists who remain committed to the demand for an overall Labour majority have become increasingly sceptical of the chance of achieving one in the foreseeable future.

There are good grounds for such fears. For, as can be seen from Table 5.3, the mean level of support for the left in the United Kingdom in the 1970s and 1980s now falls well below that recorded by the traditional (social-democratic and communist) left in many other West European states, ranking ninth out of fifteen countries in the 1970s, and thirteenth out of fifteen in the 1980s, when it exceeded only the levels reached in Switzerland and Ireland. Labour's record in terms of duration in office is even more dismal. In the whole period from 1970 to 1990, for example, traditional parties of the left *throughout* the rest of Western Europe – whether socialist or communist, whether governing alone or in coalition, and whether stronger or weaker in electoral terms – have actually governed for longer periods than has Labour in the United Kingdom.

Labour's relative decline in recent years is all the more striking in view of the fact that – contrary to popular impression – the overall balance between left and right has remained remarkably stable in Western Europe as a whole across the postwar period. In the 1950s, for example, parties of the left polled an average of 40.6 per cent of the popular vote across Western Europe, a level only marginally higher than that of the 1980s, when they polled some 38.2 per cent. If Green

Table 5.3 Average electoral support and governing record of social-democratic and communist parties* in Western Europe, 1970–90

	Average Vote in 1970s	Average Vote in 1980s	% of time a left party was in office 1970–1990
Austria	51.2	46.1	98
Belgium	29.5	29.4	52
Denmark	36.6	32.8	48
Finland	42.7	39.8	96
France	43.1	47.4	33
Germany	44.2	39.4	59
Iceland	38.5	32.4	53
Ireland	12.7	8.9	51
Italy	45.1	44.7	77
Luxembourg	43.5	37.4	58
Netherlands	35.3	32.1	38
Norway	39.8	38.3	66
Sweden	48.8	50.0	76
Switzerland	28.1	22.1	100
United Kingdom	39.1	29.2	28

* Excludes new left and green parties.

party support is also taken to be part of the broader left, then the average left vote in Western Europe in the 1980s reached 40.5 per cent, almost identical to the figure for the 1950s (see Table 5.4). There is, to be sure, substantial variation from country to country, with the overall vote for the left in the 1980s marking quite a significant increase over that of the 1950s in Germany and Italy, and quite a significant decrease in Finland, France, and Norway. But nowhere has the change been so pronounced as in the United Kingdom, and in no country has there been such a dramatic decline. In this sense the British experience is quite exceptional.

The United Kingdom is also exceptional in terms of the sheer monopoly of the left vote which is enjoyed by Labour. The history of the European left since the late nineteenth century has been character-ized by four phases of electoral mobilization, each of which has been associated with a particular ideological grouping. The first, most important and enduring of these saw the emergence of social-democratic parties, beginning in the 1880s, and lasting for three decades during which working-class politics was effectively unified within a single political formation in each of the countries concerned. The second phase witnessed the split in social democracy precipitated by the Russian Revolution of 1917, and the development of a communist movement which in certain countries won a majority position on the left. The third phase came in the 1960s, and its effects

Table 5.4 The Electoral Performance of the Left in Western Europe, 1950s to 1980s

	1950s	1960s	1970s	1980s
Austria				
SD	43.3	45.0	50.0	45.4
CP	4.3	1.7	1.2	0.7
G				4.1
All	47.6	46.7	51.2	50.2
Belgium				
SD	35.9	31.0	26.6	28.0
CP	3.4	3.7	2.9	1.4
G				6.1
All	39.3	34.7	29.5	35.5
Denmark				
SD	40.2	39.1	33.6	31.9
CP	4.5	1.0	3.0	0.9
NL		7.7	8.3	14.4
G				0.7
All	44.7	47.8	44.9	47.9
Finland				
SD	25.9	26.9	25.1	25.4
CP	22.1	21.6	17.6	13.9
G				2.7
All	48.0	48.5	42.7	42.0
France				
SD	25.9	26.9	25.1	25.4
CP	23.9	21.4	21.0	12.4
G				0.9
All	49.8	48.3	46.1	38.7
Germany				
SD	30.3	39.4	44.2	39.4
CP	1.1			
G				5.1
All	31.4	39.4	44.2	44.5
Iceland				
SD	19.5	15.0	14.8	17.1
CP	16.4	16.3	23.7	15.3
NL				7.8
All	35.9	31.3	38.5	40.2
Ireland				
SD	10.9	14.8	12.7	8.9
NL			1.4	3.9
G				0.4
All	10.9	14.8	14.1	13.2
Italy				
SD	18.0	19.4	14.4	16.4
CP	22.7	26.1	30.7	28.3
NL		2.2	3.3	4.0
G				1.2
All	40.7	47.7	48.4	49.9

Table 5.4 continued

	1950s	1960s	1970s	1980s
Luxemburg				
SD	37.1	35.0	35.4	32.3
CP	11.6	14.0	8.2	5.1
G				6.8
All	48.7	49.0	43.6	44.2
Netherlands				
SD	30.7	25.8	31.9	31.0
CP	4.4	3.2	3.4	1.1
NL	0.6	3.0	4.0	3.7
All	35.7	32.0	39.3	35.8
Norway				
SD	47.5	45.4	38.8	37.4
CP	4.3	1.8	1.0	0.9
NL		4.0	6.9	6.8
All	51.8	51.2	46.7	45.1
Sweden				
SD	45.6	48.4	43.7	44.5
CP	4.2	4.2	5.1	5.6
NL				2.9
All	49.8	52.6	48.8	53.0
Switzerland				
SD	26.0	26.0	25.7	21.2
CP	2.7	2.6	2.4	0.9
NL			0.9	3.5
G				3.9
All	28.7	28.6	29.0	29.5
United Kingdom				
SD	46.3	46.1	39.1	29.2
All	46.3	46.1	39.1	29.2
WESTERN EUROPE				
SD	32.2	31.7	30.5	29.5
CP	8.4	7.8	8.0	5.8
NL	0.0	1.1	1.7	2.9
G				2.3
All	40.6	40.6	40.2	40.5

Note: SD = Social Democrats; CP = Communists; NL = New Left; G = Green Parties. Note that only parties winning at least 1 per cent of the vote or one parliamentary seat have been included in these figures.

Source: Michael Gallagher, Michael Laver and Peter Mair, *Representative Government in Western Europe*, New York 1992, pp. 60–8.

were at once more marginal and more uneven, as smaller new left parties sprang up in a number of countries, combining a degree of commitment to Marxism with attachment to the more libertarian values which were then being voiced by the student movement. Finally, in the late 1970s and 1980s, various ecological parties emerged throughout Western Europe, which – if often only peripherally connected to the traditional politics of the left – have increasingly come to be seen as potential components of a more broadly based radical alternative.

The fragmentation of the left which has resulted from these different phases of mobilization is more or less characteristic of almost every country in Western Europe (see Table 5.4). In some cases, such as Denmark, Italy, and Switzerland, representatives of each of these four families of parties currently compete in popular elections, with a greater or lesser degree of success. Elsewhere, at least three of these party families compete. In the United Kingdom, however, and uniquely so, the left vote is monopolized by just one single strand of the left, with no substantial communist, new left, or green party managing to poll even 1 per cent of the vote.

From one perspective, this can be seen as beneficial, affording a degree of unity of purpose and strategy which is clearly not possible in the more fragmented scene of other West European countries. From another perspective, however, it is precisely this absence of alternatives which may be partly responsible for the exceptional electoral decline of the left. In the United Kingdom, the monopoly of the left which is enjoyed by the Labour Party effectively means that any disillusion with Labour as a party will be reflected in a disenchantment with the left as a whole. The two are not distinguishable. Elsewhere in Western Europe, however, disaffection from one of the parties of the left does not necessarily result in a shift to the centre or right. On the contrary, the evidence suggests that when faced with a variety of different options within the left, voters who turn away from one party of the left are more likely to transfer to another party within the same bloc rather than to transfer to a party from the centre or right, thus leaving the overall support for the left bloc as a whole relatively unchanged.[9] It is in this sense that the fragmentation which characterizes the left through-out most of Western Europe may also help to sustain the overall support for the left, whereas the concentration of left voting behind Labour in the United Kingdom may well be one reason for its current debility.

Finally, Labour's weakness compared with other traditional social-democratic parties in Europe is also highlighted by the relative thinness of its organizational implantation. Labour, which has never been a party of mass mobilization, currently supports a level of individual membership which is equivalent to just 0.7 per cent of the British electorate as a whole, as compared to the much higher average of between 2 and 4 per cent for the memberships of the social-democratic parties in Belgium, Denmark, Finland, Germany, and Norway. In

Austria almost one in eight of the electorate are members of the socialist party, while in Sweden the figure reaches one in six. Only in the Netherlands and France does the ratio of socialist party membership to the electorate fall as low as that in the UK.[10]

Labour and Electoral Reform

Conscious of the party's recent failures, and aware of the obstacles which stand in the way of its winning sole government again, Labour's National Executive has set up a working party on electoral systems, to compare the British and other voting systems, and consider reforms in elections to a variety of constitutional bodies, including the House of Commons, a possible elected second chamber, the European Parliament, and the proposed parliaments for Scotland and Wales. An interim report which assesses a number of different electoral systems was published in July 1991, and a final report, making specific recommendations for electoral reform, was considered by the party in 1993. The working party, otherwise known as the Plant Commission, has been widely hailed as a watershed in the consideration of constitutional reform by the left, and for this reason its interim report, which includes a full discussion of the arguments for and against electoral reform, particularly merits serious scrutiny.

The first thing which must be emphasized regarding the interim report of the Plant Commission[11] is that while Labour is a relative latecomer to the debate on electoral reform, the full and lengthy character of this report suggests that the party is at least finally taking the question seriously. As Plant notes in his preface to the interim findings: 'There can be nothing more fundamental in a democracy than proposals to change an electoral system and it is imperative that we evaluate the reasons for such reforms, the criteria which we believe legitimate electoral systems should satisfy, and that we examine in detail the major systems in the light of these criteria. This is our strategy in this report. Elections are central to democracy and their nature should not be determined by a few simplistic slogans.' Nevertheless, perhaps because Labour is a latecomer, the Commission itself shows signs of being sometimes poorly informed about the evidence it cites and the standards it applies.[12] That said, the more obvious empirical errors it makes are easily corrected, since there is now an extensive and widely available literature on electoral systems and their potential consequences.[13]

However, in some cases the inadequacy of the Report's information has led to seriously misleading conclusions. This occurs, for example, when the report attempts to tackle the crucial question of the degree to which different electoral systems yield proportional outcomes – that is, results where the distribution of parliamentary seats closely matches that of the popular vote. Only one of a wide variety of possible indices of proportionality is cited, and this index is applied to one recent election only in each of the countries assessed. The result is that while the Report does indeed emphasize the disproportionality inherent in the British system, it nevertheless also suggests that the United Kingdom enjoys a more proportional system than that of either France (a two-ballot majority voting system) or Spain (a distorted proportional system). In fact, the particular index invoked by the report, and frequently employed elsewhere, is not suitable for the specific needs of a comparison of the UK with other European systems. For it is an index which exaggerates the *dis*proportionality of systems in which there are many parties (such as Spain or France) and concomitantly underestimates the degree of disproportionality in less fragmented systems (such as the UK).[14] An alternative and arguably more effective measure, based only on the extent to which there is a distortion in the shares of votes and seats won by the three largest parties in the system, thus controlling for differential levels of fragmentation, and applied not just to one election but to all elections in the 1980s, thus controlling to some extent for variation over time, suggests that the British system is *substantially* less proportional than that used in *any* other West European country in this period – and that it is more than twice as distortive as the system adopted in Spain in this period, and almost twice as distortive as even the majority voting system in France (see Table 5.5).

More generally, however, and no matter what index is used, any attempt to measure the proportionality of an electoral system which is based on an analysis of the *outcomes* of elections must recognize the likelihood that voter choice will have been informed by prior popular awareness of the constraints imposed by the system, thus potentially masking powerful sources of distortion. For example, the suggestion that small parties may not suffer too badly from the distortions inherent in a given electoral system simply because they are small parties at the outset, may overlook the possibility that these same parties might have won more votes had the system been manifestly more proportional in the first place. Hence, when the Plant Report cites figures which indicate that the level of proportionality of the outcomes in British elections was much higher in the 1950s and 1960s than was the case in the 1970s and 1980s (p. 45), this may have less to do with the electoral system as such, which was certainly not intrinsically more proportional, and rather more to do with the unwillingness of many voters to waste their ballots on what was then seen to be a very weak third party.

Table 5.5 Mean levels of electoral disproportionality in West European countries in the 1980s*

Germany	.50
Denmark	.83
Sweden	.94
Netherlands	.95
Austria	1.07
Belgium	1.28
Italy	1.81
Switzerland	1.95
Iceland	2.08
Ireland	2.15
Norway	2.44
Finland	2.61
Luxembourg	2.90
Portugal	3.31
Greece	4.05
France	6.17/8.06**
Spain	6.75
United Kingdom	14.12

* The figures refer to the average deviation between the percentage of seats and the percentage votes for each of the three largest parties in the country concerned, across the different elections. The higher the figure the greater the average deviation and hence the greater the degree of disproportionality.
** The second figure refers only to the elections of 1981 and 1988 which were conducted under the majority voting system.

It is important to recognize that electoral systems *per se*, beyond simple electoral formulae, exert a great influence in their own right. The Plant Report rightly notes at the outset that 'the issues at stake between different sorts of electoral systems are not primarily technical ones, but rather raise some of the deepest questions about the nature of representation, the role of parties and the nature and scope of assemblies and parliaments' (p. 6). It also correctly indicates that there is no such thing as an 'ideal' electoral system, but that a balance must be found between alternative and often conflicting criteria – equity, clarity, stability and so on. Hence the idea that an electoral system in itself can cure a variety of different political ills, or that a change in voting procedures will necessarily lead to certain desirable consequences, is largely misconceived. As has been noted elsewhere, electoral systems provide at best 'facilitating conditions', whose impact will be mediated by a range of other institutional and cultural factors.[15]

But while the Plant Report acknowledges these truths in its framing and concluding remarks, it largely ignores them in its assessment of the existing British system, and the principal alternatives to it. Its discussion of the Single Transferable Vote in Ireland offers a case in point. The report remarks that while STV is sometimes suggested as a practicable and preferable – because significantly more representative – alternative to the current British system, it can nevertheless be criticized for encouraging 'patron-client or parish pump politics' (p. 71). No one can doubt that these are features of the Irish scene. The Report also argues that STV may not in fact encourage fairer political representation of women, or of ethnic and other minorities – identified as one of the major goals of electoral reform – since there is 'no necessary correlation' between STV and greater minority representation (p. 69).

In the STV system, voters are presented with a composite list of individual candidates, ordered alphabetically and regardless of party affiliation. Rather than choosing between different party lists, therefore, as in most PR systems, the voter simply ranks these competing candidates in order of preference, whether by party or not, giving a first preference to the most favoured candidate, a second preference to the next most favoured candidate, and so on, allocating as many preferences as she chooses. Voting takes place in multi-member constituencies, and the allocation of the seats within these constituencies to the individual candidates involves a long and often difficult process of determining the quota of votes necessary to win a seat; transferring votes (on the basis of lower preferences) from candidates whose first-preference total exceeds the quota; eliminating candidates with very few first preferences and transferring their votes (again on the basis of lower preferences) to other candidates, and so on, until all the seats in the constituency are filled.

What are the consequences of such a system? The Plant Report's deductions are contradictory. The reality is that there is no *necessary* correlation between this particular voting system and *any* of the consequences of which it speaks – whether it be the representation of minorities or the encouragement of patron-client politics. In fact, there is no necessary correlation between *any* electoral system and particular political consequences of this kind. The logic of STV, for instance, promotes competition not only between parties, but also between rival candidates from the same party each chasing their own first-preference votes within the same multi-seat constituency. In the particular case of Ireland, for a variety of contingent reasons, the *practice* is that this intra-party competition tends to revolve largely around parish-pump issues, with each of the contending candidates claiming to be able to serve the interests of a locality best – a pattern which naturally does little to further the representation of women or minority groups.

But it must be emphasized that is perfectly possible to conceive of an STV system in which rival claims were pressed not in terms of parish-pump interests, but rather in terms of gender (female candidates competing against male candidates within a given party), or even ideology (left-wing candidates competing against those from the right on the same list). In other words, appeals for intra-party first preferences could be made on the basis of individual qualities which had little or nothing to do with geography, and which might therefore well create the conditions for a more balanced pattern of representation. The point here is that while competition between candidates from the same party *is* a logical consequence of STV, the precise *form* taken by this competition is much more contingent, and there is little to be gained by simply assuming that specific Irish conditions are universal effects of it. The mechanism which promotes parochial political campaigning in Ireland could, in another setting, encourage minority political campaigning – and hence minority representation, if parties are willing to nominate minority candidates in the first place, and if voters opt for them in the second place. Reflections of this kind are familiar in the literature on STV,[16] but seem to have escaped the authors of the the Plant Report.

The same sort of arguments apply to their discussion of the present British electoral system. The Report concedes that it has various faults, but contends that it has the advantage of maintaining a direct link between the act of voting and the formation of a government. Elections held under many PR systems, as is well known, often give no single party a overall majority of parliamentary seats, leaving the formation of a cabinet to post-electoral bargaining between the different party leaders. Government is therefore decided less by the outcome of elections than by – often confidential – negotiations within the political class. Indeed in some cases, for instance in Ireland in 1989, the outcome of such negotiations can lead to the formation of a government formed by parties whose support actually fell in the election. Under the British system, on the other hand, the Plant Report maintains that 'the emergence of a government is the direct consequence of the act of voting; it is not the result of coalition building between party elites in a parliament or assembly; nor can a government be brought down by a change in the attitude of coalition partners' (p. 53).

But while this is once again usually true *in practice*, it is by no means a logical or *necessary* consequence of the working of the British system. To speak of the Conservative governments of the eighties emerging 'as a direct consequence of the act of voting' when they had polled only some 40 per cent of the vote, but won over 50 per cent of the seats, is in any case hazardous – and simply impossible if we are to recall the elections of 1951 and February 1974, when the party which gained the most electoral support actually ended up in opposition. But even setting this aside, the central point remains that the absence of coalition government in the UK, and hence of post-electoral negotiation, is due not so much to the nature of the electoral system in isolation, as to its combination with a particular pattern of party support. There is nothing in the British electoral system itself which necessarily discourages coalitions, nor anything which necessarily leads to single-party majorities. Indeed, coalitions are not only clearly conceivable under the first-past-the-post system, but, in the event of a so-called hung parliament, they might prove inevitable. Conversely, single-party majority government is perfectly possible under PR, and has often occurred, with different degrees of proportionality, in Greece, Ireland, Norway, Spain, and Sweden.

What this once again simply illustrates is that it is not only the electoral system itself which matters, but also the particular balance of political support. Neither type of system will in itself ensure minority representation, or parish-pump politics, or more stable government, or whatever, for in the end all of these factors also depend on the attitudes, behaviour, and structure of both the electorate and the party system.

The Constituency Link

The Plant Commission expresses a number of misgivings about the British plurality voting system, but chief among its advantages – more important even than the alleged link between the act of voting and the formation of a government – it holds to be the representative bond between an individual MP and his or her constituency. This is a tie of which it speaks in quite glowing, if not almost romantic terms. The Report declares that is a matter of 'common concern' that MPs should have 'organic' links with constituencies (p. 30) which can themselves be seen 'as embodying some sense of identity, of being in some sense a natural community' (p. 71). Later, in distinguishing between what it calls 'legislative' assemblies, designed to pass laws and elect and sustain governments, and 'deliberative' assemblies, intended primarily to revise and scrutinize policy (the role it judges suitable for a putative democratic second chamber), the Report concludes that a central feature of the former should be 'a clear link of accountability between a legislator and a clearly defined body of people' (p. 95). This in turn requires single-member constituencies, which define 'a clearly defined group of people to whom the member is accountable' (p. 30).

Given the transcendent importance attached here to individual

representation and accountability within a single-member constituency, it is perhaps surprising that it has been adopted by so few other
West European systems. The German system, in which half of the
members are elected on a plurality vote in single-seat constituencies,
while the other half are elected from party lists under a proportional
formula, does include this type of linkage – although within substantially more populous constituencies; and the Plant Report notes this
element of it with favour. The French double-ballot system, when
operable, also uses single seat constituencies; it also ensures – unlike
that in the UK or Germany – that the elected MP does eventually win an
overall majority of the votes in the constituency. In Italy the current
electoral reform introduces single-member constituencies for three-
quarters of the seats of the Chamber and Senate, the rest being elected
proportionally; its effects are still untried. But that is really as far as it
goes. The Irish system of STV can be discounted, since the very strong
(and possibly even 'organic') linkages which exist between individual
members and their constituencies have been dismissed by the Plant
Report as undesirably parochial.

There are two central flaws in these conventional arguments for the
British system, repeated by the Report. In the first place, the very large
proportion of MPs (some 40 per cent in 1992) who are elected by a
minority vote in their constituency poses a problem of accountability
and representativeness little different from that facing the governing
party as a whole in relation to the wider electorate. If the notion of an
individual MP's accountability to a single-member constituency is taken
seriously, it is not compatible with that of a plurality (as opposed to a
majority) system. The Report is not unaware of this difficulty, and
devotes some consideration to the Alternative Vote System, which like
STV includes first and lower-preference votes, but unlike STV uses
only single-member constituencies.[17]

There is a second and graver problem, however. It is this. The Plant
Report nowhere addresses the question of to whom, and by what
means, the accountability of an individual MP is ensured, or the role of
party within this system of accountability. In fact, the accountability of
the individal MP is simply assumed, rather than proven (or justified).
The reality, however, is that there is little, if any, evidence from the
various studies of British electoral behaviour which suggests that the
role and character of the individual MP exerts a substantial influence
on voting preferences. Rather, whether it be through a long-standing
process of psychological party identification, or through a concern with
a particular set of issues, or as a result of economic circumstance and
outlook, individual voters in the UK are primarily *party* voters, whose
response to politics is predominantly mediated by party performance

and party ideology. It is in this sense that MPs are accountable – accountable, that is, to their party, which, in turn, is accountable to the electorate. That is why the electoral success or failure of individual MPs is determined largely, albeit not exclusively, by the success or failure of the party to which they belong. British democracy is party democracy, in the same way that British government is party government. The weakness of non-party modes of representation can be seen very clearly in the complete absence of independent MPs representing mainland British constituencies in the House of Commons.

This, indeed, is the great irony of British democracy – that an ideology of individual MP accountability is so fervently maintained within what is in effect a wholly *partisan* political structure. There are, to be sure, maverick party MPs, on both the left and the right of the political spectrum; and there are also MPs who devote a considerable amount of time to the sort of constituency work which, under a different system, might just as effectively be carried out at more locally representative level. But a recent and stark example of the reality of political accountability in the Commons and the 'partyness'[18] of British democracy is the experience of former Labour MP Dave Nellist, whose tireless constituency work and prominent (indeed award-winning) role in Parliament were disregarded both by a party which expelled him, and by a local electorate which, albeit only marginally, rejected his independent candidacy in favour of that of the new 'official' Labour candidate.

But if there is in practice little to indicate a widespread popular concern with the merits or otherwise of individual MPs, there also seems little in principle to justify Plant's concern with the maintenance of single-member constituencies. The Report early on cites, but does not heed, John Stuart Mill's view that there is no 'logical link between opinion and [geographical] constituency', and hence that 'if an electoral system was to represent opinion on an individualistic basis, then constituencies had to be self-selecting rather than being pre-ordained in geographic locations' (p. 29). This is, in effect, the logic of representation in 'pure' PR systems, where both the link between voters and their representatives and the mode of accountability are mediated wholly by party – each party's voters together constituting what amounts to a 'self-selecting' ideological 'constituency'. No doubt the Plant Commission would regard such a practice as insufficiently 'natural' or 'organic'; but it is striking that it receives no real attention in the Report.

Actually, the objections to the British electoral order go even deeper here. For it can be said that this is a system which, so far from encouraging genuine accountability of the individual MP, actually militates against it – since it is one of the very few in which it is impossible to separate out a preference for a candidate on the one hand, and a preference for a party on the other. Yet such a separation is clearly essential if the acccountability of the MP is to be distinguished from that of the party. If a voter wants the party, then she is obliged to accept the candidate; if she wishes to repudiate the candidate, then she is also obliged to reject the party. The two are quite indistinguishable. Thus even if there were a popular demand for the more equitable representation of women or minority candidates, this could not currently be expressed except in a way which also has an impact on the party preference of the voter.

This is not the case in the single-member constituencies in Germany, where the elector's second vote can be used to support a party whose candidate might prove an unacceptable choice for the first vote; nor is it really the case in France, where the more open first ballot can be, and often is, used to indicate a relatively unconstrained candidate or party preference. Even in the United States, where a simple plurality, single-member voting system also obtains, voters do at least have the option of participating in primary elections in order to express their preferences among the various party candidates. It is also important to recognize that choice among party candidates is also possible in a variety of PR systems, including not only STV, but also those many party-list systems in which voters have the option of changing the party nominees' order of the candidates on the list through a system of intra-party preference voting.[19] In the UK, however, where party membership is exceptionally low, and where the selection of candidates therefore occurs at a far remove from any sense of popular partici- pation, candidate and party are fused, with the choice of one wholly determining the choice of the other. Indeed in this party democracy par excellence, it would seem that the notion of individual MP accountability, so treasured by Plant, is little more than a chimera.

The Consequences of Reform

Whether Labour itself becomes converted to electoral reform, or whether it is forced into that position as a condition of acquiring Liberal backing within a future hung parliament, its endorsement will clearly be required if the British electoral system is ever to be changed in the foreseeable future. The Conservatives, unsurprisingly, are resolutely opposed to reform, and the Liberal Democrats remain too weak to effect a change on their own.

The Plant Report does favour reform, albeit guardedly. Its reluc- tance to move away from the use of single-member constituencies effectively rules out the adoption of either STV or any one of a variety of straight party-list types of proportional representation, excluding even those which allow voters to express alternative candidate preferences within the list. The Report also clearly reflects a desire to ensure stability and political authority within the House of Commons, and a concern at the prospect that a more proportional system might enable too many new parties to enter it – a feeling no doubt shared even by more committed reformers within the Labour Party. Admitting that new parties may well be squeezed out by the present British system, the document nevertheless also invokes the argument that these 'are not necessary when [the established] parties are doing their job well' (p. 63) – and adds: 'it is at least arguable that if a new entrant party does represent a significant range of public opinion, then under plurality systems parties have an incentive to incorporate those aspirations and policies in its [sic] own raft of values and policies' (p. 75). The logic of such a view is that small parties, rather than seeking a mandate of their own, can best serve democracy by flagging issues to be taken up by their bigger and more established opponents – in much the same way that the role of small firms in the marketplace should be to indicate gaps in the product ranges of the larger conglomerates. Still, whatever the limitation of current party thinking, Labour support for some form of fairer voting procedure would clearly increase the likelihood of electoral reform in the United Kingdom, and to the extent that more proportional outcomes are achieved, this might in turn transform the structure of party competition.

As yet, of course, all of this remains uncertain. The final Plant Report, which was submitted to Labour's annual conference in September 1993, endorsed the adoption of PR for elections to a new upper house, as well as for elections to devolved assemblies in Scotland and Wales, but nevertheless shied away from proportionalism in the House of Commons. Its majority opted instead for the wholesale maintenance of single-member districts, modified only by a novel counting process which falls somewhere betwen the French double ballot and the Alternative Vote. In this system, voters would indicate both a first and a second preference. Should no candidate achieve an absolute majority (50 per cent + 1) of the first preferences, then all but the two leading candidates would be eliminated; and the second preferences of those eliminated which went to either of the two leading candidates would be added to their totals, making the one with the highest combined score the winner. In the autumn of 1993, the Labour Party Conference – following a discussion of the Report – voted to commit a future Labour government to a referendum in which the

electorate would have an opportunity of choosing between maintenance or modification of the present system.

Uncertainty therefore still prevails. In the first place, there is no
guarantee that the change recommended by the majority of the
Commission would win popular approval. Secondly, there is no
guarantee that it would result in a fairer distribution of seats in relation
to votes. Indeed, the only improvement it would be likely to effect is to
reduce the chances of individual MPs being elected on a minority of
constituency votes. Thirdly, if such a system were adopted for the
House of Commons, while more proportional formulae were introduced for the upper house and devolved assemblies, the discrepancy
between the two systems could well renew pressure for further reform,
and a more equitable system for all elections. Finally, it should be noted
that even the use of more proportional rules for elections other than to
the House of Commons could in itself transform the structure of party
competition.

There are two key aspects of such a transformation of potential
concern to the left in Britain. The first is the perennial question of
coalitions, and the challenge they pose to the principle of the electoral
mandate. As things currently stand, a party enters an election with a
given programme, and if successful, proceeds to implement that
programme while in government; and since government in the UK is
single-party government, this involves few if any ambiguities. The
voter knows what is at stake and is aware of the alternatives. In coalition
situations, on the other hand, the party programme may be known, but
the extent to which it may be implemented is not, since negotiations
between the parties may result in the shelving of certain parts of the
manifesto. Voters therefore vote in the dark, without knowing which
elements of the policies they support may be jettisoned when it comes
to the stage of post-election bargaining. There is, in short, the problem
of post-electoral compromises.

In one sense this problem is both acute and intractable: the need to
negotiate coalitions means that office-seeking parties will inevitably
temper their policies in order to win government, and policies once
declared vital may slip off the political agenda. This may be regrettable,
but it can also be seen as a reasonable price to pay in order to have a
more representative parliament. Indeed, as noted above, it may even
yet happen under the present voting system, if future elections were
leave no single party with an overall majority.

In another and more important sense, however, the problem of
compromise simply reflects a shift in a terrain which is already well
established. For although the current British system rarely necessitates

post-electoral bargaining, it gives an enormous incentive to a form of *pre*-electoral bargaining – that is, to a politics of compromise that actually precedes the elaboration of a party programme. British parties are office-seeking parties, and under the present electoral system that means they must appeal to as wide a public as possible. Typically, this requires the adoption of a programme which aims squarely towards the centre ground, eschewing the sort of radical agenda which might drive potential supporters into an opposing camp. There are, to be sure, exceptions to this pattern: Thatcherism is a notable example. But the usual pressure in British politics is towards strategies that seek the centre – a pressure which has, of course, led Labour to marginalize and on occasion even expel more radical elements within the party. Indeed, when Thatcherism did move the Conservatives further to the right in the early 1980s, and Labour swung to the left, the abandoned centre was rapidly filled by the Liberal–SDP Alliance, whose impressive electoral performance served to underline the importance of maintaining a more consensual appeal. In a sense, Thatcher was relatively fortunate that her radical strategy did not cost her party too much support. While the Conservatives in 1979, 1983 and 1987 polled a markedly smaller share of the vote (averaging just under 43 per cent) than in the heyday of the more consensual Macmillan period (49.4 per cent in 1959), the efficacy of this vote was magnified by its regional concentration in the South of England and by the divisions of the non-Conservative vote – factors enhanced by the inherent inequities of the first-past-the-post system.

The normal upshot in Britain is that compromises which might otherwise characterize the rounds of post-electoral bargaining in a more proportional system now tend to occur *before* the election takes place. The result is a clear tendency to exclude radical options from the agenda completely. Where coalitions are normal, on the other hand, radical policies may well be tempered after the vote, but are at least more likely to have been presented to the electorates to begin with. It is in this sense that coalition politics could represent a not unwelcome shift in terrain, that postpones bargaining till after the election and so frees the electoral agenda itself for bolder alternatives.

The second potential concern of the left has been a fear of the fragmentation of political alignments which might result from the adoption of proportional representation. For while proportional systems do not cause fragmentation, any more than plurality systems prevent it, there is a crucial difference between the two: the latter are 'strong', that is they impose powerful constraints on voter choice, whereas the former are 'weak', and may impose only a minimum of constraints.[20] Thus if there already exists a tendency towards political fragmentation, plurality systems can do much to discourage it, whereas PR systems will tend to do little.

The decline of the aggregate Conservative–Labour vote and the growth of the Liberal Democrats and of the Scottish and Welsh nationalists, as well as the sudden but short-lived surge in Green Party support in the 1989 elections to the European Parliament, make it clear that a tendency towards fragmentation does exist in the United Kingdom. The introduction of PR would help to remove brakes on it. But the release of a more diverse range of political opinion in Britain could only be seen as an enhancement of the democratic process. Given that these parties currently accumulate more than one in every four votes in the United Kingdom – a figure that probably underestimates their potential appeal – it is difficult to see how it can be argued that they should be denied full representation.

But what would be effect of lifting the constraints of first-past-the post on the two major parties themselves? It could be feared that PR might lead to a three-way split of the Labour Party – with the creation of a small radical party of the left, and a migration of the right to the Liberals, leaving a rump even more reduced than is the Labour Party today. The likelihood of a secession to the right is impossible to conjecture; but one to the left might not prove too damaging. At the moment, Labour is almost the only social-democratic party in Western Europe which enjoys a monopoly of the total left vote (see Table 5.4, above). Elsewhere in Western Europe, the tendency is for social-democratic parties to be flanked by at least one more radical alternative, whether communist, green, or new left. In practice the effect of these is to help maintain a more radical agenda within the public sphere, and to provide an alternative choice which helps to sustain the overall vote for a left bloc. Neither of these consequences can be regretted, and should electoral reform lead to the emergence of an electorally credible party to the left of mainstream Labour in the UK, it might well have a similar impact.

On the right of the British political spectrum, fragmentation might also occur. Parties of the far right have mobilized effectively at recent polls in Belgium, France and Germany – and the conservative *Leghe* of Northern Italy have scored a major breakthrough. The recent successes of the Progress parties in Denmark and Norway, and of New Democracy in Sweden, are other cases in point. But while proportional electoral systems may have facilitated the appeal of such parties,[21] and secured their representation in parliament, it is naive to think that proportionalism in itself can explain their electoral success – just as it is naive, and even dangerous, to imagine that it was proportional representation in the Weimar republic that was responsible for the rise of German fascism.

For the fundamental choice in cases like these is whether it is better to try to squeeze out such parties through legal or institutional means – by maintaining plurality voting, for example, or by establishing high electoral thresholds in a proportional system – or to try to defeat them politically. If the terms of the Plant Report's discussions of the role of new entrants into politics are accepted, it could be thought preferable to let such extreme groups mobilize on an independent basis, and be challenged as such, rather than have them flag issues which are then absorbed by a larger, more effective and formidable opponent.

Conclusion

Electoral systems are at most mediating agencies. The patterns of politics always owe much more to the nature of the parties and to the type of party system. No system will *in itself* produce or prevent fragmentation, and none will necessitate or prevent coalition government, for this will also depend on the way in which the parties compete and the manner in which they organize. Proportional Austria has long maintained a less fragmented party system than has the majoritarian UK. Majoritarian France has had more experience of coalition government than has Ireland, while the proportional parliaments in Norway and Sweden have had nearly as much experience of single-party government as Westminster.

It is for this reason that the debate over constitutional and institutional reform, which is a feature not only of modern politics in Britain, but also in Belgium, France, Israel, Italy, and Japan, needs to go beyond questions of electoral reform, and address the role of political parties themselves. Modern democratic governments are, in the main, party governments, and modern democracy is largely party democracy. But the traditional dominance of parties in representative systems of government – not least the British – is now under challenge. The mass party, which once provided the crucial linkage between the citizens and their government, is slowly but inexorably drifting away from the society of which it was part. Membership in parties is declining in almost all Western democracies, even if this is more evident in terms of the ratio of party members to the wider electorate than in absolute numbers. Electoral strategies rely increasingly on personalized campaigns and privileged access to the mass media, rather than on any real sense of partisan mobilization. In most countries parties depend increasingly heavily on public funds for their resources, and are often to such an extent nested within the state that they may be more suitably defined as official institutions rather than as representatives of civil society.[22]

The linkages between parties and people are waning, and with them the legitimacy of parties themselves. It is striking that the new movements of the far right not only flaunt an unconcealed xenophobia: they also ventilate hostility towards what they typically denounce as the privilege, patronage, and self-serving pursuits of the traditional party elites. This is a refrain that strikes a chord with many contemporary voters. Within the last year it has been used to great effect by the National Front in France, the Freedom Party in Austria, and the various *Leghe* of Northern Italy, all of which have unfurled cogent complaints about the cartelization of the party system as a cloak for the promotion of racist and neo-fascist policies.

In Britain, as in most Western democracies, the parties clearly require revitalization. For while partisan divisions in Britain are probably more acute than in many other European countries, and the intensity of adversarial exchanges in the Commons discourages any sense of an elite cartel, the parties remain extraordinarily remote. Party membership is now and always has been lower than that in almost any other European country; the social presence of parties is now and always has been more muted than that in almost any other country; and the extent of active, participatory democracy, both inside the parties themselves as well as within the wider political system, is now, as in the past, minimal. British parties sustain themselves on the basis of their role in Westminster. With the possible exception of the Liberals, they are essentially parliamentary affairs, whose connection to the wider society is largely confined to the need for periodic electoral endorsement. But as parliamentary sovereignty itself becomes eroded, or is transferred to supranational European institutions, so too may the position of the traditional parties atrophy. No amount of electoral engineering will in itself cure this deeper disorder.

Notes

1. See the important study by Arend Lijphart, *Democracies: Patterns of Majoritarian and Consensus Government in Twenty-One Countries*, New Haven 1984, which identifies the United Kingdom as the paradigmatic case of majoritarian democracy. While the British style of government is exceptional by European standards, it does nevertheless bear many similarities to the practices in countries such as Australia, Canada, and New Zealand, which imported many of the constitutional features of the Westminster system.

2. These figures and those reported in Table 5.5 come from a data collection on Democracy and Competition which has been gathered in collaboration with Stefano Bartolini of the University of Geneva.

3. See Michael Gallagher, Michael Laver, and Peter Mair, *Representative Government*

in Western Europe, New York 1992, pp. 75–8. More generally, see Emil Kirchner, ed., *Liberal Parties in Western Europe*, Cambridge 1988.

4. For a full discussion, see Stein Rokkan, *Citizens, Elections, Parties: Approaches to the Comparative Study of the Processes of Development*, Oslo 1970, pp. 72–168. The theme is also addressed in Peter J. Katzenstein, *Small States in World Markets*, Ithaca 1985, pp. 150–6.

5. See Stefano Bartolini, 'The European Left Since World War I: Size, Composition, and Patterns of Electoral Development', in Hans Daalder and Peter Mair, eds, *Western European Party Systems: Continuity and Change*, London 1983, pp. 139–76.

6. Interestingly enough, however, the British government did introduce the Single Transferable Vote (STV) form of proportional representation as part of the constitution of the Irish Free State in the 1920 Government of Ireland Act as a means of encouraging the allegiance of the Protestant minority in Ireland, and, even later, in 1973, introduced the same system for provincial elections within Northern Ireland as a means of encouraging the allegiance of the Catholic minority. Thus while the *principle* of proportionality as a means of minority representation has been accepted by Westminster governments, it has never been seen as relevant to the pan-British electoral context.

7. See the full discussion in Perry Anderson, 'Origins of the Present Crisis', *New Left Review* 23, January–February 1964, pp. 28–53, recently reprinted in his *English Questions*, London 1992, pp. 15–47.

8. See, for instance, the recent extensive discussions in Robin Blackburn, 'The Ruins of Westminster', *New Left Review* 191, January–February 1992, pp. 5–35, and in Perry Anderson, *English Questions*, pp. 302–53.

9. See the discussion in Stefano Bartolini and Peter Mair, *Identity, Competition and Electoral Availability: The Stabilisation of European Electorates, 1885–1985*, Cambridge 1990.

10. For up-to-date figures on France, see Colette Ysmal, *Les Partis politiques sous la Ve République*, Paris 1989, p. 163; for all other countries see Richard S. Katz, Peter Mair, et al., 'The Membership of Political Parties in European Democracies, 1960–1990', *European Journal of Political Research*, vol. 22, no. 3, 1992, pp. 329–45.

11. The report was published by the *Guardian* in July 1991 as Volume 3 of Guardian *Studies*.

12. Such as, for instance, the claim by the Report (on p. 10) that the modern French voting system was established under the impact of World War II, even though the present majority system was not adopted until the inauguration of the Fifth Republic in 1958; or when it repeats (p. 59) the somewhat conventional mistake about Italy maintaining a system of compulsory voting; or, when evaluating the impact of electoral systems on the stability of governments (pp. 36–7), the Report relies for its evidence on comparative data published as long ago as 1975, which fail even to indicate the relative duration of the various governments' terms of office under the different electoral regimes.

13. The most comprehensive recent English-language studies include Vernon Bogdanor and David Butler, eds, *Democracy and Elections*, Cambridge 1983; Andrew McLaren Carstairs, *A Short History of Electoral Systems in Western Europe*, London 1980; Bernard Grofman and Arend Lijphart, eds, *Electoral Laws and Their Political Consequences*, New York 1986; Arend Lijphart and Bernard Grofman, eds, *Choosing an Electoral System: Issues and Alternatives*, New York 1984, and Rein Taagepera and Matthew S. Shugart, *Seats and Votes: The Effects and Determinants of Electoral Systems*, New Haven 1989. A very clear and readable review of the main alternatives to the British system can be found in Vernon Bogdanor, *What is Proportional Representation?*, Oxford 1984.

14. See Arend Lijphart, 'The Political Consequences of Electoral Laws, 1945–85: A Critique, Re-Analysis, and Update of Rae's Classic Study', *American Political Science Review* vol. 84, no. 2, 1990, pp. 481–96.

15. See Giovanni Sartori, 'The Influence of Electoral System: Faulty Laws or Faulty Method?' in Grofman and Lijphart, pp. 43–68, which offers perhaps the best single discussion of the importance of the political and institutional contexts within which electoral systems operate.

16. See, for instance, the comprehensive analysis in Michael Gallagher, 'The Political Consequences of the Electoral System in the Republic of Ireland', *Electoral Studies* vol. 5, no. 3, 1986, pp. 253–75.

17. Given that the Liberal Democrats are probably the 'least disliked' alternative as far as both Labour and Conservative voters are concerned, at least in England, they would also be likely to receive the transferred second preferences of both Labour and Conservative candidates when either was eliminated from the contest under the Alternative Vote System, and hence they might be expected to do particularly well as a result of such a reform. This is particularly so given that the Liberal Democrats lie in second place in a large number of constituencies. In the event of votes not transferring, of course, which occurs when voters indicate a first preference only, then the victorious candidate in a single-member constituency could well be elected without an overall majority, thus helping to maintain a practice which electoral reform is intended to correct.

18. This is the term used in the context of a more general analysis in Richard S. Katz, 'Party Government: A Rationalistic Conception', in Francis G. Castles and Rudolf Wildenmann, eds, *Visions and Realities of Party Government*, Berlin 1986, pp. 31–71.

19. See the discussion in Richard S. Katz, 'Intra-Party Preference Voting', in Grofman and Lijphart, pp. 85–103.

20. See Sartori, 'The Influence of Electoral Systems'.

21. Indeed, the main reason why Socialist President Mitterand pressed for the introduction of a proportional system in the French legislative elections of 1986 was in order to help ensure that the Front National would win representation in parliament, so reducing the share of the seats won by the traditional parties of the right, and thereby reducing the likelihood that a strong government of the right could be formed.

22. See Richard S. Katz and Peter Mair, 'Changing Models of Party Organization: The Emergence of the Cartel Party', paper presented to the ECPR Joint Sessions, University of Limerick, 1992.

6

France: Triumph and Tragedy

George Ross and Jane Jenson

The legislative elections of March 1993 closed an era for the French left. During the 1960s and 1970s, virtually all sections of it had claimed to represent different and more daring forms of progressive politics than mere social democracy. 'Social democrat', in fact, was a term of opprobrium used to disqualify those who failed to demand a 'rupture with capitalism'. Then after 1981 its leader, François Mitterrand, became the first two-term President of the Fifth Republic and its parties controlled parliament for ten out of twelve years. A dramatic change in outlook ensued. In power the French left altered course towards structural adjustment – austerity and monetarism – to improve the competitive capacity of the country.

In March 1993 the bill came due. Parliamentary elections brought the worst results in modern history. All left groupings together won barely one-third of the vote, and the Socialists (nearly 40 per cent in 1981) dropped below 20 per cent. Plainly, this defeat represented a strong popular desire to punish the left for its deeds and misdeeds. The worst deed was mass unemployment – officially 10.5 per cent, but in reality much higher, in a society marked by increasing levels of urban insecurity and racist hostility to immigrants. But there was also a terrifying scandal of official indifference to hospital use of HIV-contaminated blood, and a cloud of suspicion around campaign funding. The left in power had come to seem a caste of careerist technocrats clinging to office. Traditional linkages of representation between parties and people had broken down. French trade unions had become the weakest in the advanced capitalist world. The Socialist Party, giving up any pretence of popular organization, seemed more like an advertising agency for feuding presidential hopefuls. Ideas, projects, dreams of another and better

158

society had vanished, replaced by fatalism about a world out of control.

There are common strands in the fate of the French left, which weave it into a wider history. Through the seventies and early eighties it promoted an ambitious reformist project, based on the assumption that the traditional resources of a national state could be mobilized to accelerate economic growth and redistribute its fruits. That strategy soon foundered on the rocks of the global economy. It then tried to use what public leverage remained to make national firms more competitive in international markets, relying now on budgetary, fiscal and monetary policy to set the necessary economic parameters and – where possible – limit the social costs. The results, even where successful, inevitably undermined its own popular base. 'Flexible' working practices weaken the labour movement and erode working-class identities already attenuated by post-industrial shifts of occupational structure and consumer culture. Formerly loyal left voters become volatile. Seeing no more than marginal and conjunctural differences between right and left, they vote on grounds of the moment, when they care to vote at all. None of this means that the left cannot win elections, of course. Voters will punish the right as well as the left for their deeds and misdeeds. But such transformations do mean that a long moment in the left's history, and not only in France, is over.

But the story of the French left nonetheless remains in certain respects unique. History, since 1920 and especially since the Cold War, had fixed a deep divide between Socialists and Communists. Given the electoral system of the Fifth Republic after 1958, success demanded that the left find ways to mute or overcome these divisions and make effective alliances. The balance of forces between the PCF and PS was such that through 1981 the strategic puzzles of managing these divisions within the left pointed it towards strongly radical projects. The logic of radicalization was further exaggerated by the fact that the left as whole never held power during the long postwar boom. It was the right that presided over the economic and social modernization of the country in the sixties, and then continued in office into the international downswing of the seventies. Political marginalization nourished a distinctive culture, and ultimately strategy, of opposition on the left. Intellectually, its world was unfettered by routines of government or constraints of managerial 'realism'. The result was that when the left finally came to power in the eighties, it arrived with a sweeping programme for social change, of a kind not seen in Western Europe since the forties. At the same time, the constitutional framework of the country gave it exceptional latitude: control of an imperious presidential executive, and a huge majority – 70 per cent of the Assembly – in the legislative. Rarely have a strong programme and a strong state been so conjoined in postwar Europe. But fate also decided that this combination would be put to the test of a global recession enveloping all national states, and obstructing any radical projects. Confronted with this quite new challenge, the French left had to respond either with enough creativity to sustain its original aims, or agility to abandon them without destroying itself. In the end, it was able to do neither. To see why the victory of 1981 had turned to ashes by 1993, it is necessary to look back at the trajectory that brought it to office, after so many years of opposition.

The Pains of Modernization: 1945–68

In the late 1940s France still had many of the features of an agrarian, protectionist and empire-oriented society, of nineteenth-century stamp. More of the active labour force – nearly 30 per cent – was in farming and forestry than industry. Over the next two decades, this world was obliterated.[1] In these years economic growth was sudden and rapid: GNP grew from an index of 100 in 1938 and 109 in 1949 to 333 by 1970 and 400 by 1975. Industry as a whole expanded, traditional branches were replaced by modern sectors, productivity shot up, and service employment exploded. There were striking changes in consumer habits. The French built houses, installed central heating and indoor plumbing, and bought refrigerators, washing machines, television sets and automobiles at a tremendous pace. Foreign trade shifted decisively away from France's former colonial empire towards Europe and the advanced capitalist world.[2]

The wind behind this swift voyage to modernity was statist. An economic transformation of France occurred, not for the first time, more despite than because of French capitalists. Exasperated by the inertia of the traditional *patronat*, administrative elites pushed ahead with a partly-planned modernization after 1944. When the absence of any politically stable majority in the Fourth Republic became an obstacle to their designs, they bypassed parliament for state agencies wherever they could.[3] The advent of the Fifth Republic, transferring power away from the legislature to a presidential executive and the higher civil service, eventually created a legitimate framework for the pursuit of a strong *dirigiste* strategy: indicative planning, industrial policies, mobilizing public incentives and resources, and manipulation of credit. In this space, new generations trained in the prestigious and efficient National School for Administration (ENA) colonized the executive and political class itself. General de Gaulle, a genuine charismatic leader, put his political weight behind the technocrats' strategy. This consummate nineteenth-century statesman needed twentieth-century instruments for his geopolitical ambitions. France required independent military high technology to take its strategic distance from the USA, and advanced industry to help build the Franco–German core of an autonomous Europe that could one day undo the Yalta settlement.[4]

Progress in the early Fifth Republic was nonetheless profoundly contradictory. The modernizing coalition of statist technocrats, forward-looking political elites and fractions of capital had to compromise with sluggish sectors of business, the petty bourgeoisie, and peasants. Moreover, change was carried out with little regard for its social consequences. The General himself wavered between reliance on the efficacy of soothing nationalist rhetoric and advocacy of Catholic-corporatist notions of participation, which crucial parts of his own political coalition opposed.[5] The technocrats shared the contemporary conceit that economic growth and sound management would dissolve social conflict. Modernizing fractions of capital had a simpler outlook, adamantly refusing any concessions to labour without open class warfare. Much of the *bien pensant* peasantry and petty bourgeoisie desperately wanted French society to remain in the nineteenth century.

Labour was excluded, an object of modernization. Aggregate growth figures considerably outstripped wage increases.[6] Development was often based on the transformation of a rural labour force into semi-skilled operatives, a profoundly disorienting experience for those who lived through it. Backed by a supportive state and faced with weak unions and an under-regulated labour market, employers saw no reason to grant substantially better pay or conditions to their workers. Nor did the Gaullist regime show much awareness of the need to modernize institutions like schools and universities, the legal system or the police. The General was a precociously skilful performer on television. But the political culture of official France oscillated between a technocratic authoritarianism and an archaic paternalism.

The Communists Squander Their Chance

The starting-point of the modern French left flowed from the workings of Gaullist power. By the early 1960s the consolidation of a conservative parliamentary majority around the General had re-polarized party politics, narrowing the strategic options of the non-Communist left and increasing the pressures for collaboration between Communists and Socialists. At that time, the PCF commanded the support of about a fifth of the electorate, and the loyalty of the majority of the working class; it controlled the largest trade-union federation and possessed an army of militant members; it enjoyed substantial power in local government, and wide ideological influence. By contrast, its traditional Socialist rival – the Section Française de l'Internationale Ouvrière (SFIO), having immolated itself in Cold War manoeuvres and bloody colonial repressions during the Fourth Republic, was now in free fall. Its vote was scarcely half, and its membership a mere fraction, of that of the PCF. After a decade of talking Marxism and doing the work of the right, French Socialism had little credibility.[7]

The opportunities presented by the structures and pathologies of Gaullist modernization thus initially fell to the Communists. The PCF's first quandary was choice of strategy. Its repertory held but two: unity of the left as practised in the period of the Popular Front, or militant autonomy – the strategic posture of its 'class against class' years between 1928 and 1934, and again during the Cold War.[8] The party had traditionally picked the strategy of a united front whenever it judged full participation in electoral politics either possible or desirable. Such was the case when the party began to perceive that its isolation might end in the early 1960s.

A united front meant arriving at some understanding with the non-Communist left. In its original form, it had been conceived as a means to achieve important, but limited, reformist goals. Like the Leninism from which it was derived, the strategy was profoundly centralizing – a vision of change effected by politicians controlling and altering the state. Proponents of renewing this approach – over which the party leadership was initially divided – could point to the tremendous outpouring of popular support it had fostered in the Popular Front and Resistance–Liberation years. On the other hand, the mobilizing forces of hostility to fascism and admiration for the USSR, so important for its success in the 1930s and 1940s, were of scant relevance in the 1960s. There was another difference too. In the earlier period, the aims of the united front had been fairly modest: specific adjustments in French diplomacy and limited domestic reforms.[9] Even these had proved hard to achieve. Now the party's declared objective was a socialist transformation of France – a task of a different order.

The facile assumption that a strategy from the thirties could be dusted off for the sixties was accompanied by a belligerent refusal to admit that French society had changed in the interim. Beginning in 1955, general secretary Maurice Thorez issued a series of pronouncements restating the claim that French workers were suffering both relative and absolute pauperization – thus in effect telling Communists to ignore rather than analyse the obvious consequences of economic growth around them.[10] Official hostility to birth control, in the name of a patriotic natalism, signalled similar blindness to social changes transforming the family and labour force.[11] Worst of all, the PCF leadership – which had approved Soviet suppression of the Hungarian revolt – refused to heed any call for a de-Stalinization of its own organization, in which a rigidly undemocratic centralism persisted unabated. Thorez's last purges, of precocious Eurocommunists in 1961 and 'pro-Italian' students slightly later, eliminated from the party precisely those currents which might have proposed better alternatives for it.[12]

Yet despite this combination of unimaginative and destructive responses to the changes in the world around it, electoral and institutional developments in the aftermath of the Algerian war strongly favoured the PCF's turn towards alliance politics. If the Communists had lost about a quarter of their postwar electorate during the consolidation of the Fifth Republic, their vote then held steady at around 22 per cent in the early 1960s, while Socialist support plummetted. The SFIO's electoral nosedive, and the abolition of proportional representation under de Gaulle, forced the Socialists to reconsider their hitherto absolute refusal of any understanding with the Communists. So, for all its inability to rethink its own positions in any larger sense, the PCF could move in slow but sure steps towards its immediate objective – an agreement with the non-Communist left around a 'common programme' that would reflect as much as possible of the party's own vocabularies and purposes.

The 1965 presidential campaign gave the PCF its chance. When the Socialists failed to field an anti-Communist politician – Gaston Defferre – who had been positioning himself for the role of a centrist candidate, François Mitterrand promptly presented himself as a candidate standing for unity of the left. An ambitious veteran of the Fourth Republic, Mitterrand had among other posts been minister of the interior and minister of justice during some of the worst years of the Algerian war. But when de Gaulle came to power with the backing of the army in 1958, he was one of the rare centre-left leaders who refused to rally to the new regime. His presidential bid skilfully finessed the deadlock among Socialists and centrists over whom to put up against de Gaulle.[13] Even though Mitterrand made few programmatic concessions to the PCF, his willingness to end Communist isolation was enough for the party's new general secretary, Waldeck Rochet. Mitterrand's well-judged campaign, loyally supported by the PCF, won 45 per cent of the vote in the run-off. The scale of this success made it clear that de Gaulle had become vulnerable, and a more formal alliance of the left possible. In the next two years, there was gradual progress towards clearer agreement and closer electoral coordination.

The dramatic upheaval of May–June 1968 upset all previous calculations. Every established party floundered amidst this seismic shock to French society. But the PCF was challenged most deeply by what looked like a virtually revolutionary situation, and was found most acutely wanting. The student rising on the streets of Paris included many former leaders of its own campus organization among the militants of the movement, purged for deviations from the party, and now intensely hostile to it. Caught by surprise, the PCF's claims that legitimate student discontent had been perverted by *gauchiste* agitators playing the game of monopoly capital, if not in the pay of the police, only discredited it. The party's own response to the sudden breakdown of authority in the capital came through the CGT, which called for a general stoppage.[14] The result was far beyond anyone's expectations – the largest strike in the history of modern capitalism, unleashing a wave of factory occupations across France, and threatening to topple the regime. But party and union alike had little more idea what to do with the explosive energies of workers than of students. Eventually the CGT bargained away the great strike for substantial, but entirely conventional, concessions on wages, hours and working conditions – and bailed out General de Gaulle in his hour of danger.

The crisis of 1968 revealed how out of touch French Communism had become with the social forces of opposition gathering under Gaullist rule. Its inability to cope with the student movement was the most spectacular symptom of this failure to adapt. But its handling of labour was in its own way another. The CGT adopted an uncompromising stance towards modernization, denouncing capitalism with unfailing verbal militancy and mounting strikes whenever it could. But, keeping to lines laid down by the PCF, the CGT let workers understand that a new social order would come down from above, when the left had achieved political power, and that meanwhile they should concentrate on traditional economic demands in the workplace – whose pursuit made the day-to-day practice of the CGT look like that of moderate unions anywhere. Furthermore, because the confederation believed that simple ideological themes were needed to unify the working class, it tended to downplay local struggles which did not fit them, and to overlook the aspirations of new categories within France's changing workforce. It thus easily appeared stodgy and bureaucratized – failings which redounded to the advantage of the CFDT, its ex-Catholic ally and rival.

From Gaullist Modernization to Crisis

The crisis of 1968 changed the political world of French capitalism. De Gaulle's abrupt resignation a year later deprived it of charismatic authority, and both weakened and redefined the dynamic of modern-ization.[15] Georges Pompidou, the General's successor, was less vision-ary and more conservative. He sought to attenuate *dirigisme* and give business more freedom of manoeuvre in markets at home and abroad. Prompted less by doctrinal liberalism than by a pragmatic moderation of statism, the new regime responded to the increase in trade-union power since 1968 by trying to depoliticize labour relations. Pompidou's first prime minister, Jacques Chaban-Delmas, first devalued the franc to undercut the rise in wage costs since 1968 and then undertook a mild social democratization from the right. Guided by Jacques Delors, his left Catholic advisor for social affairs,[16] Chaban encouraged decentral-ized collective bargaining and a neo-corporatist incomes policy in the public sector.

This turn was resisted by both capital and labour, and much of it was soon discredited.[17] Business was now facing insistent pressure from a combative working class during a period of rapid economic expansion. Pompidou's presidency saw a paroxysm of high investment and growth, exceeding the already formidable rates of the de Gaulle years. Now, however, the boom was accompanied by rapidly rising real wages and rates of inflation. Corporate profits began to decline. In these conditions, efforts to force up productivity often triggered industrial conflicts, as newly inducted workers and semi-skilled operatives rebelled against speed-up and harsher working conditions.[18]

Clouds were already gathering before 1973. French capital, dragged into the twentieth century by the state, had modernized without decisively bettering its competitive position. The economy was now, however, far more dependent on international trade. When the benign environment of the long world boom suddenly petered out, and much fiercer conflict over market shares became general, French business – ignoring its handicaps and hoping difficulties would be temporary – was initially slow to react. The first oil shock brought little awareness of the minefield that French capitalism had begun to cross. Government and employers both acted as if the new situation was but another cyclical downturn susceptible to short-term Keynesian correction. The result was a rapid rise in unemployment, accelerating inflation, and the end of the old tempo of growth.[19] French industry created fewer new jobs, while state capacities to do so were squeezed by rising benefit payments and declining tax revenues. But since it took some time for the growth of unemployment to weaken organized labour, strikes continued to be quite frequent. In this climate, it is not surprising that the French left resumed its political advance.

Sidling to Success: 1974–81

In 1968 the PCF had squandered its greatest opportunity since the War. In the aftermath, initiative passed back to its rivals. In 1971, the hitherto divided and reduced non-Communist left was regrouped – under the impulsion of François Mitterrand – into a new Parti Socialiste at Epinay.[20] The freshly-minted PS was a federation of competing factions within a cleverly designed structure, in which strength inside the party depended upon support mobilized outside it, encouraging each tendency to develop its own politics and discourse. This pluralism allowed the PS to appear to be almost all things to all people, reaching out to the left and to the centre simultaneously. What held it together in a common purpose, however, was Mitterrand's leadership of the party. His strategy remained left unity. In June 1972, negotiations between the PS and PCF led to the signature of a joint programme.

Apart from its vagueness on issues of defence and foreign policy (where the two parties agreed to disagree), the Common Programme was in most respects a close replica of policies the PCF had long advocated. The new coalition pledged itself to expand welfare benefits and raise wages, nationalize large swathes of industry, democratize management at firm level and planning at national level, increase the rights of trade unions and enhance participation generally. The document was somewhat milder than traditional Communist plat-forms, but its radicalism was still startling in any comparative perspec-tive. Mitterrand's acceptance of it was, however, carefully calculated. His aim was to strengthen the electoral hand of the Socialists at the expense of the Communists, as a springboard to winning the pre-sidency. The Common Programme was an instrument to that end rather than a commitment in its own right. By moving leftwards and yielding to the PCF on issues of programme, he was purchasing a certificate of good radical conduct which would help to blur political distinctions between the Socialists and the Communists. His gamble was that this would attract both soft sectors of the PCF electorate and dissident younger middle strata, seeking a new home after 1968, to the PS.

The price of this wager was to bind the PS to a stronger set of reforms than certain of the party's factions would otherwise have wanted. Mitterrand was well aware that the French left, including his own Socialist Party, was a mixture of two political cultures. For one the Liberation-period ring of the Common Programme was just right. For the other it was old-fashioned. But the road to power, he reckoned, meant choosing the first culture. This was the option that would ensnare the Communists, allow the PS to raid the PCF electorate, and yet pick up votes from a discontented centre. Mitterrand understood that the logic of union was such that while the left as a whole was likely to grow in strength, one party's gain would come at the other's expense.

On its side, the PCF leadership realized that Communist prospects within a united front depended on a rapid modernization of its own postures. So the party's theoretical stance was wrenched away from the miserabilist absurdities of the recent past. Its organization was loosened, as recruitment standards were relaxed and more space opened for rank-and-file discussion. Its international affiliation was modified: painfully and partially, distance was taken from the Soviet model. The result of these changes was that members flocked in, particularly from the new middle strata, and interest in the party's politics and leaders grew significantly. By the mid 1970s the PCF had acquired a more legitimate standing as a broad party of the French left than at any other point in its history.

But the balance of advantage was nevertheless shifting towards the PS. In the 1973 legislative elections the PCF still outpolled the PS – but it would be the last time. A year later, Mitterrand – at the head of a united left – came within 1 per cent of defeating the candidate of the right, Valéry Giscard d'Estaing, in the presidential election of 1974. A very small margin separated the French left from gaining power in circumstances that would – in retrospect – have been far more favourable than they later became. At the time, the dynamic of unity still seemed promising enough. But was the PS now benefiting disproportionately from it? Once Giscard was installed in the Elysée, the PCF leadership started to hesitate. From the outset of the party's turn towards a united front there had been substantial internal opposition to the dilution of workerist purity which the new strategy was bound to bring. Sectarian reflexes were now reinforced by psephological fears within the obscure but very real debates at the top of the party. The upshot was an unstable compromise, as the party tried to find ways to undercut the growth of PS electoral advantage by asserting an updated PCF radical identity. This led first to a year of attacks on the Socialists as unreliable partners and then – lurching in the opposite direction – to a hectic embrace of Eurocommunism.[21] For a time the PCF became a very lively place to be, recruiting more and more members. But the turn to Eurocommunism sharpened internal conflict, as pro-Soviet elements within the leadership – hostile to criticisms of the USSR – moved into an alliance with opponents of the united front, supported by Moscow.[22] Pressure began to build up inside the party for a break with the Socialists. The PCF, however, had no viable alternative strategy. Reasserting a vaguely modernized 'class against class', go-it-alone stance was a sure recipe for declining mass support in the France of the seventies. The strife between the two wings of the party simply pulled the PCF in incompatible directions, resulting in a series of incoherent public positions and strategic mistakes over the next decade.

Meanwhile, the Socialists were engaged in their own manoeuvres. At the Assises du Socialisme in 1974 the PS joined with the Rocardian wing of the PSU (the small Parti Socialiste Unifié) and delegates from the CFDT to give a strong *autogestionnaire* thrust to Socialist politics, emphasizing workers' control rather than state direction of the economy. Most *autogestionnaires* were well known to be suspicious of the Common Programme and hostile to the PCF. Mitterrand nevertheless resolved to coopt them into his camp without altering his strategy, calculating that their inclusion would broaden the electoral base of the PS and give him a freer hand in dealing with the PCF in a governmental situation virtually everyone sensed would come soon. The PCF was understandably irked. Formally, however, unity still withstood these strains.

In 1977 municipal elections indicated that the united left had achieved an electoral majority in the country. Within another year, it looked as if the legislative elections of 1978 would finally bring the French left to national power, albeit in cohabitation with a President of the right. But the local polls had also shown the PS gaining a clear-cut advantage in the inter-party competition of the left. Eurocommunist innovations had failed to halt the PCF's relative loss of ground. The result was to destroy the unstable equilibrium in the party leadership, as the forces hostile to the alliance with the PS gained the upper hand. In the summer of 1977, the PCF suddenly abandoned left union. Fifteen years of political work were abandonded, as the party turned on the Socialists, savagely attacking them for allegedly reneging on the Common Programme. The immediate consequence was that the left, seemingly more interested in mutual recrimination and character assassination than governance, lost the legislative elections of 1978.

But this self-inflicted defeat did not affect the two parties of the left equally. Mitterrand and the PS, presenting themselves as *unitaires pour deux* and standing by the Common Programme, salvaged their reputation. Blame for the disaster fell overwhelmingly, and under-standably, on the PCF. The lurch towards a French Brezhnevism destroyed its credibility in the eyes of a large part of its electorate, and of its own membership.[23] In the next three years it lost a quarter of its voters and a third of its members. More than two decades of work for a union of the left had converted many Communist militants into passionate believers in it, and attracted hundreds of thousands of new members, particularly from the intelligentsia and urban middle strata, into the party. The sudden break with the Union de la Gauche, decreed from above and accompanied by a return to miserabilist demagogy, galvanized these forces into an unprecedented inner-party revolt.[24] The PCF leadership set out to obliterate this dissent, using the full armoury of its authoritarian controls. The result was to drive activists who remained committed to unity out of the party by the tens of thousands, along with the virtual totality of the Communist intelligentsia. Those who stayed were the most hidebound and *ouvriériste* of the faithful, by definition those least capable of creative initiatives. The PCF's turn was a moral and organizational catastrophe from which it has never recovered. After 1978, it sank steadily towards a secondary station in the French left.

The consequences of the rupture between the PCF and PS soon made themselves felt in the trade-union movement. The CGT's efforts to promote unified action with the CFDT yielded to competitive bids from both sides for general actions to improve the electoral prospects of the parties that they supported. Over-politicization of industrial action was accompanied by worsening relations between the two federations, as the CGT openly took the PCF's side and the CFDT, less openly, that of the PS. While the PCF imposed its new line on the CGT and the CFDT retreated from its earlier radicalism, union membership and mobilizing power, already slipping by 1977–78, declined rapidly – with the CGT suffering most.[25] The backlash against the union of the left was not confined to the Communist Party.

Among the Socialists, Mitterrand was now attacked by Michel Rocard as an 'archaic' figure too attached to 'old left' politics, in a campaign backed by the fashionably progressive Parisian press and intelligentsia, which swung behind Rocard's announcement of his candidacy for the presidency. To remain leader of the PS, after a tough struggle, Mitterrand had to recompose the factions behind him by giving more weight to the left CERES group, which then imposed on the party a programme considerably more radical than the leanings of most of the PS membership.

But for all the travails of the left, the right in power faced acute difficulties of its own. The postwar boom was over, leaving a train of economic maladjustments, which the political situation made hard to manage. The margin of conservative dominance was very narrow – with all its warts, the left still hovered on the edge of a majority. It was clear that sectors like steel and shipbuilding needed drastic restructuring, yet the right could do little out of fear for the electoral consequences of major layoffs. High rates of inflation had to be brought down, but the government could not risk the unpopularity of a stiff deflation. The trade deficit had to be reduced, but not by resort to devaluation. Even after the second oil shock in 1979, the impending presidential elections in 1981 constrained the right to political caution. The living standards of French workers – those with jobs – continued to rise, along with social spending. Official talk of austerity, when Raymond Barre became prime minister, was not matched by comparable action. The absence of an effective deflationary programme, combined with administrative controls to minimize unemployment, meant that capital could not 'purify' itself in classical fashion; while an overvalued currency cut back the export prospects of an industrial base that was often only just competitive. At a time when capital elsewhere was reassessing its postwar strategies, much of French business was still asleep at the wheel.

In this climate of malaise, policy disputes and personal rivalries divided the right. Hoping to capitalize on discontent with Giscard's rule, Jacques Chirac came out as Gaullist candidate against him in the presidential elections of 1981, and after being beaten into third place by Giscard, offered only luke-warm support to him in the run-off. Mitterrand, running for the PS, had won just over a quarter of the vote in the first round – Marchais, for the PCF, only 15 per cent. But in the second round, enough disgruntled centrist voters abstained or switched to give Mitterrand victory. The victory came to much of the left as a 'divine surprise'. But it was greeted with great popular celebration, and changed the political atmosphere in the country overnight. Without further ado, the new President dissolved the Assembly and when legislative elections were held a month later, they produced a large majority for the left.

The results showed the complete transformation in the balance of forces between the two parties of the left. The PS secured 37.5 per cent of the vote – the PCF, with 16.1 per cent, was below half the Socialist total. The electoral system converted this ratio into a seven-to-one predominance of Socialist over Communist deputies in the Assembly, where the PS gained a large absolute majority of seats. Rough equality of position four years earlier had become crushing PCF inferiority. The party which could have negotiated a government on equal terms with Mitterrand was now a dispensable adjunct to his rule. To ensure himself against Communist sniping, and tie the hands of the CGT against temptation, Mitterrand offered the PCF four ministries. After all its tirades against 'social democracy', the party signed on to the new 'presidential majority', hat in hand – not as a partner, but as a hostage.

The Left in Power

The Socialist government which now ruled France had exceptional assets at its command. The constitution of the Fifth Republic gives enormous power to any President with a majority in the Assembly. Mitterrand, whatever else might be said of him, was a strong and skilled politician, now in complete control of a party making up nearly 60 per cent of the deputies. The right was in acrimonious disarray, torn apart by the way Giscard had fallen. The left had a long-prepared and wide-ranging programme at its disposal, for which it had received a decisive popular mandate. France, though buffeted by the strains of the seventies, was the second largest and richest economy in Europe, and its one fully independent nuclear power.

The circumstances, however, in which the Socalists had come to power contained hidden dangers from the start. The Common Programme had been effective as an instrument of mobilization and as a source of hope. But its specific proposals were neither widely understood nor supported. Many of the measures to which the left was pledged remained slogans rather than actual designs for reform. The PS elected in 1981 was itself considerably to the right of a platform whose origins went back to 1972 – its elites well colonized by ambitious civil servants more interested in power than principle. The international environment, above all, was far less favourable to a radical experiment in France than in the mid seventies, when the left so narrowly missed office. By 1981, the world economy was not only in a deep recession. The cumulative response to its difficulties was a swing to the right that had already swept the UK and USA, and would soon extend through most of Northern Europe, bringing with it a return of neo-liberal orthodoxies not seen since the twenties. The diplomatic setting had also taken a sharp turn for the worse. With Reagan's presidency, a new Cold War had set in, dominated by a massive American military build-up, and mobilization of NATO to confront the USSR, perceived as an expansionist threat. Within France itself, the ideological climate had changed abruptly in the late seventies, with the widespread conversion of once *soixante-huitard* or *marxisant* intellectuals to Cold War verities, rediscovered as the bombast of a 'new philosophy'. Neither the economic, diplomatic nor cultural setting was favourable to a government of the left, for all the institutional levers at its disposal.

The Mitterrand Experiment: 1981–84

The Socialist vision of reform derived from the original commitments of the Common Programme. There would be extensive nationalizations of the core monopoly sector of the French economy, and major changes in industrial relations to increase workers' control at firm level. Greater popular involvement from below, and new leadership of public corporations and planning institutions from above, would foster a national mobilization of research and innovation. These would make French industry more dynamic and competitive in foreign markets, and allow it to reconquer domestic markets. More rapid and equitable economic growth would in turn permit an expansion and democratiz-ation of social programmes.

This was in many ways a classical social-democratic vision of an earlier period, when confidence in a progressive postwar reconstruc-tion was at its height, in the late 1940s.[26] Its fundamental premiss was that the national state had sufficient power over its economic environ-ment to control and redirect capital flows into appropriate channels. The strategy had, however, a peculiarly Gallic twist. For underlying it was a massive dose of Jacobin optimism that change could be legislated from the centre, reflecting the self-confidence of France's enlightened technocrats in their own managerial abilities. But at the same time, the scheme assumed – not without contradiction – that electoral victory and legislative action to promote social participation would unleash a flood of popular enthusiasm, carrying the regime forward to new successes and further reforms.

Once the legislature was secure, Mitterrand was as good as his word. For a year, France was the scene of a barrage of reforms without precedent in post-reconstruction Europe. The scale of nationalization was sweeping: 90 per cent of the banking sector and a third of industry, including thirteen of the country's twenty largest corporations, were taken over by the state, making it responsible for 60 per cent of all industrial and energy investment in France. Labour reforms increased trade-union control of working conditions, mandated annual wage bargaining, and protected 'rights of expression' on the shop floor. A boldly redistributive social programme was enacted to stimulate demand: family allowances for more than one child were raised by 40 to 50 per cent, pensions by 17.5 per cent, housing benefits for the low-paid by 50 per cent, the minimum wage by 15 per cent. A shorter working week, longer holidays, early retirement and work-sharing were introduced. Bigger budgets and greater prominence were given to research and development, cultural activity, gender equity and national education.

Yet in just under a year, this grand reformist momentum had foundered. Mitterrand's government had underestimated the depth of the corporate sector's weaknesses – many of the conglomerates nationalized had been close to insolvency. It had failed to devalue the franc, for misplaced reasons of prestige. Above all, it had ignored the likely impact of the surrounding deflationary environment on its dash for growth. The result of its major stimulus package was a massive balance of payments crisis, as domestic output failed to keep pace with rising incomes, inflation accelerated and demand was absorbed by a flood of imports.[27] Faced with an unsustainable trade deficit – the current account went from balance in 1980 to a deficit of nearly 80 billion francs two years later – Finance Minister Jacques Delors imposed stringent austerity – *rigueur*, in his words – after June 1982. The franc was devalued, reforms were halted, taxes increased, ambitions for growth scaled back to near zero, and measures taken to de-index wages from inflation. At first, the government took pains to keep its commitment to redistribute income towards the poor. In consequence, both blue- and white-collar middle-income earners, the voters upon which the left most depended, bore the brunt of *rigueur*.[28]

This new austerity was not enough. With the IMF in the entryway if not quite at the door, the government completed its policy turn in spring 1983. The precipitating event was again a currency crisis, as the trade deficit with Germany continued to undermine the franc. The Socialist regime was now faced with a fundamental choice: either to realign the franc within the European Monetary System (EMS), which involved accepting German constraints on French budgetary policy, or pulling out of the EMS altogether, with potentially ominous implications for the European Community. For a short period there was intense debate and conflict within the government. CERES, the Communists, and some important Socialist ministers and advisors to the President[29] argued that the French economy should be uncoupled from EMS, using Italian-style forms of tacit protection to redress the trade balance, pursue an active industrial strategy and sustain the domestic market. Delors, supported by the weight of centrist opinion, contended that this was the path to nationalist adventure and disaster: the competitive discipline of full European integration had to be accepted, whatever the short-term social cost within France.

After initial hesitation, Mitterrand came down decisively for Delors. The result was a revaluation of the German mark to save immediate French face, and a fundamental alteration of direction in France. Abandoning a vision which had given priority to the interests of labour and the poor within a strategy for national regeneration, the PS – the PCF refused to follow, quitting office in 1984 – henceforward turned towards a quest for international market share, in which domestic social issues would be secondary.[30] 'Modernization' meant the invention of a new discourse. The Parisian daily *Libération* greeted it in

the Beaujolais season of 1983 with the irreverent headline 'le Mitterrand nouveau est arrivé.' A cult of entrepreneurial ingenuity, the
centrality of the firm and the dynamism of profits increasingly
displaced an older vocabulary of redistribution, social equity and
justice. The task of France's mixed economy was now to streamline,
rationalize and high-technologize itself for battle with the Americans,
Germans and Japanese. Nationalized firms, once envisaged as agencies
of social justice and collective control, were re-dedicated as lean and
mean multinationals. Socialists began to defend the decision-making
and allocative rationality of the market with a new enthusiasm.

The rhetoric reflected a rapid and dramatic turnabout in policy. The
Socialist government moved resolutely to reduce inflation, in a spirit of
de facto monetarism and devotion to a strong franc. Budget deficits
were cut and the share of public spending in GNP sharply reduced,
squeezing social programmes. In 1984 the state backed away from
investment in the Lorraine steel industry and refused to bail out the
Creusot-Loire conglomerate: public funds would no longer be used to
maintain employment levels in declining sectors. Nationalized firms
with a mission to become competitive on the world market were no
exception: the public sector led the way in shedding tens of thousands
of jobs.

The social consequences did not take long to make themselves felt.
Unemployment climbed steadily, as rust-belt regions like the Nord–
Pas-de-Calais and Lorraine were abruptly de-industrialized, and large
numbers of young people – victims of demography, seniority and
tenure rules – could not break into the labour force at all. Meanwhile,
stock-market reforms were fuelling the biggest boom on the Paris
Bourse in recent memory.[31] On the shopfloor the Auroux laws,
intended to democratize the firm, became something very different, as
trade-union weakness, changing employer strategies and governmental shift turned strident capitalist opposition into benign tolerance.
New rights of expression and communication within the firm often
played into the hands of employers seeking to engage workers in
Japanese-style dialogue to circumvent unions and promote 'flexibility';
while new forms of representation tended to transform activists into
quasi-functionaries whose myriad official tasks kept them from the
outreach needed to sustain union support.[32]

Checked on the socio-economic front, could the reforming impetus
of the Socialist government recoup on civil and cultural terrain? There
was a genuine attempt to mitigate the authoritarian harshness and
hauteur of the French state. Legal reform was long overdue, and here
the left was considerably more liberal than the right. The death penalty
was abolished and the relationships between police, courts and the

public overhauled. Some progress was also achieved in the protection of women's rights and the regulation of reproduction. These advances, however modest, still provoked a backlash exploited by the revanchist right. Regions were granted greater autonomy from Paris – a change that was certainly needed, but hardly a radical one: its main immediate effect was to provide a staging area for the building of conservative provincial machines.[33] Efforts to reform the school system were stymied by clashes with religious opinion – the left wasting inordinate energy fighting a century-old battle over church–state relations, and then failing ignominiously to further prevail.[34] The opportunities lost here were repeated, more dishonourably and even more disastrously, in the media – where Socialist 'modernization' of television opened the gates to crass commercialism and political manipulation.[35] The record in foreign policy was no more distinguished. De Gaulle's assertion of French national independence had its roots in the experience of Free France and the Liberation. Mitterrand's outlook was formed by the Fourth Republic, when Atlanticism was one price of a ministerial career. After 1981, Paris moved closer to Washington than it had been under Giscard. Mitterrand proved one of Reagan's most dependable allies, playing a prominent role in urging West Germany to accept the deployment of Euromissiles, even at the cost of alienating the SPD. Subordination to the US then precluded France from leading any response to the emergence of Gorbachev in Russia, as de Gaulle might have done. Mitterrand got little in exchange from Reagan, whose monetary policy – sky-high interest rates and an over-valued dollar – exerted relentless downward pressure on the French economy. Nor was the role of the Socialist government in North–South relations any less conventional than in East–West. Despite rhetoric about solidarity with the Third World, and the presence in government of figures – Jean-Pierre Cot or Régis Debray – who had meant it, France continued to be a leading arms exporter to the South, post-colonial gendarme in Africa, and nuclear tester in the Pacific.

Managing the Change: 1985–89

The scale and sharpness of the change of policy after 1983 inevitably put an acute strain on the regime's structures of support. Management of the transition to the new course without loss of power now became the main test of Socialist rule. This was not easy: no one can renounce a programme and outlook consecrated by decades without risk. But changes in the landscape of the French left, which might in other conditions have threatened its survival, paradoxically facilitated the shedding of the past. For the turbulent period since the early seventies had culminated in a dramatic collapse of many of the sources and institutions of an older radicalism.

The most striking example was the fate of French Communism. The PCF gained nothing from its initial participation in office; and when it withdrew, it proved unable to benefit from opposition. What had once been a formidable complex of organizational and ideological power, for half a century supplying the left – for better or worse – with much of its mobilizing outlook and energy, suddenly shrunk to a beleaguered and involuted rump of a party. Within the space of a few years, the PCF lost well over half its voters and by 1986 polled less than 10 per cent of the electorate. Positions in local government (traditionally very important in maintaining party organization) dwindled; membership fell to half the levels of the late seventies; bitter internal conflict wracked those who remained.[36]

The trade unions, meanwhile, underwent steady attrition. Partisan conflicts refracted through the union movement, dividing the CGT and CFDT; the impact of economic crisis on core sectors of industry weakened labour yet further. Despite an allegedly friendly government, the major confederations continued to lose strength in the eighties, while the CFDT began to pull away from any left identification and mimic the moderation of FO, the third-force union. By the mid 1980s union membership covered only just over 10 per cent of the labour force – a lower figure than in the United States. The overwhelming majority of these were concentrated in a public sector targeted for cutbacks and a rigid incomes policy.[37] French trade-unionism had become the weakest of any major society. Strikes became rare, labour activists very thin on the ground, workers less and less able to resist employers or the state. The division of national income between profits and wages shifted strongly towards profits. Yet ideologically the unions were unable to fight back against campaigns labelling them as selfish corporatists: in the mid eighties a book entitled *Toujours Plus* was a runaway bestseller.

The intellectual eclipse of the culture of the left was even more complete. The Parisian intelligentsia had abandoned Marxism wholesale before the Socialists came to power. But other ideologies of the left continued to have their adherents. Now these too were transformed or jettisonned. The evolution of many *autogestionnaires* who were advocates of decentralized revolutionary action in the early 1970s was emblematic: a decade later, they had decided that the solution to France's problems lay in the revitalization of 'civil society'. Proudhon and Rosa Luxemburg gave way first to Nietzsche and then to Tocqueville and Adam Smith.

In a negative sense, all these changes smoothed the way for the drastic turn of the Socialist experiment after 1983. PCF decline freed the PS from pressure to its left. Trade-union shrinkage allowed rationalization at the expense of labour. Repentant intellectuals eagerly assisted centrist normalization.[38] But none of this was enough to provide a positive momentum for the regime – a project attractive enough to retain its support, against more confident opposition from the right. The mainsprings of left mobilization were broken. What could replace them? Mitterrand had won the presidential elections of 1981 by a small margin, and his coat-tails had pulled the PS to a majority in the Assembly. Two years later the municipal elections inflicted severe losses on the left, and marked the breakthrough of Le Pen's Front National on the right. By late 1984 the government was in serious political trouble. What the left stood for, beyond austerity, had become quite unclear, while its economic policies were hurting many of its voters very directly.

This was a situation – of social disorientation and ideological vacuum – that placed a great premium on the manipulative skills of one man, François Mitterrand. Intricate political manoeuvring was, however, precisely his forte. The term of the presidency was seven years; of the Assembly five. This meant that Mitterrand would almost certainly have to 'cohabit' with a parliamentary majority of the right after 1986. Cohabitation had never occurred. Given that the President had constitutional prerogatives in important areas of power, particularly foreign and defence policy, Mitterrand would inevitably cross swords with any right-wing government armed with its own claims to a fresh mandate. The PS had a powerful interest in Mitterrand's success in such a duel. If he could emerge victorious in the presidential election that would follow in two years, the party might once again benefit from a parliamentary dissolution and return to power in the Assembly in 1988. Perhaps more than ever before, then, everything depended upon Mitterrand's personal and political skills. From 1984 onwards he carefully began to position his pieces.

The President's first priority was to limit the scope of the left's probable defeat in the 1986 elections. An initial step was to appoint a new prime minister, Laurent Fabius, the youngest man ever to hold the job. In his late thirties, Fabius was the model of the elegant technocrat: cultivated, wealthy and glib – a far cry from the cloth-cap workerism and old left passion of his predecessor Pierre Mauroy. Images had begun to count a great deal in French politics; changing them was now one of Mitterrand's main resources. The more important move was an electoral change: the introduction of a measure of proportional representation designed to reduce the possible majority of the right in the Assembly, and allow the National Front to threaten its flank.

Treating the rise of Le Pen's racist movement as a tactical pawn, the change was calculated to maximize the chances of preserving Mitterrand's own and his party's power.

However high their price, Mitterrand's deft manoeuvres achieved their goal. By the time of the legislative elections of March 1986, the turn to financial orthodoxy had borne conventional fruit: inflation had fallen below 5 per cent, the trade balance was in surplus, and investment had picked up. This was far from enough to reverse the political tide: the left's vote tumbled from 54 to 43 per cent. But because of the new rules, which gave the National Front 32 seats, the moderate right gained only a bare parliamentary majority. The playing field between Mitterrand and the right had been made as level as possible, given the electoral disfavour into which the left had fallen. Mitterrand could now use all his political gifts and presidential resources to outmanoeuvre the right and embarrass the new prime minister, Jacques Chirac, his most likely opponent in 1988.

The performance of Chirac's government helped him. Despite the mild recovery it inherited, its policies failed to create jobs or restore substantial growth. Mishandling of student demonstrations in late 1986 deflated its political credit. The stock-market crash of October 1987 scattered its economic hopes. The divisions between Gaullists and Giscardiens were not buried, but aggravated by the pressure of the new right led by Le Pen. The result was official cacophony – hard-line neo-liberalism, old-fashioned Gaullist corporatism, tough law-and-order talk pandering to racism, and conservative christian-democratic paternalism, competing with each other. In these conditions, Mitterrand had little difficulty in exposing the limitations of Chirac, whose changeability and lack of longer-term purpose became notorious.[39]

The presidential elections of 1988 presented a new Mitterrand to the country. If in 1981 he had been the bearer of much-needed fundamental change, now he was a rock of middle-of-the-road stability, 'tranquil strength', everyone's *tonton* (uncle). Mitterrand focused attention on his persona, refashioning it to project the image of a sage elder who understood all, and whose experience would guide a troubled France towards safer harbours. His policies were studiously vague – platitudes about the role of the President, the importance of the welfare state, and France's destiny in Europe. Beyond pious sentiments, the message was that Mitterrand's opponents were unstable, without firm ideas, and eager to perpetuate partisan wars which the French wanted to end. The campaign was a demonstration model of Socialist 'new politics', and the result was satisfactory. Mitterrand won by a wide margin, taking 54 per cent of the vote in the runoff against Chirac's 46 per cent.

Victory secured, Mitterrand called new legislative elections. This time Socialist candidates were marketed much more as supporters of the President than as bearers of a specific programme. At most, the PS claimed superior management competence – 'with a human face' – for restructuring the French economy in changing world markets. Mitterrand's gamble had paid off.

Is Management Enough? 1988–93

Mitterrand's capacity for long-term calculation had not been simply electoral. The President was well aware that the turn of 1983–84 was not enough for the gigantic operation of making the French economy fully competitive. For that a much larger architectural design was necessary. His strategic choice was to promote a renaissance of European integration. The effect of the turn had been to bring France back into the EC mainstream, restoring harmony with Germany – the traditional axis of European construction. It was no accident that the politician responsible for the fateful decision of March 1983, Jacques Delors, became president of the European Commission in late 1984.[40] In his new post, Delors immediately set to work on a masterful scheme for relaunching the momentum of European integration. By the end of 1985 the European Council had agreed the Single European Act, and soon afterwards the ambitious package of financial, agricultural, regional and social measures to be known as Delors–I. Beyond the programme for a single market, to be completed by 1992, lay new agendas for monetary and political union. By 1988, the Community's new dynamism was a central fact of European political life.

Mitterrand's reorientation towards the EC rested on a multiple structure of calculation. Economically, the Single Market would offer French companies a wider space to operate, and oblige them to rationalize through economies of scale and new technologies, making them more internationally competitive. Politically, the pooling of selected dimensions of sovereignty might create a regulatory Europe – perhaps with some social-democratic traits – capable of standing up to American and Japanese power. Diplomatically, such a closer union could become a new theatre for French leadership in Europe, since Germany – whatever its economic dominance – could not assume political primacy, and Britain disqualified itself by Thatcher's hostility to the Community. Ideologically, a powerful European framework might change the domestic political game in France, perhaps providing a way out of the dilemmas of the left created by the collapse of older projects, organizations, and constituencies. On the one hand, the EC could be a convenient way of avoiding political responsibility for difficult decisions: blame for austerity measures might plausibly be transferred to Brussels. On the other hand, if the European option struck fire at home, it might provide mobilizing fervour for the left to replace the causes jettisonned by the PS in the early eighties.

The complex field of European manoeuvres Mitterrand kept for himself, as the high ground of his second presidency. For the lower level of domestic administration, he picked Michel Rocard, a politician he disliked intensely, as the first prime minister of his new term.[41] The choice had two implications. It signified the delegation of internal affairs to a government held at arm's length from larger strategy; and at this level a willingness to try out the most prominent exponent of the 'new politics'. Rocard had long denounced the traditional ambitions of the left as dangerously out-of-date. France had limited choices as a medium-sized mixed economy in an open international market. It was the duty of the PS to be frank about this, and to base its appeal on political tolerance and transparency, managerial creativity and social compassion, the resources of civil society and not the Jacobin impulses of the state. Class identities were no longer relevant. Opinion polls, public-relations techniques, professional use of television were the ways to reach an electoral market peopled by mobile individuals on the alert for the right product.

Rocardianism presented itself as a politics of feasible reformism. In his first speech to the Assembly, Rocard rejected large goals as unattainable, stressing the benefits of tackling tangible and local problems instead. His government committed itself to opening a series of 'workshops' – *chantiers* – where concrete reforms could be tried out. These came to include a 'Minimum Income for Economic Reinsertion', to help those rendered jobless by necessary restructuring to avoid social 'exclusion';[42] much-publicized measures to address urban prob-lems, coordinated by a new ministry of cities; and, more obscurely, a reorganization of career structures in the civil service. The message was that, despite the constraints on France's freedom of action, modest things could still be changed.

More significant than these reforms, however, were the macro-economic policies of the administration. Their centrepiece was dedi-cation to sound money and price stability, to render France competitive with Germany. The pursuit of a strong franc dictated high interest rates that limited the possibilities of reducing unemployment, which remained stuck at around 10 per cent of the labour force. But economic growth had returned across Europe, and French GDP rose satisfactorily by over 4 per cent in both 1988 and 1989, although this dropped to just over 2 per cent in 1990 as recession set in again. But against the background of this relative prosperity, Rocard's three years at the helm – until May 1991 – were a placid period.

While Rocard attempted to fill the domestic scene, Mitterrand pursued his European strategy. For a time, all went well. In 1989 Delors submitted plans for an Economic and Monetary Union and negotiations to rewrite the Treaty of Rome, with firm backing from Paris. In 1990 Mitterrand and Kohl persuaded other EC states to initiate parallel talks on 'Political Union', a vague conception revolving round the idea of a Common Foreign and Security Policy. Eventually a Franco–German military corps was created, indicating the extent to which Mitterrand had shifted – in contrast to the line of his first presidency – to a more Gaullist vision of Europe's relations with the United States. By 1991, the Community was moving down the slipway towards the most ambitious advance in European integration since its foundation, the commitment to a single currency set out in the projected Treaty of Maastricht.

At this juncture, however, everything started to go wrong. In the spring, Mitterrand dismissed Rocard and replaced him with Edith Cresson. It had become customary in the Fifth Republic to change prime ministers halfway through presidential terms – the usual reason being that the political credit of the incumbent was exhausted, and a new face needed to dissociate the President from mid-term problems and prepare for the next legislative elections. Rocard, however, had maintained his popularity, and could well have been allowed to continue. The explanation for his dismissal lay elsewhere. Rocard's very success meant that allowing to stay on would almost certainly have given him an insuperable lead in the race within the PS for succession to the Elysée, which had already begun. Firing him, on the other hand, would give Mitterrand and the many anti-Rocardian PS leaders time and space to block this prospect. The decision was a bad misjudgement, indicating a basic loss of touch. Cresson, appointed as the first woman prime minister in French history, quickly proved to be a political liability. Prone to spectacular public gaffes and sniped at by her rivals in the PS, her government quickly became a shambles, as recession deepened, and President and party alike hit a nadir in the polls. Within little more a year, she was replaced by Pierre Bérégovoy, the long-standing minister of finance. But the Cresson fiasco proved a turning-point, from which the domestic credit of the PS was not to recover.

The decisive blows to Mitterrand's strategy, however, were external. The framework of his European calculations had been the existing Community. The sudden unification of Germany in 1990 blew these parameters apart. Aware that the absorption of East Germany by the

Federal Republic would transform the traditional balance of power within the EC, Mitterrand tried to shore up Hans Modrow's short-lived government in Berlin – the first of a series of clumsy missteps in adjusting to the new situation in Eastern Europe. Kohl was soon to follow suit, with ill-starred German initiatives in Yugoslavia heedless of French reservations. Both partners continued to press for a Treaty of European Union to be signed at Maastricht, but a common foreign policy was actually further away than ever, while Britain frustrated the hope of any real social dimension to the new Treaty. The rapid expansion of Community competences into new policy areas had underlined the opacity and elitism of the EC's workings, exposing its 'democratic deficit'. But here Mitterrand was scarcely more sensitive than Major. Keenly interested in using European Union as a vehicle for the pursuit of French international grandeur, he was basically uninterested in democratizing its legislative structure, to even the mild extent favoured by the Germans. The result of negotiations was an impenetrable set of drafts and deals, at once confused and evasive, too complex for anyone save experts to decipher, and finally signed in a mixture of haste and fatigue at Maastricht.[43]

The one clear-cut commitment of the Treaty was to a deflationary convergence of all EC states towards a single currency. This was going to be unpopular enough on its own. But more explosive than the ultimate prospect of a European monetary authority modelled on the Bundesbank, was the immediate stance of the actual Bundesbank itself. Confronted with a huge budgetary deficit, the result of the refusal of the Kohl government to raise taxes sufficiently to pay for German unification, it raised German interest rates to the highest level since the Depression. At a time when the world economy was already in recession, this icy douche to investment and employment chilled Europe to the bone. In France Bérégovoy's pledge to maintain at all costs the stability of the exchange rate forced French rates of interest up, without any compelling internal reasons, and the number of unemployed with them – yet even so, waves of speculation battered the franc. The grand European strategy of the mid eighties had backfired, as the French economy was punished for German mismanagement.

When the Danes then rejected Maastricht in the referendum of June 1992, Mitterrand took the gamble of calling a referendum on the Treaty in France, although there was no constitutional need for one. His decision undoubtedly reflected principled devotion to a European project which owed much to his own labour. But he also calculated that since current polls showed nearly 70 per cent of the electorate nominally in favour of Maastricht, and the right seemed divided over the Treaty, a yes vote could be transformed into plebiscitary support for his presidency. The master of such manoeuvres, however, had aged. Contrary to his expectations, as soon as the Treaty was seriously debated, popular resistance to it grew. The entire pro-European establishment, left, centre and right, had to struggle down to the wire on 20 September to win a very narrow majority (under 52 per cent). The disaster of outright rejection, disavowing Mitterrand and tor-pedoing European Union, was averted. But the result was nonetheless a symbolic defeat for Mitterrand, and an ominous portent of what the upcoming legislative elections might have in store for the PS. Those who voted for the Treaty mainly came from the wealthy and well-educated sectors of the population. Maastricht had been resound-ingly rejected by what had once been the core constituencies of the left. Fearing more unemployment, less social protection, and surrender of national ability to shape a better future, poorer, less educated, more proletarian France voted against the treaty.

Six months later, the PS faced the electorate at the polls. Bérégovoy's government had done little to improve its prospects. Unemployment was now at its highest level since the War – 10.5 per cent. The party had long presented the unpleasing spectacle of rival clans quarrelling over future presidential prospects – a battle-ground of 'elephants', as they came to be called, rarely fighting over ideas or principles, but rather for position and influence. It was now tainted by scandal too. Fabius and his health officials had refused to take responsibility for a tragedy of hundreds of unnecessary deaths, caused by contaminated blood, and manipulated the judiciary to avoid legal charges. Mitterrand himself was touched by others: insider trading by friends, illegal wiretapping of newspapers, dubious machinations by the secret services. Politically, most damaging of all were a series of indictments of leading Socialists for fraudulent campaign fund-raising – typically, faked invoices to PS municipalities for fictitious services, with the money kicked back to the party. To many, the Socialists looked increasingly like a gang willing to do anything to stay in power.

Electoral retribution, predicted for some time, was drastic when it came. In the March 1993 elections the PS lost half its support at a stroke, its total vote falling to 17 per cent; while its parliamentary strength dropped from 258 to 53. The right, fighting a united campaign, swept into office with a parliamentary majority of nearly 80 per cent in the Assembly.

Conclusions from Two Failures

The French left lived the last acts of a great drama in the 1980s. The logic of postwar capitalist accumulation did not completely dictate the

scripts, whatever the current enthusiasts for liberal economic reduc-
tionism may claim. It was not the case that economic constraints left no
other options than those taken. Nor, on the other hand, were the
scripts inspired by either social-democratic treason or Stalinist perfidy,
as favourite leftist reductionisms might have it. To be sure, the French
left had to design its choices around large economic and social-
structural trends – but it had choices. The steps toward the tragic
outcome of the 1990s must thus be seen as two sets of strategic options
which deepened the difficulties of creating a juster society in France,
rather than surmounting them.

In 1981 a French left came to power which had never made peace
with consumer capitalism in the postwar period. The Communists,
junior partners in the new governing coalition, remained committed to
the socialist transformation of France. The Socialists, a mixed bag of
political factions, scorned the meliorism of social democracy and
advocated a rupture with capitalism. Might not this combination give a
French lead to Europe once again, by managing to 'exit the crisis from
the left'? In power, the French left did embark on a programme of
radical reformism without equal in the post-reconstruction world. A
decade later, it is important to remember this. But that course was
abruptly abandoned in 1983–84, when the French economy was
drawing water in an extraordinarily harsh international sea. The
failure of this option was not just an accident of circumstance. The
leading actors had made decisive choices – by omission and commission
– long before 1981, which closed down a range of possibilities
afterwards. In particular, the break-up of the union of the left had
transformed the balance of forces behind the Common Programme,
and fatally weakened its original dynamic; while neither party to it had
given serious thought to the scale of the difficulties confronting it in the
condition of the French economy and the constraints of the world
recession. But choices made after 1981 excluded other possibilities that
still remained – popular mobilization was deliberately eschewed, and
the limits of temporary protection never tested. The experiment had
selected a political style that was unlikely to resist the pressure of
external crisis.

As the first left exited the stage after 1984, a very different one
entered. The dream of social democracy in one country was soon
forgotten. What had once been a broad progressive movement with its
centre of gravity in the working class was – partly for political, but
mainly for social reasons – rapidly decimated. With it went the idea of
redistributing wealth and power to transcend capitalism. The basic
premiss of the second, 'modern' left was that the country's new setting
in an open globalized economy placed ineluctable constraints on any

government. Once the French understood this, popular concern would focus on the efficiency and creativity of those in charge of the narrow choices which remained. Then a new set of loyalties could be aroused by lucid and competent administration, promoting solidarity and advancing reform within the modest limits of the possible. Only one grand design remained – the gradual construction of a European Union. It was quite unclear, however, if it was a grand design *of the left*.

The new strategy assumed that traditional loyalties built around community, workplace and local association had declined, creating an individualist electorate for whom political 'products' had to be tailored by sharp polling and shrewd packaging. Personalities would matter more and issues less, in a presidential and televisual politics. The long-standing tension between 'traditionalists' and 'modernizers' among the Socialists dissolved, as the shift of the mid 1980s led to a complete embrace of modernism. In 1993, the party reaped what it had sown: voters treated as fickle atoms reacted in some measure like them. But the electoral rejection of the PS was also quite intelligible in more traditional terms. What the party promised – up-to-date management with a human face and a European future – differed very little from what a modern centre-right could offer; only its prospectus came shop-soiled with rising unemployment, urban insecurity and visible corruption. It is not surprising that the conservative alternative seemed preferable.

If the sociological changes brought by post-industrialism and globalization were inevitable in France, as elsewhere in the West, the failure of the French left to understand or adjust effectively to them remains striking. Two successive strategies have come to nothing in the past decade. The cumulative consequences have been devastating. The political landscape of the left in France is for the time being a desolate scene. The PCF remains immured in its ghetto, with about a tenth of the electorate. A shrunken PS, many of whose voters have switched to the right, is trying to regroup under Rocard. Meanwhile, the opportunist populism of the National Front attracts dispirited workers and the chameleon-like Greens graze on what was once firm left turf. In this wreckage, the claims of the French left to a political temper distinct from the meliorist compromises of Northern Europe are over, and the cult of mere modernity has proved empty progress. It must be hoped that the shock of defeat will stir more independent thought and inventive politics once again.

Notes

1. For figures, see André Gauron, *Histoire économique et sociale de la Cinquième République*, Volume 1, Paris 1983 and Jean Fourastié, *Les Trentes glorieuses*, Paris 1979.

2. Imports from the old empire declined from 25 per cent of total trade in 1949 to 6 per cent in 1973, and exports from 38 to 9 per cent – while imports from advanced industrial societies grew from 55 per cent to 75 per cent and exports from 47 to 75 per cent.

3. For a discussion of the role of these technocrats see Richard Kuisel, *Capitalism and the State in Modern France*, Cambridge 1981.

4. Lacouture, *De Gaulle*, Volume 3, Part II is especially good on de Gaulle's geopolitical pretensions.

5. Ibid., chapters 21–25.

6. Real wages went up only rather slowly until the later 1960s: Gauron, *Histoire économique*, Graph 1, p. 31.

7. For the record of the SFIO, see Hugues Portelli, *Le Socialisme français tel qu'il est*, Paris 1980, especially chapter 3; Daniel Ligou, *Histoire du socialisme en France depuis 1900*, Paris 1961; Roger Quilliot, *La SFIO et l'exercice du pouvoir*, Paris 1972.

8. There is a large literature on the PCF in the Cold War period. See Philippe Robrieux, *Histoire intérieure du Parti communiste français*, Volume 2, Paris 1981, chapters 4–6; Annie Kriegel, *Les Communistes français: Portrait d'un peuple*, Paris 1968; Irwin Wall, *French Communism in the Era of Stalin*, Westport 1983. Two sharply contrasting official accounts are the Thorezian *Histoire du Parti communiste français*, Paris 1964, chapters XII-XIII and Roger Bourderon et al., *Le PCF, étapes et problèmes*, Paris 1981, chapter 7 by Roger Martelli.

9. For this, see André Donneur, *L'Alliance fragile*, Montreal 1984.

10. These articles were republished as *La Paupérisation des travailleurs français*, Paris 1961.

11. Birth control was denounced as a Malthusian plot against workers by capital and the Americans. See Jeannette Vermeersch. 'Faut-il choisir entre la paix du monde, l'interdiction de la bombe atomique ou le contrôle de la natalité : Contre le néo-malthusianisme réactionnaire', in *Les Femmes dans la nation*, Paris 1962.

12. Thorez saw proponents of 'Italian' ideas in France as suspect Khruschevites: Philippe Robrieux, *Notre génération communiste*, Paris 1977. For the student purge, see Hervé Hamon and Patrick Rotman's *Génération*, Volume 1, Paris 1987, which links the anti-Communism of the *gauchistes* of 1968 to these events.

13. The best study of his early career is Franz-Olivier Gisbert's *François Mitterrand ou la tentation de l'histoire*, Paris 1977.

14. For the role of the CGT and PCF, see George Ross, *Workers and Communists in France*, Berkeley 1982, chapter 7.

15. Lacouture, *De Gaulle*, chapter 27 discusses the last 300 days of the General; see also Georges Pompidou, *Pour rétablir la vérité*, Paris 1982.

16. Delors, who would have been a Christian Democrat had there been a plausible DC in France, had worked for the French planning apparatus and the Catholic trade unions in the sixties. After 1968 he threw in his lot with the Gaullist left – hence his sojourn with Chaban: see Gabriel Milesi, *Jacques Delors*, Paris 1985.

17. The CGT refused to accept an incomes policy for the public sector, despite a guarantee of indexed wage increases, and managed to persuade the CFDT to follow suit. Ultimately, however, it was conservatives in the legislature who brought down Chaban in 1972.

18. For the evolution of wages and profits, see Jean-Claude Delaunay, *Salariat et plus-value en France, depuis la fin du XIXe siècle*, Paris 1984, esp. pp. 221 ff; for industrial tensions, see Robert Boyer, 'Wage Labor, Capital, Accumulation and Crisis, 1968–82', in Mark Kesselman and Guy Groux, eds, *The French Workers' Movement*, London 1984.

19. For contemporary alarm, see Stoffaës, *La Grande menace industrielle*, Paris 1978, chapter 3, and Alain Cotta, *La France et l'impératif mondial*, Paris 1978, part II, chapter 1.

20. For this history, there is a large range of sources. They include: R. W. Johnson, *The Long March of the French Left*, London 1982; David Bell and Byron Criddle, *The French Socialist Party*, Oxford 1984, chapter 3; Jacques Kergoat, *Le Parti socialiste*, Paris 1983. For some of the flavour of the smoke-filled back rooms, see A. Du Roy and R. Schneider, *Le Roman de la rose*, Paris 1982.

21. The best source on this period is François Hincker, *Les Communistes au carrefour*, Paris 1981; for documents and discussions of the time, see PCF, *Le Socialisme pour la France*, Paris 1977, and Jean Favre, François Hincker and Lucien Sève, *Les Communistes et l'Etat*, Paris 1977.

22. Jean Fabien's *La Guerre des camarades*, Paris 1985, publishes a long letter sent by the CPSU to the French leadership in March 1977 in which it threatened to undermine Marchais and, perhaps, split the PCF altogether, should 'anti-Sovietism' continue. Pressure like this must have galvanized die-hard forces in the Central Committee.

23. Purporting to be based on documents held by a leading figure in the PCF, Jean Fabien's *Guerre des camarades* claims that Moscow was responsible for the break-up of the union of the left. While it is clear that the Soviet leadership was hostile to it, the PCF's turn cannot be explained *only* in these terms – the logic of the domestic situation was strengthening internal opposition to it.

24. We have written ethnographically about how this period was lived 'from below' in the Paris party: Jane Jenson and George Ross, *The View From Inside: A French Communist Cell in Crisis*, Berkeley 1985.

25. For the CGT, see Ross, *Workers and Communists*, chapter 10 and George Ross, 'The CGT', in Kesselman and Groux, *The French Workers' Movement*; for the CFDT, Hamon and Rotman, *La Deuxième gauche*, and René Mouriaux and Guy Groux, *La CFDT*, Paris 1989.

26. Mitterrand's programmatic pledges drew heavily on the *Projet Socialiste* of 1980 which had been written by CERES, the most left-wing fraction of the PS: for its roots in the period of Resistance and Liberation, see Jean-Pierre Rioux, *La Quatrième république, I. L'Ardeur et la necessité*, Paris 1980.

27. The best general analysis of the crisis is Alain Lipietz, *L'Audace ou l'enlisement*, Paris 1984; see also the more econometrically informed Alain Fonteneau and Pierre-Alain Muet, *La Gauche face à la crise*, Paris 1985, and Peter A. Hall, *Governing The Economy*, London 1987.

28. See CERC, *Constat de l'évolution récente des revenus en France*, Paris 1984.

29. The ministers included future premiers Laurent Fabius and Pierre Bérégovoy, and the advisors Jean Riboud, head of Schlumberger and a close friend of the President.

30. The best account of the conflicts inside the government at this critical juncture is Philippe Bauchard, *La Guerre des deux roses*, Paris 1986; see also Pierre Favier and Michel Martin-Roland, *La Décennie Mitterrand*, Volume 1, Paris 1990, part 4.

31. Daniel Singer, *Is Socialism Doomed?*, New York 1988, provides a good left critique of the thrust of government policy, and the extent to which it took measures the right had never dared.

32. For the original intentions of the Auroux Laws see Jean Auroux, *Les Droits des travailleurs*, Paris 1981, and for commentary Duncan Gallie, 'Les Lois Auroux: The Reform of French Industrial Relations?', in Howard Machin and Vincent Wright, eds, *Economic Policy and Policy-Making under the Mitterrand Presidency, 1981–1984*, New York 1985, pp. 205–21. Subsequently, the government made strenuous efforts to break up corporatist arrangements in state firms like Renault.

33. For details on decentralization see the articles by Yves Mény and Catherine Grémion in George Ross et al., *The Mitterrand Experiment*.

34. By the 1980s, Catholic schools had often become safety valves for middle-class parents seeking to shield their children's prospects from the effects of deteriorating public schools – hence the strong defence of them. The influence of the teachers' union and lay tradition inside the PS pushed the party into a politically imprudent conflict. For a shrewd overview, see Antoine Prost, 'The Education Maelstrom', in Ross et al., *The Mitterrand Experiment*.

35. In 1985, aware that the PS was facing difficult elections the next year, Mitterrand granted franchises to friends on whom he thought he could rely politically – in particular

the Italian tycoon Silvio Berlusconi, close to Craxi in Italy, notorious for his reliance on inane game shows and borrowed American series. When the right returned in 1986, it proceeded with equal cynicism.

36. One of us has analysed its plight: George Ross, 'Party Decline and Changing Party Systems, France and the French Communist Party', *Comparative Politics*, autumn 1992.

37. For an analysis of these trends, see Chris Howell, *Regulating Labor*, Princeton 1992, and *La Question syndicale*, Paris 1988; for more on the trade unions and the left up to 1986, see George Ross, 'From One Left to Another: *Le Social* in Mitterrand's France', in Ross et al., *The Mitterrand Experiment*.

38. On this see George Ross, 'Where Have All the Sartres Gone?', in James Hollifield and George Ross, *Searching for the New France*, New York 1991.

39. The most interesting review of this interlude is to be found in Philippe Bauchard, *La Crise sonne toujours deux fois*, Paris 1988; see also Favier and Martin-Rolan, *La Décennie Mitterrand*, Volume 2, Paris 1992, part 8.

40. Delors was appointed at the Fontainebleau summit of the European Council, chaired by Mitterrand, in June 1984 – where French initiative was decisive in resolving issues that had paralyzed the Community in the early eighties, in particular the British rebate and Spanish/Portuguese membership.

41. There are a number of books on the relationship between Mitterrand and Rocard: among them, Jean-Paul Liégois and Jean-Pierre Bédeï, *Le Feu et l'eau*, Paris 1990, and Robert Schneider, *La Haine tranquille*, Paris 1992.

42. Serge Paugam, *La Société française et ses pauvres*, Paris 1993, discusses the RMI, particularly in part 3.

43. See George Ross, 'After Maastricht', *World Policy Journal*, summer 1992.

7

Italy: A New Agenda

Tobias Abse

Italy is a country apart in the panorama of the postwar European left. For its history exhibits a singular paradox. No other Western society has so consistently thrown up radical popular movements from below, in a pattern of turbulence that has again and again surprised observers; and none has had such a long and unbroken record of fundamentally conservative rule. For forty-five years years Italy has been the land of social insurgency and political immobility. The principal formation of the left, the Italian Comunist Party, remained excluded from office in Rome long after even its French counterpart – a much less accommodating force – was readmitted to government in Paris, and a Socialist Party – to which it was now much closer – was firmly entrenched in Madrid. In the political earthquake of 1993, the regime that dominated Italy for half a century finally broke up. For a brief moment, the heirs of the PCI – and not a few of their opponents – believed that they were at last poised to govern the country. In the event, the outcome of the collapse of the old order has been the very reverse. Far from bringing the left to power, the Second Republic has given birth to a regime of the radical right. Descendants, not of Gramsci and Togliatti, but of Mussolini are ministers in Rome today. How has this bitter dénouement come about? No answer can be separated from the long-term development of Italian Communism since the War.

From the Resistance to the Centre-Left

Although the Italian Communist Party had been founded in 1921, it only became a mass formation in the 1940s. Its transformation from a relatively small, if dedicated, organization into a major political and

189

social force was essentially the result of the profound upheavals that marked the years 1943–45; in calmer circumstances Togliatti's political skills – notable enough – would have counted for very little. The mass strikes in the spring of 1943 signalled the rebirth of Italian working-class militancy, after nearly two decades of enforced quiescence under Mussolini's dictatorship, and weighed critically on the decision of the king and the army to break with the Duce after the Allied landings in Sicily. The forty-five days of monarcho-military dictatorship between 25 July and 8 September 1943 enabled the Communists, who had helped foment the strike wave, to regroup in conditions of semi-legality and profit from the gradual release of political prisoners. But it was the period of German occupation between September 1943 and April 1945 that was crucial to the Communists' capture of first the ideological and then the political primacy of the Italian left. The PCI rather than the – formally larger – PSI, from which it had originally seceded, played the predominant role in both the military activities of the Resistance and the great strikes of March 1944 – the most success-ful anywhere in Nazi-occupied Europe.

Electorally, the Socialists were still the first party of the left in 1946 but the Communists had far more committed activists and were much less prone to paralysing internal divisions. Whilst Togliatti curbed rather than encouraged the revolutionary dreams of the Northern Resistance, he was adept in channelling the energies of the masses mobilized by it into his own project of 'progressive democracy' – in essence little more than the Popular Frontism first advanced in 1935. The PCI participated, along with the PSI, in the first coalition govern-ments led by the Christian Democrats after the war. The Communists remained in office until De Gasperi expelled them in May 1947, despite the failure of these cabinets to deliver the kind of reform Togliatti had claimed would distinguish a progressive from a more conventional kind of democracy. However, the marked political polarization of the Cold War elections of April 1948, in which a joint Communist–Socialist list confronted the Christian Democrats and their allies, erased the memory of the party's record of inaction. Paradoxically, the left's unexpectedly severe defeat – it polled 31 per cent against the DC's 48.5 per cent – strengthened rather than weakened the identification of the more revolutionary workers and peasants with the PCI. The semi-insurrectionary general strike of July 1948 that broke out in spon-taneous response to the assassination attempt on Togliatti, which the party had some difficulty in calling off, served to demonstrate that even the most radical militants could not conceive of a politics beyond the boundaries set by the existence of the PCI.

Throughout the fifties, as the Christian Democrats consolidated their political hegemony and the governmental alliance that had emerged victorious in April 1948 hardened into a regime, the Communists remained the symbolic focus of all the rebellious aspirations of a working class deprived of bargaining power within the factories. The relatively moderate programme of the party had little significance within the subculture into which the PCI – and the PSI, now its junior partner – were driven by the pressures of the Cold War. It was not until Khrushchev's secret speech of 1956 that Nenni moved to distance the Socialists from the Communists, and it was another seven years before the Christian Democrats decided that the PSI was sufficiently decontaminated to be an acceptable partner in a centre-left coalition. In 1960, the Tambroni government relied instead on parliamentary support from the MSI – provoking major street riots that, for all their violence, emphasized the continuity of the tradition of anti-fascist Resistance identified with the PCI. Meanwhile, the economic miracle of 1958–63, with its spectacular growth rates and tidal waves of migration from the South, led to a resurgence of strike activity in the North.[1] Against this backcloth, the more intelligent elements within the DC felt the time had arrived to absorb the more moderate wing of a divided workers' movement and bring the Socialists into the government. Nevertheless, the formal entry of the PSI into Moro's cabinet did not occur until December 1963. Thereafter the slow-down in growth rates and recalcitrance of conservative sectors of industry and the state apparatus ensured that the PSI obtained very little in the way of reforms between 1963 and 1968, while the PCI's credibility as an apparently intransigent opposition only increased.

The Student Revolt 1967–68

Such was the scene when a general social crisis overwhelmed Italian society at the end of the sixties. Its decisive event was the workers' rebellion that reached its peak in the autumn of 1969. But the immediate catalyst of factory unrest was the movement in the universities.[2] The Italian student movement preceded the French movement of May 1968 by over a year. The first occupations, at the universities of Pisa, Bologna, Cagliari and Camerino, took place as early as January 1967, and in February the radicalization spread to Turin and Naples. With the beginning of the following academic year, in November 1967, the movement became generalized throughout the Italian university system, with occupations in Trento, Milan, Genoa, Turin, Venice, Padua and elswhere. In January 1968 Pisa reasserted its role as the storm-centre of student protest, and in February the vast majority of Italian students were swept into the struggle. The conflict escalated into a confrontation with the state as well as with the university authorities. The most serious single incident was the street-fighting of 1 March 1968 in Valle Giulia in Rome, when five hundred students and a large number of policemen were injured. By the end of the academic year nearly three thousand students had been charged with offences against the state.

The outbreak of such widespread revolt amongst a previously conformist and seemingly privileged section of society owed a lot to the breakneck expansion of the universities. There were twice as many university students in 1968 as there had been in 1951. The expansion in enrolment had not been accompanied by any commensurate increase in the number of graduates turned out by the system. In 1968, for example, out of the 500,000 students enrolled in Italian universities, only 31,000 graduated – a failure-rate in good measure due to impersonal and authoritarian teaching and overcrowded libraries, laboratories and lecture rooms. The Italian universities, instead of remaining an efficient machine for the reproduction of a narrow economic and cultural elite, as they had been before 1945, had started to produce an ever larger marginal intelligentsia with little prospect of gaining employment of the kind that they and their ambitious parents had dreamt of. The ideology of the student movement of 1967–68 rapidly radicalized. Under the heady influence of the Chinese Cultural Revolution (misread as spontaneous and libertarian), the Vietnamese Tet Offensive and the French May, the mass of the militants moved from challenging the structures of the traditional university to confronting those of the Italian state itself. The PCI was completely bypassed in this process. The students, who in the past had normally been associated with the political right, had moved to the extreme left without ever experiencing the full impact of Communist orthodoxy.

The Workers' Rebellion 1968–70

The Italian student revolt was virtually unique in lighting a fuse amongst the working class. The campus movements in the United States, Britain or even West Germany proved ephemeral or isolated by contrast. Even the legendary French May fizzled out once the PCF and the CGT allowed de Gaulle to drive a wedge between the students and the working class. The Italian case was different because of a massive rebellion amongst the factory workers of Northern Italy in 1968–69 which shook the power of the bosses for at least a decade. This eruption was characterized by a spontaneity alien to the Communist Party tradition derived from the Stalin era, and therefore initially represented almost as much of a threat to the trade-union leaderships as it did to the industrialists. The demands of the workers often focused on control over the production process rather than on wages, and insofar as they concerned wages they tended to transcend sectionalism, taking such unexpectedly egalitarian forms as the call for flat-rate increases for all grades within a given factory – a kind of demand that had not surfaced since the Biennio Rosso of 1919–20. The first sign of these pressures bursting through the traditional organizations of the working class came not in a stronghold of left-wing militancy but in the traditionally passive and Christian Democratic region of the Veneto, where the CGIL was almost non-existent. In April 1968 thousands of police had to be brought in from all over the province to quell a sudden violent upsurge of working-class militancy in Valdagno. In Turin, FIAT workers started to press for an immediate reduction of the working week to forty hours and the abolition of compulsory overtime. At Porto Marghera workers refused to delegate day-to-day strike organization to trade-union officials and instead set up an assembly on the model of the contemporary student gatherings.

By the spring of 1969, the FIAT plants in Turin had become a hub of the revolt.[3] There Southern immigrants had traditionally been given the worst jobs, and been parked in the poorest housing, with least adequate public transport.[4] That year FIAT was forced for the first time in its postwar history to take on an enormous number of new workers, without going through the time-consuming vetting procedures by local police and priests that it had used to keep trouble-makers out of the plants. The result was that some workers who had more education than usual or who had come into contact with trade unions in West Germany could act as yeast amongst the mass of unskilled labour from the Mezzogiorno. The upheaval that transformed the situation at FIAT for almost a decade started in March, when workers at the Mirafiori plant refused to obey a management order to speed up production. In April, for the first time since 1948, the whole FIAT works came out on strike. Fifty days of continuous struggle culminated in the dramatic events of 3 July 1969, when the trade unions called for a general stoppage in Turin to protest against the high rents in the city – which then led a massive outbreak of street-fighting between workers and police. The agitation that had started in FIAT at Turin, Montedison at Porto Marghera and Pirelli in Milan became a nation-wide phenomenon from September 1969 onwards. Five and a half million Italian workers, more than a quarter of the entire labour force, were involved in strikes that autumn. A total of 520 million worker-hours were lost as a direct result, an impressive figure by any standards. In November 1969, twenty million Italians joined a general strike that forced the government to reform the pension system.

The new contracts won in 1969 and early 1970 represented very considerable gains for the Italian working class. The Confindustria's agreement with over a million metal and mechanical workers set the pace. It included a reduction of the working week to forty hours over two to three years; limits on overtime, and recognition that it was an exceptional rather than a normal part of the working week; the right to hold up to ten hours of assemblies each year during working time, inside plants with more than fifteen workers; recognition of union representatives, and their right to eight hours a month with pay for union duties and additional time off without pay; rank-and-file ratification of union contracts; the right of workers to defend themselves in the event of disciplinary action; and largely egalitarian wage increases exceeding the rate of inflation. Given the draconian conditions traditional in Italian factories – blacklisting, political surveillance, summary dismissal for talking on the assembly-line or glancing at a newspaper during the lunch hour, 'exile departments' to isolate militants from the rest of the workforce – these changes represented a massive shift in the balance of power on the shopfloor. They were just the beginning. When forty-three other category contracts came up for renewal in 1970, the successes of the previous year were equalled or in some cases surpassed.

One of the major achievements of the Italian workers' movement of this period was the development of new forms of workplace representation – a system of rank-and-file delegates and councils. Towards the end of 1969, it became accepted practice for workers from a homogeneous group to elect a delegate in a secret ballot in which both union members and non-members had voting rights and the delegates did not have to belong to any union. The unions then decided to choose their own (newly permitted) workplace representatives from amongst the ranks of these delegates, and set up factory councils composed of them. By 1972 this had become the normal union structure in the large plants of Northern Italy – a transformation which led to a rapid expansion of union membership. Total enrolment in the three confederations (CGIL, CISL, UIL) rose from 4.5 million in 1968 to 6 million in 1973. Last but not least, the scale of labour insurgency forced the centre-left government to pass the Statuto dei Diritti dei Lavoratori of 1970, drafted by the Socialist lawyer Giugni, which stands to this day as the most pro-union industrial relations act in Western Europe. Codifying many of the gains of the 1969–70 contracts as legal rights, it allowed unions to bring hundreds of cases for wrongful dismissal and other actions against employers. The ensuing body of legal interpretation, most of it in the unions' favour, created a new juridical basis for industrial relations in Italy.[5]

The PCI Response 1967–70

How had the PCI responded to this great upheaval? Initially, the party was rather bewildered by the tumultuous events of 1967–69. Its first reaction to the campus ferment was to focus its attention on the traditional student associations, which were being rapidly swept away by the new movement in the universities – then to call in vain for a 'mass union organization'. But in April 1968, the approach of a general election alerted the party to the need to win votes from the large numbers of radicalized students. Longo, as general secretary, formally welcomed the role of the student movement in politicizing young people and, declaring that the party must address 'the more general problems of the Italian revolution', received Oreste Scalzone – a future leader of the Autonomia – in his office at the Botteghe Oscure. Amendola, leader of the party's right, reacted angrily to these overtures, publishing a famous article entitled 'The Communists and the Student Movement: Necessity of a Struggle on Two Fronts', in which he pointed out that the movement's general political positions were opposed to those of the party: it was much further to the left and influenced by the Chinese polemics.

Despite Amendola's objections, however, Longo's flexibility seemed to pay off electorally. In May 1968 the PCI increased its vote from 25.3 to 26.9 per cent, while the PSIUP – a left-wing breakaway from the PSI in protest against its coalition with the DC, won 4.5 per cent. The next months saw a series of overwhelming events: the explosion of workers' struggles in Italy, the May–June revolt in France, the Soviet invasion of Czechoslovakia. When the party congress met against this background at Bologna in January 1969, it seemed to many that the PCI was taking a turn to the left. But although Amendola's chances of succeeding Longo as leader of the party had faded, his rival on the more radical wing of the party, Pietro Ingrao, did not benefit. Enrico Berlinguer, the Sardinian aristocrat who emerged as heir-apparent, owed his promotion in good part to his skill at finessing the opposition between them – informing the congress that 'the experience of the last months shows that it is possible to promote simultaneously radicalization, the widening of our bases and social alliances, unitary trade-union initiatives and even partial agreement between the most diverse democratic forces'. The relatively small left within the party, whose inspiration had been Ingrao, criticized the official positions adopted at Bologna, judging them inadequate as a response both to the Soviet crushing of the Prague spring, and to the social rebellions that had broken out in the West, and started to publish an independent journal to promote their own ideas, *Il Manifesto*. In it, Lucio Magri, Rossana

Rossanda, Luigi Pintor, Aldo Natoli and others argued for a much sharper rejection of Brezhnevism, and a bolder attack on Western capitalism – not based on vague hopes of winning over the middle strata for 'advanced democracy', but on the visible insubordination of the working class and its real allies: technicians and intellectuals on the one hand, and marginalized strata on the other. This challenge to official doctrine was met with disciplinary threats by the PCI leadership; and when the Manifesto group stood firm, it was expelled from the party in November 1969 – Berlinguer leading the condemnation of it at the subsequent congress. The net effect of the 1967–69 upheaval on the PCI was thus to remove the one force within it which responded positively to the new social movements among workers and students.[6] This cleared the way for a rightward shift of the party as a whole.

Outside the party, meanwhile, a galaxy of tiny revolutionary groups had been spawned by 1968. An Italian far left was born, surpassing in numbers and momentum that of any other West European country. Three main organizational curents came to dominate it, each with about 15,000 members: Avanguardia Operaia, Lotta Continua, and the Manifesto. The energy and devotion of the young militants in these groups were formidable, fired by direct contact with the massive and continuing unrest in plants and cities across the land. But from 1970 onwards, it became apparent that the role of the far left in protest movements and industrial struggles had no common measure with its ability to achieve an electoral breakthrough that would consolidate it as a national force and seriously discomfit the PCI. The total poll of the various groups never exceeded 2 per cent in these years. Their agitation, often very effective at social flashpoints, only hardened the conservative reflexes of the mass party dominating the political scene – the object of their unrelenting polemics.

Origins of the Historic Compromise

The widespread turbulence of the late sixties had, of course, come as an acute shock to the privileged classes in Italy, and the strata dependent on them. One immediate sign was a sharp rise in the neo-fascist vote – the MSI jumping from 5.8 per cent in 1968 to 10.7 per cent in 1970. The result was a cannon-effect on Christian Democracy. The DC, fearing to lose part of its clientele permanently to the MSI, moved to the right in its turn. The centre-left, agonizing since 1968, expired in these conditions. After the 1972 elections the DC formed a government without the Socialists, and adopted a stance of increasingly intransigent reaction under Fanfani. It was against this background that the PCI proclaimed the need for a 'historic compromise', in the autumn of 1973. Berlinguer's articles in *Rinascita* which provided the theoretical justification for this strategy were ostensibly a reaction to the downfall of Allende. There is no reason to doubt the alarm with which the PCI leaders viewed the defeat of Popular Unity in Chile. But the foundations for a 'historic compromise' had been laid long before by the party, and the final unveiling of the policy was a response to the political situation in Italy rather than to events in Latin America.

The origins of the conception can, in fact, be traced back to the final phase of Togliatti's career, when he started to speak of the need for a 'new majority', some years before his death in 1964. This watchword was deliberately left open to three distinct interpretations: an alliance of the PCI with the whole DC; an alliance with only a part of the DC; or a majority that excluded the DC altogether. Togliatti had tended to favour the first of these, an option that became increasingly pronounced after the centre-left came into existence. But this was not perceived as such by the rank and file of the PCI. The phrase could continue to mean one thing to the traditionalist base of the party, and another to the increasingly revisionist leadership, in a classic instance of the PCI's *doppiezza*. In the later sixties many Communist militants assumed that a new majority would be created once the left-wing minority of the DC had been split off from the rest of the party, and joined forces with the PCI. But the dominant view amongst the leadership, albeit privately held, was that an agreement should be sought with Christian Democracy as a whole. By 1970 the official position of the party, in its public statements, was in favour of an understanding with the centre and left of the DC.

At just this moment, however, the DC as a whole started to move to the right. The reaction of the PCI leadership was not to try to block this movement, but to shift rightward itself in order to keep in touch with its prospective partner. By the summer of 1972 Natta – later Berlinguer's successor – was criticizing even the centre-left government for having on occasion been guilty of an 'abstract maximalism' which had made certain sections of society feel insecure. It was now that the notion of an 'emergency government', including all the 'democratic parties', entered PCI vocabulary. The stage was thus set for the proposal of a long-term concordat between Christian Democracy and Communism, as the two fundamental forces in Italian society, that Berlinguer christened the 'historic compromise' in September 1973. The spectre of Chile – a 'vertical fracture' of society into two camps at war with each other, as the PCI leader presented it – was invoked to render this prospect palatable to the party's rank-and-file. In fact, the Chilean situation was so remote from Italian realities that this justification soon receded. A more frequent argument, in subsequent years, referred to the dangers of the 'strategy of tension' of the far right in Italy. An organic entente with Christian Democracy, reassuring the propertied and middle classes, was – the PCI contended – necesssary to isolate and neutralize the neo-fascist fanatics in the wings of the political scene, by denying them the climate of social fear in which they might thrive.

The menace of black terrorism was real enough. The years between 1969 and 1984 were marked by five major indiscriminate terrorist bombings by the neo-fascists, quite apart from uncounted selective political murders and assaults on individuals. Fascist violence was throughout this period far more random, psychopathic and nihilistic than even the worst actions of the Red Brigades. Yet the Italian state has rarely arrested and imprisoned the fascist bombers, and on the few occasions it has done so they have escaped from its gaols with monotonous ease.[7] Today, the historic leadership of the Brigate Rosse, Prima Linea and to a lesser extent Autonomia Operaia are behind bars. Those responsible for the fascist massacres are not. The escape of such notorious ringleaders as Freda and Ventura comes instantly to mind. In parliament itself, the MSI has been represented by at least three deputies, including Pino Rauti, involved in either terrorism or coup attempts or both. Neo-fascism has never been a force unambiguously separable from the structures of the Italian state, since many of these emerged largely unreconstructed after the Second World War. The Christian Democrat politicians who presided over it, honeycombing it with their party's appointees, have consequently always been within brushing distance of black intrigue at its lower or higher levels.

Thus not merely were the perpetrators of the massacre of Piazza Fontana in Milan – designed to provoke popular fear and backlash against the 'hot autumn' – never tracked down, enquiries into it invariably running into obstacles within the ministry of the interior; but the discovery of the P–2 lodge at the end of the seventies revealed the extent of the complicity among fascist financiers, cabinet ministers, chiefs of the armed forces, journalists and deputies, for ends that still remain obscure but certainly involved corruption and violence.[8] Nor were these relations between the worlds of black gangland and establishment politics the only dark side of Christian Democrat rule. The financial operations of cliques like those around Sindona or Calvi – themselves men with P–2 associations – linked the criminal personnel of the Mafia to Vatican dignitaries like Monsignor Marcinkus, and thence to DC politicians close to the Curia.[9] It was this intricate web of ambiguous contacts and surreptitious liaisons, stretching across a vast institutional area of Italian life, which made the PCI's actual record of exposing black terrorism – whose threat it invoked to legitimate the historic compromise – so intermittent and ineffectual. For there was no way that it could prosecute a really vigorous campaign against its perpetrators and backers, without colliding with powerful interests in the very party it was seeking to conciliate. Any force determined to halt the strategy of tension, or to uproot the Mafia, was misguided – to put it mildly – to delegate these tasks to the Christian Democrat elite or the existing Italian state apparatus.

In this sense, the activities of the far right were at most a secondary element in the calculations of the historic compromise. The primary reason for the PCI's fateful turn in the early seventies lay elsewhere. For the thinking behind the strategy of a full-scale partnership with Christian Democracy, it is necessary to look at the electoral situation in which the PCI found itself. This was always the central reality for the party, once the Italian political order had been stabilized after the war. The PCI was the largest Communist party in Western Europe. But the combined electoral strength of the Italian left was quite modest, particularly after the Social Democratic split-off from the PSI in 1947. At the height of the unity between the PCI and the PSI, in 1948, the two parties together scored only 31 per cent. A decade later, the figure had increased to 37 per cent. By the mid sixties, the PCI's own vote was still a little more than a quarter of the electorate, and the Socialists had parted company with it to join the DC in the centre-left – a development the PCI could do nothing to prevent. By the early seventies, however, the whole political landscape had been changed by the social eruptions of 1967–69, and the PSI – divided and uncertain of direction – was being edged out of government by the DC. This was the basic context in which the PCI now cast its strategic die. Confronted with the upsurge of the new social movements, and the exhaustion of the centre-left, it tacitly gave up attempts to rebuild its alliance with the PSI, and opted to woo the DC instead.

This decision was the real nub of the historic compromise. Its rationale was essentially a parliamentary one. The PCI had to seek a coalition if it was to be able to enter government. What lay behind its preference for Christian Democracy? There was a long history of rivalry between the two main parties of the Italian labour movement, only partly transcended during the years of the Cold War, and newly revived in the centre-left period. The PCI had a number of reasons – good and bad – for distrusting the PSI as it emerged into the seventies. The Socialists had shown opportunism in the formation of their coalition with the Christian Democrats, and weakness in the exercise of it. They had reunified with Saragat's Social Democrats, and then split from them again. There was the beginning of corruption in the party (though still nothing to be compared with the DC). At the same time, the party was democratically organized, and the plurality and vigour of its internal life was anathema to the bureaucratic regime at the Botteghe Oscure. Coolness towards the PSI, combined with *sotto voce* criticisms that its roots in the workers' movement were fast dwindling, was a feature of Berlinguer's leadership from the start. On the other hand, from 1972 onwards the PCI stressed ever more pointedly the 'popular' character of the DC, arguing that it could not be compared to bourgeois parties in other Western countries because of its mass base among Catholic workers and peasants, as well as majority support from middle strata throughout the country. In reality, the DC's share of the working-class vote was not higher than that of the CDU in West Germany, the Gaullist party in its heyday in France, or the Conservative Party in Britain. The ability to attract a significant popular electorate is a *sine qua non* of a successful conservative politics in any advanced capitalist sociey. What was peculiar to Italian Christian Democracy was less its proletarian electorate, than the parasitic character of so much of its middle-class following, above all in the South, where it has always relied heavily on forms of clientelism that involve malversation of state benefits and collaboration with the Mafia or Camorra.[10] Ideologically, of course, Christian Democracy emphasized its 'social' vocation and pastoral sensibility – themes to which the PCI showed increasing indulgence, evoking the cultural affinities between Catholic and Communist traditions wherever it could. The PCI had, in fact, voted to ratify the Lateran Pact, drawn up between Mussolini and the Vatican, in 1947 while the PSI had voted against it. So there was a significant precedent for a bid to outflank the Socialists to the right, by reaching an agreement directly with the DC.

But the social or moral points of contact between Catholic and Communist worlds, however much they figured in the rhetoric of official speeches, were the adornments rather than the core of the calculus involved in the option for the historic compromise. Two factors were decisive in the PCI's choice. A common front with the Socialists would still leave the left well short of a parliamentary majority – amounting to a bloc of something over 40 per cent of the vote. To gain the extra voters needed to pass the 50 per cent mark would require a concerted and sustained opposition politics, aimed at shaking loose key electoral fixtures of the postwar settlement – detaching constituencies from the centre and right by coherent campaigns over the medium run for a juster and more equal society. Haunted by the memory of 1948, when it had been driven into a ghetto with the Socialists, the PCI lacked any will for such a course. A bloc with the DC meant exactly the opposite. It involved no major change in the customary electoral landscape, and if it could be realized would yield a large parliamentary majority immediately. The country would not have to be stirred up, and the party would not have to wait. For all its projection of a very long-term virtually millennial strategy, much of the mentality of the historic compromise was that of the safe and short-term horizon. The option seemed to promise quicker results, with fewer risks, than the role of a confident and combative opposition accumulating forces for a real alternation of office.

Secularization 1972–81

Ironically, no sooner had the PCI proclaimed its goal of seeking a durable compact with Christian Democracy, allegedly in keeping with the deepest aspirations of the Italian masses for a national recon- ciliation of the two principal forces in the country, than its misreading of their actual mood became obvious. The issue which revealed the gap between the party's eagerness to reach an accommodation with the DC, and a growing popular desire to break with the kind of obscurantism it stood for, was appropriately enough divorce. Significantly it was a Socialist deputy, Loris Fortuna, who had introduced a divorce bill in 1965, during the early days of the centre-left, without immmediate success. In the changed climate of 1968 the Fortuna bill was revived and with PCI backing became law in December 1970. The Vatican and the DC promptly sought to reverse the law by organizing a referendum on it, in the belief that a profoundly Catholic nation would reject the evil done by anti-clericals and atheists in parliament. The PCI, which had supported the Fortuna bill without enthusiasm, was acutely embarrassed by this development, and did everything to avoid the referendum in which it feared not only defeat, but a bitter split between Catholics and non-Catholics that might wreck the chances of the historic compromise. Thus it accepted the dissolution of parlia- ment in 1972, one year before the end of its prescribed term, as a way of postponing a test which it felt must imperil its efforts to improve relations with the DC. But with Fanfani at the helm there was no escaping the referendum, which was finally held in May 1974. After a campaign in which the Socialists and the extra-parliamentary left, particularly Lotta Continua, were much more vigorous in defence of secular values than the Communists, the PCI was startled to find that divorce was approved by no less than 59 per cent of the electorate. The referendum was a clear-cut demonstration of the cultural changes brought on by the revolts of the late sixties, and the emergence of feminism in the early seventies.[11] It signalled an ongoing secularization of Italian society at variance with the whole ethos of a concordat between official Catholicism and Communism, and showed that sociological trends could work strongly in favour of radical lay politics.

The PCI's reluctant and laggard role in the battle for divorce was to be repeated in the struggle over abortion which followed it. Because of the church's hostility to contraception, Italy had a massive abortion rate for decades; the gap between the preaching of a celibate priesthood and the lived experience of large numbers of Italian women was by no means a product of 'modern decadence', as the Papacy presented it. The Radicals, a small civil-rights party moving to the left in this period, wanted to abolish all restrictions on abortion by repealing the fascist laws which outlawed it. The DC supported a new and very limited abortion law out of a fear that the only alternative would be the Radical proposal. The other parties put forward their own proposals, none of which was acceptable to the feminists, who were working alongside, but by no means in total agreement with, the Radical Party. In December 1975, fifty thousand women marched in Rome in favour of the legalization of abortion. This purely female demonstration provided the first evidence of a mass feminist movement in Italy. The UDI, a women's organization linked to the PCI, refused to participate. However, when in April 1976 a hundred thousand women gathered for a second march through Rome, the UDI decided to join in, realizing that the movement could no longer simply be denounced. Meanwhile, the Socialist Party had committed itself to a change in the law of the type demanded by the Radicals and the feminists. Over half a million signatures were collected for an abortion referendum, and the only way that Moro's government could avoid it was to call a general election instead. After the polls, parliament continued to work for two years drafting legislation on this issue – the Christian Democrats proposing one wrecking amendment after another in their efforts to weaken the law, and the Communists going along with many of these. In January 1978, feminists and UDI members mounted a joint protest against the PCI's compromises with the church at women's expense. The party's desire to placate the Vatican led it to lose control of the UDI, which eventually cut its links with the PCI altogether. Finally, in June 1978 parliament passed a rather liberal abortion law. The DC, the MSI and the Vatican campaigned against the law and, having learnt nothing from the divorce referendum, put the matter to the electorate. The vote in favour of the law in May 1981 proved to be even higher than on the less highly charged issue of divorce, a staggering 68 per cent.

National Solidarity 1976–79

For all its resistance to the worker and student rebelliousness of 1967–69, and its equivocation over the divorce referendum of 1974, the PCI paradoxically profited from both as an electoral force. In the absence of any credible political alternative to its left, and under the impact of rising unemployment as the world economic recession took hold, large numbers of voters pinned their hopes for real and far-reaching reforms, at last, in Italy's corrupt and antiquated social order on the one major party untainted by responsibility in office for it. The events of 1967–69 had set off a rolling 'organic crisis' of Italian society, in Gramscian terminology, which was neither desired nor promoted by the PCI, but became the most important factor in its spectacular electoral advance of 1975–76.[12] The party was able to reap the political benefits of protest movements which it had at first opposed and then sought to moderate. The regional polls of June 1975 were the first in which 18 to 21-year-olds could vote, an extension of the franchise that might itself be viewed as a consequence of 1968. There were over five million new voters who had come onto the register since 1972, the largest single increase in the history of the republic. Italy's economic performance in 1975 was the worst of the decade, and the young were most affected by the increase in unemployment. The PCI gained 32.4 per cent of the vote, 5 per cent more than in 1972. There was a change in numerous local and regional governments. Piedmont and Liguria now joined Emilia–Romagna, Tuscany and Umbria as red regions. Rome, Naples, Florence, Genoa and Turin acquired Communist mayors. The general election of 1976 reinforced the trend. The PCI vote reached 34.4 per cent, a figure never polled by it before or since in a general election. In the weeks leading up to the vote the dream of a *sorpasso* – of the PCI overtaking the DC as the largest single party in the country – exerted an immense pull over many sections of the left, including those with some reservations about the party.

The outcome of the 1976 elections meant that the historic compromise ceased to be a speculative project mooted in the recesses of the Botteghe Oscure, and became a practical possibility. The new arithmetic in the Chamber of Deputies meant that a majority formed purely from the DC and the minor parties of the centre and the right (Republicans, Social Democrats, Liberals) was no longer possible. The PSI made it clear that it would not enter any government or parliamentary majority that did not include the Communists, since it did not want to be blamed for supporting austerity measures whilst the PCI monopolized opposition to them and made further inroads into the Socialist vote. As a result, the Christian Democrats could not form a government without the support of the Communists or at the very least their abstention. The DC was desperately anxious to obtain the trade unions' cooperation in keeping down the cost of labour and raising productivity, and believed that if it showed some willingness to discuss its policies with the PCI, this would lead to a less conflictual relationship with the unions. On the other hand, its freedom of manoeuvre was limited by American fear of the very word 'Communist', and Washington's unambiguous message that it did not want the PCI in the Italian cabinet. It was therefore effectively pre-ordained that the most the PCI could actually hope for was a place in the majority rather than seats in the government. Such a coalition, in which the party took a subordinate position, was presented by the PCI as a government of 'national solidarity'. In view of the later justification of this conception by Berlinguer and others, it should be noted that the 'emergency' it was originally supposed to address was not the later terrorist threat to Italy's democratic institutions, which in the abstract might seem to have cut across normal political divisions, but the economic crisis that was impairing the efficiency of Italian capitalism, the kind of question on which the right and the left in a properly functioning political system would have had major disagreements.

The 1976 elections were followed by the customary governmental crisis, but once this melodrama was over, Giulio Andreotti formed an entirely Christian Democrat cabinet, which enjoyed the abstention of Communists, Socialists, Social Democrats, Republicans and Liberals. This regime continued to draw direct or indirect support from the Communists from August 1976 until January 1979. It was popularly known as the Andreotti–Berlinguer government, regardless of the differing convoluted labels attached to it by the various political parties. For the purposes of a short-term stabilization of Italian capitalism, it gave a reasonably creditable performance. During these years the lira and the balance of payments improved; by 1979 Italian economic growth at 5 per cent was second only to Japanese. On the other hand, inflation and unemployment remained acute problems. The immediate crisis was overcome by the imposition of sacrifices that fell especially heavily upon the working class. In October 1976 the government introduced a classic package of deflationary measures of the kind that the IMF normally suggests. The interest rate was pushed up by 3.4 per cent to discourage borrowing, and a large number of government-controlled prices – petrol, heating, oil, gas, tobacco, postal charges and rail fares – were raised, hitting the poorest groups hardest. Factory workers were anyway one of the few groups whose income tax was extracted at source, while shopkeepers, restaurant-owners, lawyers and a mass of the middle-class occupations freely defrauded the fiscal authorities. Five statutory holidays were abolished, indicating the desire of the employers and the state to claw back gains incorporated in the 1972 statute. The PCI made only token demurrers, allowing the austerity package to pass more or less unchanged.

The historic compromise thus took shape as a conventional regime of DC patronage and deflation. 'National solidarity' eliminated all substantial dissent or opposition from parliamentary politics. A monolithic 'constitutional arc' of the six principal parties dominated the Chamber. Not a single significant reform issued from an arrangement in which, as came to be widely remarked, the division of labour was all too clear: the Christian Democrats made the history, the Communists made the compromise. The political consequences for the country were disastrous. For it was never likely that all the unrest left by the turmoil of the late sixties would peter out under this dispensation. Ultimately the price of a blocked political system proved to be a spiralling dialectic of violence and repression that ended in the lunacy of red terrorism. The beginning of this process was less dramatic than its conclusion. It started with unrest among the newest generation of students, which then spilled out of the campuses into sections of urban youth, from petty-bourgeois, marginal or working-class backgrounds. From the outset, the movement of 1977 was a far more ambiguous phenomenon than the student upsurge of 1967–68 or the workers' revolt of 1968–69. The change in the economic conjuncture had a great deal to do with this difference. The movements of 1967–69 had occurred against a background of prosperity at the end of the long postwar boom, and mobilized the factory proletariat of the North – in a sense the Italian labour aristocracy. The revolt of 1977 was a product of the depression. Its – much smaller – popular component came from young unemployed: relatively secure factory workers were unwilling to put their jobs at risk in the middle of a slump. The protests started as a predictable reaction to the frustrations of the Andreotti–Berlinguer government. Geographically, the rebellion had two main bases, Bologna and Rome. At the time, both of these were run by Communist-dominated municipal administrations, but neither had significant concentrations of factory workers. Failing to forge real links with the industrial proletariat in the Northern cities, the movement reciprocated the hostility of the PCI towards it with a violent animosity of its own, and soon displayed manifestations of such naivety, self-regard and nihilism that it paved the way for the terrorist groups. These in turn played an important role in weakening the organized labour movement in the face of the counter-offensive by the employers and the state apparatus, who had long been waiting for an occasion to roll back the gains of 1969–70.

The trouble started in February, when a hundred fascists invaded the University of Rome and shot at demonstrators protesting against the government's new education bill. The following day thousands of students mobilized outside the MSI's Roman offices. The police responded by opening fire on the crowd. These events provoked a wave of campus occupations in Rome, Palermo, Bari, Milan, Turin, Venice, Bologna, Florence, Pisa, Cagliari and Naples, generating the impression of a renewal of the student movement of the sixties. But within a few weeks, a minority belonging to Autonomia Operaia had provoked violent clashes with Communist marshals on the Rome campus; an innocent member of Lotta Continua had been shot in the back by police on the Bologna campus, followed by street fighting and a a state of siege; and an unarmed young feminist was gunned down by riot squads during a demonstration to celebrate the anniversary of the divorce referendum in Rome.

The original student unrest of early 1977 was a confused but authentic expression of the alienation and despair of large masses of Italian youth, a protest against the climate of economic crisis and political conformism that marked the regime of national solidarity. Its initial expressions anticipated many elements of later British punk culture – a penchant for the deliberately but harmlessly bizarre that took the form of fantasmatic identification with 'Indians' (American rather than subcontinental). But the movement very quickly fell under the sway of the spokesmen of Autonomia Operaia, an amorphous descendant of earlier workerist currents of the far left, which was responsible for the introduction of fire-arms into subsequent demonstrations. Its theorists now argued that vast new layers of the population, including university students and the permanently unemployed, should be defined as a proletariat – while factory workers constituted a privileged group apart. Insofar as Autonomia Operaia acquired any mass base in the ranks of employed labour, it was among such marginalized and badly paid groups as hospital workers in Rome. But the intoxication of its leaders was such that they could incite the unemployed against production workers, as if these were their adversaries. Autonomia Operaia developed into a singularly unpleasant phenomenon, whose most hardened members practised *terrorismo diffuso* – low-level thuggery – against opponents of the kind usually associated with neo-fascist squads. But the chaotic and anarchic character of the movement meant that it swept up many younger activists who were never involved in this brutality, but were trying to register a passionate protest against what they saw as their own lack of any future in Italian society.

Meanwhile, a quite distinct form of terrorism had burst on to the political scene. The Red Brigades were a dogmatic, militarist, substitutionist sect that had been formed in the aftermath of the student movement of the late sixties. Acting in the name of, but without consulting the working class, they were committed to armed actions from the start, but did not kill anybody until June 1974 when they assassinated two MSI militants outside the party's branch office in Padua. Their really vicious phase started after the imprisonment of their founder Renato Curcio in 1976.[13] The BR recruited in part from former Left Catholics, in part from disillusioned Communists, as well as some without any political past. The group was always very small in size, but its discipline and single-mindedness made it seem disproportionately effective. After a series of shootings and hold-ups in 1977, its kidnapping and subsequent killing of Aldo Moro in 1978 convulsed Italian politics. Moro had been negotiating with the PCI the terms of its relationship to the government when he was seized in broad daylight in the middle of Rome. Universal outrage at the murder of Moro found expression in a general strike called by the PCI in May.

In these conditions, there was a rapid hardening of the already repressive dispositions of the Italian state. In December 1974, the DC minister of the interior Reale had introduced a bill to tighten Italian security legislation. Then, the Socialists and Communists had defeated a clause empowering the police to keep suspects incommunicado for 48 hours. In May 1975, when the Reale law was finally passed, the PCI voted against the entire bill, calling it a severe blow to civil liberties which would open the way to repression of the workers' movement. By 1977–78 the party had changed its mind. It not only supported yet harsher amendments of the Reale law, but further police legislation that allowed interrogation of suspects without the presence of a defence lawyer. When the Radicals forced a referendum for a repeal of the Reale law in June 1978, the PCI campaigned all-out for its retention. In February 1980, the Chamber passed still further laws curtailing civil liberties in Italy. The police could henceforward hold suspects with little or no evidence, detaining them for forty-eight hours without charge, while a magistrate's order could imprison them for more than ten years without trial. Telephone tapping, entry into offices and homes, closing of political organizations, sweeping searches through blocks or buildings, were all given wide new latitudes. Only the Radicals, the PDUP and a few maverick Socialist deputies opposed these measures.

The abuses of the repressive machinery set up in these years, and the participation of the PCI in a general punitive panic, were highlighted in the case brought against the leaders of Autonomia Operaia. In April 1979, the police arrested Antonio Negri in Padua, on the instruction of local magistrates closely associated with the party. In all probability,

Negri could have been linked with specific acts of violence by the Paduan *Autonomi*, which would have carried a very heavy prison sentence in the event of conviction. But respect for the rules of evidence was thrown to the winds, as Negri was charged with plotting an insurrection in Italy since 1969, commanding the Red Brigades, and master-minding the kidnapping of Moro, and held in jail for four years without trial. Eventually, the Radicals elected him to parliament in 1983 to draw attention to the situation. Once his parliamentary immunity was taken away from him by the Chamber, Negri fled to France, leaving his angry co-defendants to await heavy sentences the following year. The Padua trial reflected discredit on its organizers and sponsors alike. The magistrates' attempt to conflate the Autonomia with the Red Brigades suited the tactical book of the PCI, but lacked any basis in social fact. The gulf between the two kinds of extremism was, in fact, one of the reasons for the BR's failure. Their membership was always far smaller and more isolated than many of the politicians eager to mythologize it would admit. It rapidly collapsed once it was exposed to the confessions of the *pentiti* – supergrasses – and the blitzes of the *carabinieri* under General Della Chiesa.

Counter-Offensive at Fiat

In January 1979 the PCI withdrew from the parliamentary majority, complaining that Andreotti had not honoured his promises of reforms. This was indeed true – even a solitary and ill thought-out rent law had created as many problems as it solved, notably failing to remedy Italy's housing shortage. However, the PCI's immediate aim in withdrawing from the government was to bargain for cabinet posts. The DC, feeling that the worst of the crisis was over and there was no longer need of Communist support, called its bluff. The result was a general election in June. The Communist vote fell sharply: down from 34.4 per cent to 30.4 per cent. The Radicals, who had acted as the real party of opposition in these years, trebled their poll – gaining about 7 per cent in Rome and Turin: mostly young left-wing voters dismayed by 'national solidarity'.

The PCI did not change its line. At a central committee meeting in July, Berlinguer asserted the continuing validity of the historic compromise, calmly arguing that it would be social-democratic to subordinate the party's strategy to electoral considerations. For another year it persisted in its old course, in the hope that despite everything joint rule with Christian Democracy might come to pass. But the DC, which emerged unscathed from the polls, was in no mood to make concessions to a party just weakened by them. The balance of forces had altered in the country. The decisive change was in industry. Business was now ready to hit back. The epoch that had begun with the hot autumn of 1969 ended in the autumn of 1980. In September FIAT announced that it was going to sack fourteen thousand workers. The metalworkers' union FLM responded by calling an indefinite stoppage, which in fact lasted thirty-five days. This was the longest strike in a major Italian industry since Liberation. The struggle began well. The PCI declared its sympathy and Berlinguer went to the factory gates, even offering to support an occupation. Workers from other cities joined the picket lines and money poured into the strike fund. Secondary industrial action, albeit of a symbolic kind, was mounted with a one-day general strike in Piedmont and a one-day national strike of the FLM. Then on 14 October 1980, thirty to forty thousand FIAT supervisors, guards, technicians and office workers marched through the centre of Turin behind a banner claiming the FLM did not represent them. A few hundred production workers, mainly Piedmontese, joined in. That night the the union surrendered to FIAT, signing an agreement which allowed the company to lay off twenty-three thousand workers rather than the original fourteen thousand.

The union leadership, including some of the highest-ranking officials of the Confederation as well as the FLM, immediately met the factory council delegates and the FIAT workers to discuss the accord. The reaction of the delegates – perhaps not surprisingly, given the rapidity of the volte-face – was violent: Pierre Carniti, the secretary of the CISL, and Giorgio Benvenuto, the secretary of the UIL, narrowly escaped being beaten up. The union leaders called for a show of hands at the various Turin FIAT plants and declared that a majority at every factory had approved the agreement. In fact, the meetings were held in extremely confused circumstances and if there was a majority, it was probably for rejection. The union leaders maintained that their decision was based on a realistic assessment that the strike was about to crumble. But the critical decisive factor seems to have been the march of the forty thousand. The unions clearly panicked at seeing such a large hostile force on the streets of Turin, and were worried about their future relationship with the technicians.

The essence of the confrontation at FIAT, like that of the British miners' strike in 1984–85, its nearest analogue, was political and not economic. If FIAT had simply wanted to reduce the labour force, the management could have accepted one of the union proposals for rotating lay-offs. Since FIAT had an average natural wastage rate of twelve thousand workers a year, this would have been quite sufficient for the avowed purpose of the management. But its real aim was to reclaim the control over the labour force and production process it had lost in 1969. FIAT used its victory with complete ruthlessness. The twenty-three thousand people expelled from the plants were not picked at random: among them were a disproportionate number of political militants, women, young people and disabled workers, all categories held to be in some way deviant. For the survivors, the atmosphere in the plants changed radically. FIAT lost only one million work-hours in strikes in 1981, compared with 13.5 million the previous year. The workers once again became afraid of redundancies and of the supervisors. The famous sociological phenomenon of the *rifiuto del lavoro* vanished very rapidly in the face of the new factory discipline. Absenteeism, which had ranged between 14 and 18 per cent before the strike, fell to between 3 and 5 per cent – below that of even the notoriously subservient Japanese car-workers, whose average rate is about 8 per cent. Productivity jumped 20 per cent in a year and the company returned to a much sought-after profit. In the first eighteen months after the strike, FIAT pressed home the attack, closing several plants and continuing to lay off workers, often as many as forty thousand at a time for short periods. Robotization was now introduced on an increasing scale. By the mid eighties FIAT could boast the most technologically advanced auto plants in Europe, and had reconquered its slipping position in international markets. The price for this victory of the powerhouse of Italian capital was paid by the Italian working class as a whole. Turin, stronghold of the workers' revolt of 1968–69, and hot-bed of militancy throughout the seventies, has ever since been quieter than Milan. But the crushing defeat suffered by the Turinese workers in 1980 was a turning-point for Italian labour as a whole. The events at FIAT set the bitter tone of the years that followed.

Craxi in Power

For the PCI, it was no longer possible to act as if nothing had changed. Berlinguer's response to the FIAT strike was the signal that the PCI had finally accepted that 'national solidarity' was over. A month later, the leadership took the opportunity of public reaction to the earthquake in Campania – once again revealing the calamitous negligence and corruption of local DC administration – to announce that it was henceforward going into outright opposition. This so-called second *svolta di Salerno* was greeted with relief by many of the party's rank and file, who had never been happy with the policy of amity towards Christian Democracy. No coherent alternative course, however, was found. While the base of the PCI welcomed the break with the ruling coalition, much of its officialdom continued to hanker for some new way of rejoining it; Berlinguer attempted to mediate these contradictions with a rhetoric of militant moralism, while the party trod political water.

Economic conditions worsened sharply in the slump that set in after 1980. In June 1982 the Confindustria announced that it was unilaterally cancelling the *scala mobile* as of January 1983. Prolonged negotiations followed, culminating in a cost-of-labour accord signed by the unions, employers and government which cut protection against inflation, and allowed firms to increase labour flexibility – two major victories for the employers' association. By now the harsh economic climate had not left the ruling coalition immune. The elections of June 1983 saw a major shift within the *pentapartito*. Amidst the recession, the DC dropped from 38.3 to 32.9 per cent – the heaviest losses in its history. The PSI vote by contrast rose to 11.4 per cent. This result paved the way for Bettino Craxi to assume the premiership. For the first time, the PSI now occupied the centre of the Italian political stage – its leader dominating government for the next four years as few prime ministers had done since the mid fifties. The PSI of the eighties, however, was a very different creature from the party the PCI had cold-shouldered a decade before.

Craxi had become leader of the Socialist Party in 1976, in a reshuffle which seemed at the time to be merely a reaction to the party's poor electoral performance in the elections of that year. At first he looked like previous Socialist leaders, merely the head of one of the largest currents within the party, in which there were traditionally periodic adjustments in the composition of the various leading bodies as the followings of the different currents expanded or contracted. But soon it became clear that he was determined to transform the party in his own image. Craxi came to believe that the PSI's route to success lay in presenting itself as a modernizing, secular party of an anti-communist stamp that would be acceptable both to Northern industrialists and to large sections of the urban middle classes and intelligentsia in cities like his home town Milan. Under the historic compromise, he was able to capitalize skilfully on the natural resentment within the PSI at being squeezed out of decision-making by the alliance between the two largest parties. During this period it was common for PCI leaders in nominally red cities or regions to spend more time consulting with the DC opposition than with their PSI colleagues. Craxi understood better than the Communists that Italian society was moving in a secular, rather than conciliar, direction, and that any party which took up progressive lay issues would find growing social forces behind it. The PSI had voted to revoke the Concordat in 1947, and had taken the lead in the campaign for divorce in 1972–74. It now adapted to the demands for legalization of abortion (initiated by the Radicals), and even occasionally displayed some concern for civil liberties during the years of emergency. Craxi's own concern with these issues was entirely tactical. His later dealings with the Banco Ambrosiano and protection of P–2 members, in old-fashioned DC style, soon made this all too plain.[14] But at the time this line seemed to give external credence to the PSI's claim to be more libertarian in outlook than the PCI, even while Craxi himself was quietly imposing a new authoritarian regime within his party. All the PSI's currents were wound up and organizational power was concentrated overwhelmingly in his hands. By 1981, it was apparent that serious opposition to Craxi's methods and policies would not be tolerated. The *Gleichschaltung* was accompanied by an ideological mutation. In 1976, it had still been a nominally Marxist party. Craxi replaced the hammer and the sickle with the carnation as the party's symbol, and not merely abandoned the party's traditional language, but sponsored an all-out assault on it in the name of market values and Western freedoms. As the PSI became his political machine, its press became increasingly pro-American, and its intellectuals Italy's nearest counterparts to the *nouveaux philosophes* in France.

Once the two protagonists of the historic compromise had suffered their respective forms of attrition – the PCI in opposition again, the DC losing electoral ground – Craxi could thus come forward as the strong man capable of steering the country into a disciplined modernity. The cutting edge of this appeal was now directed not against religious obscurantism but against classical socialism itself, presented as a backward totalitarian faith; ceasing to have any real critical charge against the state, instead it targeted labour as the principal obstacle to the rationalization of Italian capitalism. Craxi's peculiar achievement was thus to turn secularization as a mobilizing force against the traditional identity of the working-class movement itself, while promoting an ideology of market individualsm that struck a deep chord in Italy's increasingly conformist intelligentsia. The PCI's failure to adopt any combative secular stance during the seventies thus cost it dear. The ultimate effect of its pursuit of historic compromise with the DC was to release the PSI from any social constraints from below or to its left, and allow it to occupy the position the PCI had sought for itself as the privileged partner of Christian Democracy. Italian Communism missed the boat of secularization, which took an acridly right-wing turn from the end of the seventies onwards, to the profit of the politician the PCI most disliked and feared.

Once installed in the Palazzo Chigi, Craxi lanched the most sustained attack on working-class organization and living standards that Italy had seen for thirty years. With a rhetoric at times not far from Thatcher's, the new government gave absolute priority to the battle against inflation. Together, Craxi and the Confindustria demanded a second and deeper round of cuts in the *scala mobile*. The trade-union confederations could not agree on a negotiating position, each going its own way. Craxi, never a man to miss an opportunity to show his strength, rapidly issued a government decree slashing indexation by 38 per cent. The UIL, CISL and Socialists in the CGIL accepted it; only the Communists and the far left in the CGIL were opposed. But widespread resistance surged up from below. Weeks of strikes, mass demonstrations and workers' assemblies culminated in a rally of 700,000 people in Rome in March 1984. Much of the initiative in arousing popular anger and reviving the fighting spirit of delegates' councils came from Democrazia Proletaria, the one far-left organization to survive the wreckage of the late seventies, and emerge as a small but serious organization with some influence in the working class in the eighties.

The PCI, responding to the mass sentiment of its base in the industrial triangle, joined the DP in talking out Craxi's first *scala mobile* decree in parliament, and then threw its whole weight behind the huge March demonstration in Rome. This militancy, long unseen, was in part prompted by the awareness that the DP was gaining ground in the factory councils of Northern cities, encroaching on PCI influence. On the other hand, the party was also subject to pressures from the right through the CGIL, in which the Socialists kept their place, and whose general secretary, Luciano Lama, emerged as the most outspoken leader of the PCI right. The union bureaucracy, concerned to avoid a split in the CGIL, was now the principal transmission point for accommodation to the PSI. Lama made no secret of his dislike for the party's stance on indexation. The result of this larger, contrary force was that the PCI allowed Craxi's second decree cutting the *scala mobile* to pass in parliament, claiming that to have blocked it for six months was already a major victory for the working class, and that a deal might now be struck.

Unimpressed by this retreat, Democrazia Proletaria proceeded to collect signatures for a referendum on the *scala mobile*. The PCI, after a brief moment of euphoria in the 1984 Euro-elections when the sympathy vote following Berlinguer's death on the hustings had placed it narrowly ahead of the DC for the first time, fell back to around 30 per cent of the vote in the 1985 local elections, and would probably have liked to avoid the referendum. But rank-and-file pressure made a compromise with Craxi on the issue impossible, and in June the referendum was duly held. The result was 45.6 per cent for the protection of indexation, and 54.4 per cent against – the most narrowly fought contest since the referendum on the monarchy. The PCI's reaction to Craxi's victory was an act of penitence, as it virtually threw itself at the feet of the DC in the elections for a new President – voting for Cossiga, the Christian Democrat candidate, a notorious minister of the interior of the late seventies, on the first ballot. Since all five parties of the ruling coalition were officially committed to Cossiga, the PCI could expect no concrete concessions for its cooperation – merely the satisfaction of being respectable once again, an accepted component of the consensus to elect a new head of state.

Once firmly in the saddle, Craxi moved purposefully towards his long-term goal – reduction of the PCI to subordinate status, as the second-ranking rather than largest party of the left, allowing him to discard the DC and head a Socialist regime like that of Mitterrand in France, supported by a dependent Communist Party as a junior partner. His first task was to strengthen the political position of the PSI within the *pentapartito*, by enlarging its area of influence in the state apparatus, and so potentially expanding its social base. Craxi was fortunate in coming to power just as the world economy was pulling out of the recession of 1981–82. Their spirits revived by victory over indexation, Italian entrepreneurs responded with energy. The mid eighties saw a new kind of consumer boom in Italy, as Craxi presided over the highest growth rates for some time – GNP rising by over 2.5 per cent a year between 1983 and 1987, compared with virtual stagnation between 1979 and 1983. The stock exchange was liberalized and financial speculation took off. A frenzied cult of material success and worldly display gripped the strata that benefited most – the *ceti rampanti* of the Northern cities, whose outlook and lifestyle were hailed by the media as the flowering of an overdue modernity.

While yuppie values spread rapidly through prospering professional and commercial layers of the population, the traditional culture of the working class was shrinking. The industrial proletariat, which had increased very rapidly in size – both in absolute numbers and as a proportion of the work-force – between 1951 and 1971, now started to contract in a belated repetition of the British, French and German pattern. The tertiary sector, which accounted for 29.7 per cent of the labour force in 1977, employed 38.6 per cent by 1985. Much of the new growth occurred, not in the industrial triangle of Milan–Turin–Genoa, but in small firms of the 'Third Italy', particularly in the Veneto and Northern Lombardy, areas under Christian Democrat hegemony where the subculture of the labour movement had never made much impact. Nationally, unionization fell by 15 per cent between 1977 and 1986, and factory councils faded into the background after the defeat of the *scala mobile*. Labour militancy in the later eighties tended to come from the amorphous COBAS (*comitati di base*) challenging the authority of the Confederal unions in the public sector – particularly on the railways, at the airports and in the schools, whose unabashed sectionalism might to some extent be seen as another symptom of the narrow self-interest encouraged by the Craxi government and its ideologues.

Meanwhile, Craxi's machine was expanding its positions within the byzantine structures of the Italian state, colonizing the higher bureaucracy, the parastatals and the audiovisual media with PSI appointees, and drawing increasing support from business, as a profitable partner to pick in the traditional transactions between public authority and private enterprise. In the glow of the boom, with ample funds now at its disposal, the PSI enlarged its clientele in the South and increased both its popular and middle-class support in the North. Between 1983 and 1987, when Craxi's election campaign trumpeted Italy's success in overtaking Britain as the third largest European economy, the PSI gained well over a million votes, while the PCI lost just under a million. The Socialists seemed on course towards Craxi's ultimate goal. Electorally and ideologically, they were getting the upper hand. In May 1988, local elections saw a further and more dramatic shift in their favour. The PCI vote fell to a disastrous 22.8 per cent, while the PSI soared to 18.1 per cent, its highest share of the poll since 1946. The smaller parties in the Socialist wake also did well, the Social Democrats getting 4.8 and the Republicans 5.1 per cent – even if this increased their short-term reluctance to be swallowed whole by Craxi. The figures added up grimly for the PCI. A French scenario looked not far off.

The Transformation of the PCI

After the death of Berlinguer in 1983, Italian Communism had floundered. If the FIAT offensive had buried the historic compromise, and popular mobilization had forced it into battle over indexation, the party leadership remained divided and uncertain of direction. Its first response to defeat in the *scala mobile* referendum was to seek a rapprochement with the PSI. Addressing the 17th Congress of the party in 1986, its new secretary-general, the classicist Alessandro Natta, called for a democratic alternative based on 'a reconciliation of the two great currents into which the workers' movement has been divided'. This was a drastic change of tone from the early years of Craxi's premiership, when it was regarded as a matter of debate whether the Socialists were any longer in a meaningful sense part of the left. The new prospect was still carefully qualified: it was not intended, Natta explained, to drive the DC into opposition, even if that could not be ruled out as 'a possible aspect of democratic normalcy'. The PCI now contained a new left current, still headed by Ingrao but now including the former Manifesto group led by Magri and Castellina, who had rejoined the party after Berlinguer had dropped the historic compromise, and a more pro-Soviet tendency led by Armando Cossutta – together making up about 30 per cent of the delegates; while on the right the *miglioristi* around Napolitano and Lama accounted for another 10 per cent. But although speeches clearly reflected the different positions, the essential votes were still cast with unreconstructed monolithism – the official theses approved unanimously by over a thousand delegates, with just seventeen abstentions. The one issue where a division was permitted, for the sake of appearances, only underlined the PCI's lack of touch. By a substantial majority, the congress endorsed nuclear power – only to find the party wrong-footed by the PSI once again, when a few months later the Socialists smartly reversed their support for nuclear energy in the aftermath of Chernobyl, leaving the PCI to lumber shame-faced behind them. The anti-nuclear referendum initiated by the DP, Radicals and Greens eventually pulled every political party behind it, save the Republicans, earning the PCI little or nothing for its contribution to the uncontroversial result.

By 1988, Craxi had been obliged to rotate the premiership back to the DC, but the political position of the PSI had never been stronger. The humiliating losses of the PCI in the spring elections put an end to Natta's leadership. His health exhausted by the campaign, he retired in favour of his deputy Achille Ochetto, a former youth leader of the party who had been close to Ingrao's left in the early sixties, and was much distrusted by the right of the PCI, which had voted against his elevation the year before. When its 18th Congress met in Rome in the spring of 1989, the PCI confronted a situation in which Craxi was already assigning it the role of either becoming the junior partner of the PSI, or being reduced to impotent sectarian isolation – with further electoral decline in view in either case. The prospect of gradual, or perhaps not so gradual, extinction if the PSI overtook the PCI in the forthcoming European elections of June 1989 concentrated the delegates' minds, producing an unprecedented willingness to accept changes that the party had resisted for decades. The mortal danger the party faced made unity imperative on this occasion.

The most striking feature of Occhetto's *corso nuovo* was an opening to the new social movements. He began his speech to the congress by dealing with ecological issues in a global context, relating them to models of industrial development with the firm assertion that 'green, if it is not red, is an illusion'; and went on stress the importance of women's issues, proclaiming: 'We are the only political force that has employed sexual difference as the overall criterion of social and human relations.' Warmly applauding Gorbachev's role in the USSR and international arena, Occhetto appeared to be shifting the party to a position close to that of the left in the SPD. Announcing the definitive abandonment of democratic centralism, he instituted a secret ballot in votes to leadership elections, and ensured a sweeping turnover in the composition of the central committee. Over half the members of the new body were newcomers from the younger generation that had felt the force of 1968 and 1977 – Occhetto's closest allies, such as Massimo d'Alema, were in their forties; 30 per cent of the places were reserved for women, who also secured the same proportion of seats in the inner redoubt of the leadership, the *direzione*. The ideas of Ingrao's left on feminism, ecology and internal democracy seemed to have finally been accepted. Occhetto's filial embrace at the end of the old man's speech, full of welcome to the new social movements and scepticism about the Socialists, amidst the enthusiastic applause of the delegates, appeared to many as the symbol of a fresh start.

Craxi was predictably dismissive about Occhetto's innovations, as no real departure from the totalitarian heritage at all. His arrogance was unbridled when elections in a few Southern towns in May gave the Socialists 18.7 per cent and the Communists 17.1 per cent, taking this as evidence that his party was set to overtake the PCI in the European elections. Two weeks later, the Chinese leadership staged its brutal attack on the student occupation of Tienanmen. Seizing the opportunity, Craxi led the most savagely anti-Communist election campaign since 1948, identifying the PCI with the CPC, as if Occhetto was personally responsible for the massacre in Beijing. But this cynical operation misfired. In the European polls of 19 June the Italian electorate showed its revulsion, actually awarding the PCI a small increase over its 1987 performance – up 1 per cent to 27.6, while the PSI took only 14.8 per cent. The combined forces of the PCI, PSI, DP and the Greens won 49.9 per cent, as against the DC's falling 32.9 per cent, making the PCI's long-term chances of creating a left alternative look electorally credible.

Craxi's continual charges that the PCI had not changed its spots, remaining the creature of a discredited Comintern tradition, nevertheless had their effect on Occhetto. When the East German crisis broke in the autumn, he decided the party could no longer afford even nominal connection with the Communism collapsing in Central Europe. Within twenty-four hours of the Berlin Wall coming down, he seized the emotional moment to announce in a speech at the Bolognina that he intended to change the party's name. What Italy now needed was a

'Constituent Assembly of the Left', beyond traditional formations, capable of unifying every progressive force in a common project. Occhetto's sudden initiative caught everyone outside his inner circle, even within the PCI leadership, by surprise. Its immediate results were discomfiting. The proposal for a 'constituent assembly' found virtually no takers. The Greens and the Radicals showed no interest; Left Catholics were equally unresponsive – when Palermo's radical mayor Orlando left the DC, he founded his own organization, La Rete; the Socialists remained thoroughly hostile. The proposal to change the name of the PCI, on the other hand, ran into stiff opposition within the party.

The result was a long drawn-out debate that stretched from November 1989 to February 1991. Occhetto did not try to force the pace, reckoning that a prolonged transition would minimize the danger of a major split, by isolating Cossutta's small current from the rest of the party's left and allowing the electorate to express its approval for the new turn. These proved to be mistaken assumptions. In March 1990 Occhetto got 67 per cent support at the 19th Congress for the principle of changing the party's name, but the regional and local elections in June were a popular rebuff to the still nominally united PCI, which lost 6 per cent of the vote while the Socialists and Greens made gains. Internal wrangling intensified as the prospect of the Gulf War loomed. Occhetto eventually opted for a nuanced opposition to Desert Storm, partly to try to keep the bulk of the left within the party, to the indignation of the right, which wanted outright support for Bush. But the basic dividing-lines had crystallized within a few weeks of the Bolognina address, and the 20th Congress at Rimini in February 1991 only confirmed them.

Once again Occhetto won a majority of 65 per cent on the key vote, for acceptance of the name to be adopted by the new organization – Partito Democratico della Sinistra, a title intentionally avoiding any mention of 'socialism' or 'labour', modelled on American example. Ingrao and Cossutta united behind a common motion of opposition, which won the support of 30 per cent of the delegates. The proponents of the PDS were aware that the Cossuttiani would in all probability split off, on the whole looking forward to their departure as enabling the PDS to present a more modern image to public opinion. But it was generally assumed that the rest of the opposition, having borne witness to their views, would resign themselves to party discipline with varying degrees of enthusiasm and form a minority current within the new organization.

As expected, Cossutta walked out of the congress and announced the formation of a Movement for the Refoundation of Communism in early February. What was not expected was the size of the grassroots revolt against the PDS. Rifondazione had gained 110,000 members by the beginning of March, 125,000 by early April and 150,000 by the end of the year – in more than 600 sections spread across the country, a substantial party with real roots in society.[15] Obviously not all Rifondazione members were former PCI activists – Democrazia Proletaria dissolved itself to enter the new movement and a number of small far left groups and individuals expelled from the PCI over the previous quarter century decided to put differences aside in order to preserve an Italian communist tradition.[16] But the vast majority came from the PCI. They included the Manifesto left, whose leaders Magri and Castellina joined in April. The scale of the secession had surpassed all calculations. As has so often happened when left-wing parties split in two, a large proportion of the former PCI membership joined neither party, abandoning active involvement in politics altogether. Natta himself was a case in point. Italian Communism had officially enrolled some 1,300,000 in 1990. By the end of 1991, the PDS numbered only about 400,000, with a level of commitment generally less than that of Rifondazione.

The mutation of the PCI had not gone according to plan. From the outset, Occhetto's path was dogged by mishaps. The PDS's first week approached virtual farce, as Occhetto failed to win enough votes to be elected secretary under rules he had himself drawn up, because of deliberate abstentions by the right to punish him for allying with the left against the Gulf War. All of D'Alema's skill and tact were needed to extricate the party from this embarrassment. Unseemly litigation with Rifondazione over rights to the symbol and property of the PCI followed. Post-socialist intellectuals, assiduously wooed into the party, truculently walked out of it. When the test of national elections came in April 1992, the result was little short of catastrophe. The PCI had obtained 26.6 per cent of the vote in 1987 – its lowest score since 1963. The PDS ended up with 16.1 per cent – finally putting the PSI, which held steady at 13.6 per cent, within range to overtake it. Rifondazione scored 5.6 per cent, underlining the net loss of votes to the left. The DC, for its part, dropped just below 30 per cent for first time in the history of the republic. These figures left a large gap. The new force in Italian politics, making a spectacular entry onto the scene, was the Northern League. The movement led by Umberto Bossi won 8.7 per cent of the total vote, making it the fourth largest party in the country.

Tangentopoli and the Death Agony of the First Republic

With the eruption of the Lega Nord, the whole universe of postwar Italian politics suddenly began to dissolve. Within months, the republic born of the Liberation and the Cold War was in its death agony.[17] In the extraordinary upheaval that followed the elections of April 1992, the larger part of the traditional political class, and much of the bureaucratic and business elite of the country, was consumed in a series of gigantic financial scandals and criminal revelations. These events made for riveting drama, with a melodramatic cast of lurid villains and fearless prosecutors, oligarchic corruption and popular wrath. To understand them, however, it is necessary to look behind the courtroom rhetoric at the structural realities that set off the crisis of the old regime. The conditions of its collapse lay in four decisive changes which intersected at the turn of the decade.

The first of these lay in the hidden transformation of the traditional lubrications of power in Italy. In the epoch of more or less undivided Christian Democratic hegemony – the fifties through to the seventies – corruption was built into the system of political patronage on which DC electoral strength rested. But the realm of *sottogoverno*, as the name implies, was a subsidiary and parochial one – payments into party coffers in exchange for contracts, dispensation of offices and benefits in exchange for votes. Occasionally, really big bribes lined individual pockets in Rome, but these were exceptional and usually external – like Lockheed's generosity to Rumor and Leone. The DC remained a mass party, whose strength ultimately lay in its broad social base. With the entry of the redesigned PSI into the system, however, the rules changed. Craxi's party lacked deep roots in society, was smaller than its partner, and needed to make up for its disadvantages as a relative newcomer. It was therefore virtually bound to be greedier. Its origins lay in Lombardy, where its leadership was always culturally closer to the world of modern business than the DC elites, typically recruited from rural and provincial backgrounds. So it started shake-downs on a quite new, industrial scale. Given the interdependence of the *pentapartito*, however, there was no way of confining the practices and proceeds of this kind of corruption – 'Milanese' rather than 'Neapolitan' – to the PSI alone. They spread through all the governing parties, each of which anyway needed more funds than ever in the past, because of the greater costs of media-driven (rather than mass-based) electoral campaigns in the eighties. So much money was now circulating at the higher levels of the state, that personal – as distinct from party – enrichment became increasingly normal, as part of the bargain. The cost, of course, was an immense swelling of unproductive expenses at all levels of the system. The traditional parasitism of the Italian state acquired monstrous proportions. Through the years of the Craxi boom, the public debt grew remorselessly. By 1992 it had reached 109 per cent of GDP, and comprised a third of the total government debt owed within the whole European Community.

Just at this moment, the Treaty for European Economic and Monetary Union was signed at Maastricht. Under its terms, Italy was obliged to cut its public deficit to no more than 3 per cent, and its public debt to no more than 30 per cent, of GDP. Implementation of this programme – the conditions of convergence to a single currency – requires a veritable revolution in Italian public finance, and a massive purge of the clientelistic state. Senior bankers, technocrats, and businessmen who had long chafed under the *partitocrazia* now had an imperative pressure from the European Community to hand: Italy could not continue unreformed. In itself, this change of external situation would not have been enough to force any immediate internal adjustment. The elite conscious of the need for a drastic overhaul of the system still lacked political striking-force. Suddenly and providentially, however, this materialized in a popular revolt against the system from below.

The Lega Nord, initially the Lombard League, sprang up under the leadership of Umberto Bossi – a demagogue of unorthodox gifts – in the late eighties, as a protest against the corruption and maladministration of the central state.[18] Its message was both regionalist and anti-collectivist: the North of Italy was being leeched by taxes imposed by Roman politicians to feed a tentacular bureaucracy and patronize theft and crime in the South. Freed from this incubus, the North would prosper as one of the richest, low-tax, free-enterprise zones of Europe. The whole governing class should be swept away, and the state cut down and broken up into a federation of autonomous regions, if necessary with the right to secession. The economic programme of the Lega is neo-liberal: tax reduction, privatization and less welfare. Its regionalism has a racist edge that brings it much closer to Le Pen's National Front than to the gentler devolutionism of Welsh or Catalan nationalism.[19] Perhaps the closest parallel might be with organizations like the Flemish Blok, since its ethnic animus is directed as much against other members of what are conventionally regarded as the same nationality – Sicilians or Calabrians, as against millions of Africans and Arabs who have entered the country, for the most part illegally, in the past decade. Bossi's uncompromising hostility to all the established parties, expressed in a raucously demotic language that deliberately broke with the decorum of official discourse – a vocabulary of virtually impenetrable circumlocutions – soon attracted a large following. Taking root in areas which had previously been DC strongholds with a strong white subculture, like Brescia or Vicenza, the Lega spread swiftly across Lombardy and the Veneto, becoming a major force in big and small cities alike. Its arrival changed the political atmosphere in them completely.

The final decisive change was, of course, the passing of the PCI itself. Anti-communism had always been the mortar holding the bricks of Italy's political order together. The extraordinary stability of the postwar regime depended, from 1948 onwards, on the spectre of a mass Communist party outside it, unifying the propertied classes and their electorates into a protective bloc. The PCI itself, of course, had long ceased to be a revolutionary opposition. But no matter how moderate its domestic policies or how much distance it took from the USSR, it was not trusted as a reliable shareholder in Western capitalism, so long as its leadership continued to evoke the ancestry of Gramsci and Togliatti, and its rank and file to remain attached to the idea of an alternative social order. The birth of the PDS, formally burying the Communist tradition, followed by the collapse of the Soviet Union itself, laid most traditional fears to rest. The weak performance of the successor party at the polls was further reassurance. But once the cement of anti-communism was gone, the edifice of power was sooner or later bound to come apart.

On the surface, however, normalcy still reigned in early 1992. After the elections, the Christian Democrats, Socialists, Social Democrats and Liberals put together a *quadripartito*, with a rather narrower majority than they would have liked, under the premiership of Craxi's lieutenant Giuliano Amato. But almost immediately, the political class found itself engulfed in a legitimation crisis. Investigations in Milan had some months earlier revealed the involvement of local PSI politicians in various forms of petty extortion. Now the Milanese scandals grew more and more serious, with revelations of corruption leading to the national headquarters of the PSI itself, as magistrates showed a new willingness to confront politicians with evidence of their wrongdoing. For the best part of a year Craxi attempted to ride out the arrests of his close associates and relatives, implying that their misdeeds were no concern of his, and that he was victim of a conspiracy to blacken his reputation. But in February 1993 he finally accepted defeat, resigned the PSI leadership and dug in for a long battle with the criminal justice system. In the initial period of *Tangentopoli* (Bribesville), it was the Socialists who were the principal objects of popular revulsion, playing the lead role in the nightly television drama in which magistrates led politicians away in handcuffs. If Christian Democrat deputies and cadres also fell into the pit, with an increasing number of offenders trying to save themselves by incriminating their associates, it was figures like Craxi, Martelli and De Michelis who seemed the symbols of venality, and *Tangentopoli* a day of reckoning for the *rampanti* of the 1980s boom, rather than the veterans of clerical power. Then in March 1993 Giulio Andreotti, seven times prime minister and the dominant Italian politician of the last quarter of a century, received an official warning that he was being investigated by magistrates in Palermo for long-term involvement with the Mafia. Soon all the national and local notables of the Neapolitan DC, including former interior minister Gava, were implicated in an investigation into the Camorra; while the supposed reformer of the DC, former premier Ciriaco De Mita, neo-liberal hammer of the populist old guard, saw his brother arrested on charges of massive profiteering from earthquake relief funds. Liberal, Republican and Social Democrat leaders followed them into disgrace. By the summer, magistrates had filed requests for the lifting of parliamentary immunity of 305 deputies and senators out of 945. At the same time, investigators were scything through the worlds of business and bureaucracy, jailing the heads of ENI and IRI, and forcing Raul Gardini – one-time boss of the Ferruzzi empire – to suicide.

Astonishing as this spectacle has been, it should not be inflated into an 'Italian Revolution' – the favourite term of a press that has presented a series of *images d'Epinal*, in which valiant magistrates uphold the rule of law without fear or favour against criminals in high places, making a clean sweep of an infamous ruling system.[20] Without the battering-ram of the Lega, and the end of Communism, the Northern enquiries would probably have run into the sand. Italian magistrates are not the impartial arms of justice of Anglo-Saxon imagination, but a highly politicized corps of officials, often with extra-judicial ambitions, in close contact with corridor and news-room. They are also equipped with arbitrary powers of arrest and intimidation that would be unthinkable in other EC countries – many of them deriving from the Reale law. The pattern of investigations, as could be expected, proved to be selective, reflecting lowly interests as much as lofty ideals, In Milan, the folk-hero of the *Mani puliti* pool of prosecutors, the flamboyant Antonio di Pietro, has cast a paternal mantle round the figure of Carlo de Benedetti, the Olivetti tycoon, when pursued on the gravest charges by the Roman prosecutors – but who happens to be proprietor of the publishing empire, centred on *Espresso* and *Repubblica*, that has most frenetically applauded his role. On the other hand, the Roman prosecutors, confronted with corroborating testimonies of malversation against four DC ministers of the interior from their own officials in the secret service, opened investigations into two who were political dead ducks, declared the third – the present incumbent, member of a 'reforming' government – without further ado innocent, and not only refused to pursue enquiries into the fourth, but charged the witnesses with 'subversion' for giving evidence against him, 'independently of whether what they say is true or not'. The reason? The accused is none other than the President of the Republic, Oscar Luigi Scalfaro, newly elected in 1993 as a cynosure of moral integrity. In a scene straight out of *Illustrious Corpses*, the PDS – having apparently learnt nothing from its support of Cossiga – vociferously approved this new example of the rule of law, together with mainstream press and television. *Tangentopoli* has in these ways been closer to a *règlement des comptes* within the old order, in which the axis around Craxi, Andreotti and Forlani – the execrated CAF – has been destroyed, while other ornaments – Amato, Scalfaro, Spadolini – have been spared; not in itself the arrival of a new one.

The decisive thrust towards a Second Republic came from another direction. Since 1990 Mario Segni, the son of the Christian Democrat President of the Republic in the sixties, and himself a long-serving DC deputy, had been campaigning for a referendum to abolish pro-portional representation in Italy, in favour of first-past-the-post elections along Anglo-American lines. This, Segni argued, would give Italy political accountability and ideological stability: the British and American voting rules were preferable to any other, since they produced the most continuous and conservative two-party system. Technically, Segni's proposal did not fall within the scope of questions decidable by referendum, and the Constitutional Court had originally refused to authorize one. But with growing media clamour for root-and-branch electoral reform, the judges – no less sensitive to timely influence than magistrates – reversed themselves in early 1993. By now all the governing parties had rallied to Segni's proposal, amidst an orchestrated campaign from virtually the whole of the country's *bien-pensant* intelligentsia, aflame to 'normalize' Italian democracy to Westminster–Washington standards. The PDS, jettisoning past prin-ciples, promptly followed suit. Traditionally it had always defended proportional representation on democratic grounds, and even on pragmatic ones had reason to be concerned at the prospect of first-past-the-post in Italy. Yet, although avowing its own preference to be a two-ballot majority system along French lines, it nevertheless campaigned energetically for the official agenda in the referendum. With only Rifondazione, the Greens and Rete on the left and the MSI on the far right opposed, Segni's proposal duly won a plebiscitary victory.

Once the referendum had been engineered, the Amato government resigned. European concern at the Italian situation was mounting. Political instability was having adverse effects on the lira, as Italy's partners despaired of getting the strong government committed to welfare cuts and privatizations that officials at both the Bundesbank and the Banca d'Italia saw as the only solution to Italy's chronic budget deficit. The US, for its part, no longer had an interest in bailing the DC out, now that the Cold War was over. Amato had striven to meet German wishes with an austerity package in the autumn, but his cabinet – it had included four prominent ministers caught up in the web of investigations – looked an anachronism. Tougher measures and cleaner gloves were called for. In keeping with the logic of the situation, the governor of the Bank of Italy, Carlo Azeglio Ciampi, became the new premier, charged with superintending the transition to a Second Republic. To this end, it had two tasks: to pass an electoral law in accordance with the outcome of the referendum, and a budget to reduce the deficit.

Once passed through the complex grid of interests in parliament, the principle of electoral reform did not yield the exact results that either Segni or the PDS wanted. For under the law passed, while 75 per cent of the members of both chambers would be elected by a first-past-the-post system in single-member constituencies, the remaining 25 per cent would continue to be elected by proportional representation of party lists, adjusted by deduction of the winner's margins in the single-member seats (an ingenious twist devised by Lucio Magri of Rifondazione) with a relatively low threshold of 4 per cent for a party to enter parliament. The effects of this hybrid appeared difficult for any party to calculate. The logic of the new system was, however, temporarily eclipsed by the municipal polls of 1993, held under different rules. By an earlier reform, the mayors of all towns of over 15,000 inhabitants were to be elected French-style, by direct choice in two ballots. In May–June, the most striking results came in Turin and Milan. In the two most industrialized cities of Italy, Rifondazione overtook the PDS on the first ballot to become the largest party of the left. On the second ballot, the PDS in Turin allied with Segni and FIAT to defeat the respected former PCI mayor of the city, Diego Novelli, running for the Rete with Rifondazione support; in the Milan run-off, on the other hand, the PDS rallied to the Rete candidate, son of General Della Chiesa, who was defeated by the Lega. Throughout the North, Bossi's party demonstrated growing strength at the expense of the *pentapartito*.

If these results gave grounds for alarm to the business establishment, the November–December polls in Rome, Naples, Palermo, Genoa, Venice and Trieste were explosive. Christian Democracy, after forty-five years of unbroken dominance of the Italian political scene, collapsed. No candidate officially supported by the DC even secured a place in the run-off. In the North, the Lega nearly doubled its share of the vote, emerging as the largest single party. In the South, the MSI more than doubled its share, winning the most votes of any party on a national scale. But since neither the Lega nor the MSI were able to secure support from any other parties for the second round, their candidates were defeated in all major cities in the run-off. In every case, the final victor was the candidate backed by the PDS. This stunning reversal of its fortunes was not due to its own strength as a party, which remained scarcely greater than in the national elections which had gone so badly for it in the previous year, but to its ability to form coalitions behind symbolic candidates of the left or centre, according to the local balance of forces – allying with Rifondazione in Palermo, Naples and Venice, and with Segni in Rome, Genoa and Trieste. The logic of the electoral upshot was clear. If no successor force to the DC emerged, Italy would be divided into two blocs – a centre-left coordinated by the PDS, and a right irreparably split, territorially and politically, between the Lega and the MSI. Under these conditions, the new electoral law at national level, giving 75 per cent of seats to victors in first-past-the-post contests, looked likely to lever the PDS to an outright parliamentary majority in the general elections set for spring 1994, since it would everywhere have greater ability to aggregate allies than its two opponents.

It rapidly became clear that out of the debris of Christian Democracy no effective barrier to this prospect could be reconstructed. Segni, the one former Catholic leader of national prestige, squandered his position with extraordinary ineptitude virtually overnight, proving completely unable either to build a significant movement of his own, or make a decisive alliance. The DC, thoroughly demoralized, scuttled itself into a shrunken Partito Popolare Italiano, in a forlorn hope of recapturing memories of Don Sturzo. Neither group was willing to strike a deal to its right or left, while relations between them were poor. Consequently, intense fear of a left victory mounted within all the conservative forces of Italian society. It was in this situation that, galvanized by the danger of a reverse 1948, Italy's leading entertainments magnate came forward to fill the political vacuum on the right. Silvio Berlusconi, proprietor of three television channels, newspapers, magazines, publishing houses, supermarkets, real estate, advertising agencies, and the country's most popular football team, announced the creation of a new political organization, Forza Italia, managed by executives from his financial empire, and modelled on his network of fan clubs. Berlusconi's media power all but guaranteed him a significant initial rating in the opinion polls. From this base, he moved with great speed and dexterity to construct a united front of the right, capable of winning the elections. The great – hitherto insuperable – difficulty here lay in the mutual incompatibility of the Lega and the MSI, which loathed each other for their opposite attitudes to the central state and national unity. Unencumbered by any traditional constraints, Berlusconi cut separate deals with each, conceding three-quarters of Northern seats to Lega candidates, while going into regional partnership with Alleanza Nazionale – the decorously re-named MSI – in the South. Tactically, this meant sacrificing his own potential advantage to two parties likely to have fewer votes than he. But strategically, it left him in political command of the 'Pole of Liberty', as the only mediation between them. The arrangement allowed the Lega and the AN to converge without touching each other, as each fought in alliance with Forza Italia in its own region.

Once the campaign itself got under way, Berlusconi rapidly out-manoeuvred the 'Pole of Progress' arrayed around the PDS. In the ideological contest between the two blocs, he scored decisively with two fundamental claims. Politically, Berlusconi presented his cartel as a radically new force, composed of three parties untainted by the venality and collusion of the *partitocrazia* of the First Republic. The Lega and AN were, indeed, genuine outsiders in the old order. If Berlusconi himself had belonged to Licio Gelli's P2 and owed much of his fortune to his friendship with Craxi, Forza Italia – he retorted – was indisputably a fresh organization, recruiting novel talents and energies to the political scene, and should be judged as such. By contrast, the PDS was merely a recycled version of one of the central pillars of the disgraced regime – a Communist Party permanently lodged in its regional outworks and informally integrated in its national institutions. Occhetto proved quite unable to counter this argument. Since he had become leader of the PDS, the party had fallen ever more under the sway of fashionable intellectuals outside it, many of them once close to Craxi, calling for a virtually complete repudiation of both the legacy of the labour movement, and the specificities of postwar Italian democ-racy. With extensive press support from the de Benedetti empire, it was they who provided Segni with the most vehement ideologies of the drive to Anglo-Americanize the electoral system in the referendum of 1993, which they had fought together with him under the banner of an Alleanza Democratica. Their outlook is perhaps best expressed by their chosen term of abuse for the whole political class of the First Republic, significantly – if grotesquely – termed the *nomenklatura*: in other words, metaphorically identifying the old order, including such hated aspects of it as a plural party system and equitable represen-tation, with Communism.

The FDS, in putting together its 'Pole of Progress', could not exclude Rifondazione – whose likely vote was too substantial to risk losing in first-past-the-post contests with the right. The Rete and Greens were other necessary allies on the left. But the favoured partners of the PDS were the coterie of Alleanza Democratica, generals without troops who were awarded a bumper share of safe seats in Red regions, where the PDS could be sure of electing them. From their niches in the media, the AD intellectuals continued to direct their principal fire against Rifondazione, with side-complaints against the PDS for still not having broken sufficiently with its past. In these conditions, Occhetto was in no position to rebut Berlusconi's charges effectively, since his closest interlocutors were echoing them. In the stampede to disavow the postwar Republic in the name of the absolutely 'new' and 'modern', the PDS was bound to be outbid by Forza Italia, and end up looking like a shame-faced pensioner of the old system.

Worse was to come on the economic battle-ground of the contest. Following the same logic of subordination to a current conformism, the PDS strove to present itself as the firmest champion of financial orthodoxy, committed above all to cutting public spending and reducing the budget deficit, no matter what the difficulty in a time of crisis. Occhetto flew to the City of London to prove his reliability to international investors, and lost no occasion to stress the virtues of austerity. So far did this posture go that – once again, at the instigation of AD – the PDS started openly to toy with the prospect of keeping Ciampi in office if the left were to win the elections, as prime minister of the 'Pole of Progress'. A more disastrous choice could hardly be imagined. Ciampi, the greyest of conservative bankers, had just forced through an austerity budget without the slightest sense of popular needs: if any single figure represented both economic constraint and bureaucratic continuity, it was this former governor of the Bank of Italy. To adopt him as the symbol of PDS respectability was suicidal. The way was left wide open for Berlusconi to promise an active programme to combat unemployment, reduction and simplification of taxes to stimulate investment, and a rapid economic climb out of the recession. The tone and direction of his appeal was carefully modelled on that of Reagan, rather than Thatcher – prescribing not harsh medicine, but buoyant emulsion, in the upbeat mood of Reagan's televised slogan ten years earlier: 'Good morning, America'. No less demagogic than his claims of political freshness, Berlusconi's promises of economic bounty were still more effective. The timid conformism of the PDS was left cruelly exposed.

The result of these two key ideological defeats was electoral disaster. When Italians went to the polls in March 1994, Berlusconi's coalition swept to a large absolute majority in the Chamber of Deputies, winning 366 seats out of 630, and just short of one in the Senate, with 155 out of 315. This massive victory did not reflect the actual distribution of political opinion in the country. It was the fruit of the electoral engineering to which the PDS had consented. Now it was hoist with its own petard. Berlusconi's coalition had gained 42.9 per cent of the total vote, Panella, supporting him, 3.5 per cent, making a total of 46.4 per cent for the right. The left bloc received 34.4 per cent, and the centre – composed of the PPI and Segni – 15.7 per cent, together a total of 50.1 per cent. Had proportionality still operated, there would have been a centre-left majority capable of forming a government. Beyond this significant fact, however, lay a stunning transformation of the political map of the country. Forza Italia captured half the votes of the right with 21 per cent of the electorate, against 13.4 per cent for AN and 8.3 per cent for the Lega – although here too the distribution of parliamentary strength differed markedly, each party receiving a roughly equal share of the Chamber (106 deputies for Bossi, 155 Berlusconi, and 105 Fini).

The 'Pole of Liberty' won its victory after the pattern of the paradoxical union had given birth to it – triumphing simultaneously in the two regional extremes of the country, the industrial North and the abandoned South. In a landslide, it swept 73 out of 74 first-past-the-post constituencies in Lombardy, 36 out of 37 in Veneto, and 31 out of 36 in Piedmont, crushing the left in the centres of Milan and Turin, where even traditionally 'red' working-class districts fell to the right. Here, in the most advanced industrial centres of Italy, Berlusconi's claims to electoral modernity – in tandem with Bossi – received popular certification. Simultaneously, on the other hand, Forza Italia achieved its highest single vote in Sicily, where it piled up a third of the electorate, recruited overwhelmingly from the mafia-ridden clientele of the former DC; while on the Southern mainland the refurbished MSI topped the polls in Lazio, Campania, Apulia, Abruzzo and Molise. Here, the archaic terrain left by the disintegration of the DC was occupied with equal alacrity by the axis of Berlusconi and Fini. Only the traditional regions of PCI strength in Central Italy – Emilia-Romagna, Umbria and Tuscany – resisted the pincers of the right. Sociologically, the most striking single feature of the election was the capture of the youngest sector of the electorate by the 'Pole of Liberty'. Male youth between the ages of 18 and 24 voted 55 per cent for the right, compared with the national average of 43 per cent; only 25 per cent for the left, compared with a national average of 34 per cent. Berlusconi's promises to tackle the unemployment rampant in this generation were not in vain. Two other categories that went disproportionately for the right were housewives, notoriously addicted to the pabulum of Berlusconi's TV stations, and the self-employed, attracted by the prospect of tax-reduction. Here the parallels with Reaganism were very close.

The 'normalization' of Italian democracy that, in the dreams of Alleanza Democratica and PDS advisers, was supposed to arrive with a Second Republic has proved a *journée des dupes*. Italy under Berlusconi today, with its post-fascist ministers and personal union of economic power and political office, looks farther than ever from the wished-for capitalist norm – only now its deviation from the standard is unambiguously to the right, where it once always held a promise, at least, of being to the left. Once again, but this time more starkly than ever before, the heirs of Italian Communism have been the object rather than subject of a fundamental change in the country. Between 1945 and 1964, the PCI commanded the loyalty of all the most rebellious forces in Italian society, and guided their initiatives. After 1968, this ceased to be the case. Henceforward every major social or political upsurge occurred independently of the PCI or its successor, time and again taking it by surprise. The student revolt of '68, the hot autumn of '69, the divorce referendum of '74, the *autonomia* of '77, the battle of the *scala mobile* in '85, the nuclear referendum in '87, the break-up of the *pentapartito* in '92, the electoral reform of '93 – each was the initiative of other agents: spontaneists, workerists, Socialists, DP, Greens, Lega, Segni. The destruction of the First Republic was not its doing, and the construction of the Second Republic may bring its final undoing. For the moment its future, and that of the Italian left as a whole, looks bleak. Beyond the will of the parties concerned, however, the fate of progressive politics in Italy will be decided by the persistence – or passing – of the radical pressures from below of which the First Republic had such an unexampled record since the War.

Notes

1. For a detailed study of the social and political history of this period, see the judicious account – especially strong on the centre-left – of Paul Ginsborg, *A History of Contemporary Italy*. London 1990.
2. Sidney Tarrow, *Democracy and Disorder: Protest and Politics in Italy 1965–1975*, New York 1989, and Robert Lumley, *States of Emergency: Cultures of Revolt in Italy from 1968 to 1978*, London 1990, both contain fascinating empirical material about the student movement and the workers' revolt of the time. Neither Tarrow's cyclical theories, based on complex statistical analyses, nor Lumley's postmodern and post-Marxist cultural framework offers an entirely satisfactory explanation for the phenomena they describe so vividly.
3. Joanne Barkan, *Visions of Emancipation: The Italian Workers' Movement since 1945*, New York 1984, provides much valuable information about the social history of the

FIAT plants. Barkan is an American journalist, broadly sympathetic to the new left, from a position more firmly committed to feminism than to Marxism, but her book is very uneven as a work of history in the strict sense.

4. Giovanni Contini, 'Southern Immigration and Class Conflict in Turin', paper given at the annual conference of the Association for the Study of Modern Italy, London, December 1984.

5. See Giovanni Contini, 'Politics, Law and Shopfloor Bargaining in Post-War Italy', in Steven Tolliday and Jonathan Zeitlin, eds, *Shopfloor Bargaining and the State*, Cambridge 1985, p. 208.

6. The best account of the origins and evolution of the Manifesto group is the interview given by Luciana Castellina, '*Il Manifesto* and Italian Communism', *New Left Review* 151, March–April 1985.

7. According to figures originating with the ministry of the interior, cited in *Keesing's Contemporary Archives*, London 1984, p. 32755, some 432 black terrorists were imprisoned between 1969 and March 1982, compared with 1,414 red terrorists. The statistics give no indication of the length of time spent in prison by black terrorists, whether it was before or after trial, and whether those concerned were eventually acquitted or allowed to escape.

8. Amongst the 963 names on Gelli's list were thirty generals, eight admirals, the heads of two counter-intelligence services, the civilian coordinator of intelligence, the police chiefs of Cagliari, Salerno, Palermo and Treviso, the prefects of Brescia and Parma, the editor of the *Corriere della Sera*, and forty-three deputies: Paul Wilkinson, *The New Fascists*, London 1981, pp. 138–9. Wilkinson suggests that P–2 may have been involved in Piazza Fontana and chronicles MSI links with black terrorists.

9. See Rupert Cornwall, *God's Banker: The Life and Times of Roberto Calvi*, London 1984.

10. Judith Chubb and Percy Allum have written two major empirical studies, respectively of Palermo and Naples, dealing with the South in the postwar period. Both authors, by the very nature of their material, have reached broadly left-wing and markedly anti-Christian Democratic conclusions. See Judith Chubb, *Patronage, Power and Poverty in Southern Italy*, Cambridge 1982; Percy Allum, *Politics and Society in Post-War Naples*, Cambridge 1973.

11. Judith Adler Hellman, *Journeys among Women: Feminism in Five Italian Cities*, Oxford 1987, is the only full-length book in English on the Italian women's movement of the 1970s and 1980s. Lesley Caldwell, *Italian Family Matters: Women, Politics and Legal Reform*, Basingstoke 1991, discusses the issues of divorce and abortion in greater depth. Joanne Barkan, *Visions of Emancipation*, represents the most serious attempt to integrate class and gender issues within a single text.

12. The original analysis to develop this interpretation was that of Paolo Flores d'Arcais and Franco Moretti, 'Paradoxes of the Italian Crisis', *New Left Review* 96, March–April 1976, written between the two elections. The Canadian scholar Grant Amyot has subsequently employed Gramsci's terminology for this period: *The Italian Communist Party: The Crisis of the Popular Front Strategy*, London 1981, p. 207. Amyot wrote from a perspective sympathetic to Ingrao's left within the PCI, and incorporated a number of local case studies. His book is less misleading than other current general accounts of the PCI, but it remains somewhat too internalist as a history of the party.

13. For the Red Brigades, see Paul Furlong, 'Political Terrorism in Italy: Responses, Reactions and Immobilism', in Juliet Lodge, ed., *Terrorism: A Challenge to the State*, Oxford 1981. Amongst the growing literature in Italian, the two most important acconts are probably Giorgio Galli, *Storia del partito armato 1968–1982*, Milan 1986, and Giorgio Bocca, *Noi terroristi: 12 anni di lotta armata ricostruiti e discussi con i protagonisti*, Milan 1985.

14. See Saverio Asprea, *Craxi Addio*, Livorno 1984, which also furnishes some impressionistic data on PSI membership for 1979–80, pp. 97–8. Asprea was a member of the Lega dei Socialisti who left the party, and his account is a journalistic chronicle of their break with Craxi. In 1993 Asprea reissued his book with an introduction pointing out how time had vindicated his view of Craxi; very few British or American academics

who wrote about the PSI in the 1980s would be able to republish their texts in unamended form without acute embarrassment.

15. Figures taken from Ritanna Armeni and Vichi de Marchi, eds, *'Chiamateci compagni': Cronache della Rifondazione comunista*, Rome 1991, which also contains revealing comments from many ordinary militants during the first three months of Rifondazione's existence. Sergio Garavini, *Le ragioni di un comunista: Scritti e riflessioni sullo scioglimento del PCI e sulla nascita di una nuova forza comunista in Italia*, Rome 1991, provides an intellectually coherent explanation of the political differences that gave rise to the split. The persistence of a mass communist formation in Italy has so far failed to arouse the curiosity of political and social scientists whose attention has remained firmly focused on the PDS.

16. Luigi Cortesi, *Le ragioni del comunismo: Scritti e interventi per la Rifondazione*, Milan 1991, gives some indication of the attraction of the new organization for an intellectual who had broken with the PCI many years before and never joined DP.

17. Two useful accounts of the current crisis, if somewhat overtaken by events, are Percy Allum, *Chronicle of a Death Foretold: The First Italian Republic*, University of Reading, Department of Politics, Occasional Paper no. 12, January 1993, and Stephen Hellman, 'The Left and the Decomposition of the Party System in Italy', *The Socialist Register 1993*, London 1993, pp. 190–210.

18. Ivo Diamanti, *La Lega: Geografia, storia e sociologia di un nuovo soggetto politico*, Rome 1993, is the best academic study of the movement. Percy Allum and Ivo Diamanti, 'The Autonomous Leagues in Venetia', in Carl Levy, ed., *Regionalism in Italy: Past, Present and Future*, Oxford (forthcoming 1994), is a good introduction to some of the issues raised by Diamanti in his more general text. Whilst Diamanti has made the link between the Lega and a specific model of industrial development characteristic of the Third Italy clearer than most commentators, the most detailed work on this question is that of Anna Cento Bull, 'The Politics of Industrial Districts in Lombardy: Replacing Christian Democracy with the Northern League', *The Italianist*, no. 13, 1993. She demonstrates the very strong correlation between the areas of concentrated industrialization within Lombardy and those which gave the highest vote to the Lega in the 1992 general election – explaining this pattern partly in terms of the Lega's economic neo-liberalism, attractive to small businessmen, and partly in terms of the racist potential in the political subculture of these districts. The volume edited by Renato Mannheimer, *Lega Lombarda*, Milan 1991, also contains much valuable material.

19. The League's racism has been minimized or denied by its American and Scottish apologists: see Edward Luttwak, 'Italy's *Ancien Regime*', *London Review of Books*, 19 August 1993, and Joseph Farrell, 'The Lombard/Northern League: Conservative Revolution?', in Levy, ed., *Regionalism in Italy*. But Anna Cento Bull, 'Ethnicity, Racism and the Northern League', in the same volume, supplies convincing evidence of it, drawn from the party's electoral manifesto of 1992 and surveys of its voters. For racist sentiments from the League's chief theorist, Gianfranco Miglio, see his interview in *The Guardian*, 1 December 1993.

20. The title of Stephen Gundle and Simon Parker, eds, *The Italian Democratic Revolution 1989–1993*, forthcoming 1994, indicates how far the misleading notion of an Italian revolution has spread among relatively well-informed commentators.

Spain: The Survival of Socialism?

Patrick Camiller

In the past decade Spanish Socialism has enjoyed a record of electoral success without parallel among parties of the left in Western Europe. Four times victorious at the polls, it has now held office without interruption for twelve years. If, at the outset of the eighties, the rise of neo-socialist parties was a general phenomenon throughout Latin Europe, today the PS is a shrunken remnant in the National Assembly in France; the PSI has disappeared in the maelstrom of Italy's corruption scandals; the PSP has long been relegated to opposition in Portugal. The PSOE alone has established an enduring political dominance. Its achievement poses two central questions. What explains the pre-eminence of Hispanic socialism, against the background of the legacy of Franco's dictatorship; and what has been the actual record of the Socialist Party in office?

Expectations that Franco's passing would introduce a radical overturn of the social and political order over which he had presided were widespread on the Spanish left in the early seventies. Yet neither the *ruptura democrática* advocated by the major organizations of the Spanish opposition, still less the revolutionary situation predicted on the further flanks of the Socialist and Communist movements, was to be realized after the death of the dictator. The 'transition' to a new Spain, so nervously discussed and anticipated, was smoothly conducted and controlled from above. Since the contemporary character and fortunes of the PSOE have their origins in this period, it is important to ask what made it possible for Adolfo Suárez, a career functionary in Franco's National Movement, to achieve such a decorous end to forty years of military-police repression.

The key to Suárez's accomplishments is to be found in the record of Franco's long regime itself, which proved to be far more astute and successful than other European dictatorships of the twentieth century in preserving the conditions of its survival while transforming the bases of its rule. Born out of the emergency of a Popular Front government, Franco's historic mission was to crush the violent working-class and peasant turbulence that posed a clear danger to the very existence of the Spanish bourgeois and landowning classes. Above and beyond every regional, social and ideological division, the defence of private property was the driving force which unified the Nationalist crusade. This purpose was common to Portuguese and Italian fascism as well. What came to distinguish the Spanish variant, as it was slowly modulated by the Caudillo, were two things. Firstly, although German pressure secured rudimentary Spanish participation in the Axis war effort, Franco thereafter kept rigorously out of foreign or colonial adventures, of the kind that brought down not only his original sponsors of 1936 but also the Greek junta and, less directly, the Portuguese dictatorship. The quiet cession of Spanish Morocco in 1956 and Ifni in 1969 was emblematic in this respect. Secondly, and more fundamentally, whereas Salazar's rule was notable for a marked, virtually deliberate slowness of growth – consecrated by a social and financial ideology that valued stability of mores, and of money, above all other considerations – the *franquista* regime actively presided over the most sustained and explosive expansion of any Atlantic capitalist economy from the late fifties onwards. Tourism, emigrant remittances and cheap labour were the motor of a surge of accumulation which broke every European record and utterly changed the structures of the society that had once thrown up the revolutionary challenges of the Second Republic.[1] Between 1962 and 1975, GNP grew at an average rate of 7 per cent a year, as industrialization swept away most of the old rural order. A nation that was still over 40 per cent peasant in 1959 saw the workforce on the land drop to less than 20 per cent two decades later. Per capita income increased ten times over in the same period, shooting up from $300 to $3000 a year.[2] However unevenly distributed – and distribution of income was grossly skewed – the benefits of this headlong advance towards north European patterns of occupation and consumption could not but produce a political configuration quite different from that of the April Revolution in Portugal as the days of the regime neared their end. Popular anger and impatience at the oppressive police machinery, the lack of elementary rights of suffrage or association, naturally continued to be wide and deep. But vast numbers of Spaniards had gained from the material transformations wrought by the long capitalist boom, so that rejection of the political order no longer necessarily spilled over into radical questioning of the socio-economic order. For the leading echelons of big business, as for the bulk of the new middle classes which had multiplied during the years of growth, Spain appeared safer for capitalism than it had ever done before. The political scaffolding that had both concealed and allowed the construction of a stabler social edifice was an anachronism that could now be dismantled.

Yet few within the ranks of the possessors could be absolutely confident of the immediate future when Franco expired in 1975. The industrial working class of the seventies was much better off than its predecessor of the thirties. But it was also twice as numerous, now comprising some 37 per cent of the active population, and far from docile. Industrial unrest had been steadily mounting, spurred by the combination of tight labour markets and absence of political rights. Some 1.5 million working hours were lost in strikes in 1966. By 1970 the figure had reached 8.7 million, and by 1975 14.5 million. Then, in the first year after Franco's death, Spanish labour rose to the highest level of militancy in the continent: in 1976, 150 million working hours were lost in disputes, the great majority of them politically inspired. If such was the situation in the factories, the position of the exile parties offered little direct reassurance either. Both the PSOE and PCE – the traditional spectre of the Spanish right – were committed to rupture with the whole institutional legacy of Francoism, the former even seeming to menace sweeping programmes of socialization. There thus appeared to exist no predictable or reliable channels for containing the potential aspirations and energies of the masses, once police controls were lifted. Moreover in one region, Euzkadi, the armed resistance of the nationalist ETA had set a disturbing example for the rest of the country and spectacularly intervened in central political affairs with the assassination of Franco's chosen successor, Admiral Carrero Blanco, in 1973.

Nevertheless, amidst these uncertainties, the front-line sections of Spanish capital were in no doubt that a Euromodernization of the country's political structures was not only a desirable but an inevitable consequence of the social changes that had taken place since the Civil War. Well before the turmoil of 1976, the industrial workforce had become increasingly unionized in the Workers' Commissions and the UGT, which were now central to shopfloor wage-bargaining and indeed often courted by employers anxious to secure productivity agreements. For the banks and big business, the only alternative to a subordinate integration of labour into national politics would have been a Pinochet-style decapitation of the workers' movement for another generation – a course that Spain's insertion into the European economy, including the vital tourist trade, rendered virtually unthinkable. Their objective, symbolized by the drive for EC membership, was to anchor Spanish capitalism in a parliamentary system of the West European type, in such a way that the flow-tide of working-class radicalism would not leave any permanent mark on the new political settlement.

The Dismantling of Dictatorship

It was this task that Suárez, appointed premier by King Juan Carlos in the summer of 1976, carried out with great ability in the next three years. Suárez had first to win over the mainstream official right to political reform and then in a second stage to impose its agenda on the mass workers' parties. He was aided in this process by the hybrid character of the *franquista* regime itself, of which he had been a familiar. The Nationalist forces which won the Civil War always remained far more heteroclite in outlook and origin than the fascist fronts in Germany, Italy and Portugal. As monarchists, Carlists, Falangists, Catholics and career officers jostled for position, acquiring relative dominance at various junctures in the forties and fifties, no thoroughgoing organizational or political unification ever occurred below the person of the Caudillo himself. By the time of the postwar boom, this mixed establishment allowed the entry of quite new elements into the regime – above all, the Opus Dei technocrats who managed Spain's economic liberalization in the sixties. The result was a growth of informal or semi-formal opposition groups within the Spanish bourgeoisie, whose personnel was not separated by hard-and-fast lines of division from that of the regime itself – leading members often taking up posts in the state apparatus, while former state functionaries could cross over to these outlying *frondes*. The regime was thus surrounded by an indeterminate 'buffer zone' extending into more or less liberal or enlightened bourgeois circles in civil society.[3] The dictatorship was, in this sense, never an isolated fortress within Spanish society – the very term 'bunker', reserved for its most unyielding sector, tacitly points up the mesh of connections between the rest of the administration and the capitalist 'public sphere' it had helped to bring into being.

Here lay the secret of much of Suárez's initial breakthrough. He was able to construct, quickly and easily, a cabinet containing leading figures from the buffer zone who simultaneously represented guaran-tees of continuity with the past and promises of a normalized future – mainly self-styled Reformists and Christian Democrats. A Law of Political Reform, introducing universal suffrage, was then pushed through a recalcitrant Cortes and ratified by referendum in December 1976. Legalization of non-Communist political parties followed in

February 1977, and the dissolution of the National Movement in April. However, the success of Suárez's project – and the overall credentials of the new order – evidently also required the legalization of the Spanish Communist Party. This step was hard for the army to swallow, but Suárez met less resistance than he had expected and was able to carry it through in April 1977, once the PCE leadership had agreed to abjure the cause of the Republic, and accept Franco's restoration of the Bourbon dynasty. In July the Cortes was dissolved and general elections staged, on the basis of an electoral system bent to over-represent the less urbanized provinces which had been the strongholds of the CEDA right in the Second Republic – Soria, for example, had one deputy per 34,000 voters against Madrid's one per 136,000 – and designed to grant a large premium to the biggest party. Suárez's newly created Union of the Democratic Centre (UCD), with 35 per cent of the vote, took 47 per cent of the seats in the new Assembly. This triumph of political artifice was then completed with the Moncloa Pact of October 1977, which tied down trade-union freedom of action in exchange for pledges of welfare and other reforms, and finally with the adoption of a new constitution in early 1978.

Within a little over a year, Suárez had smoothly piloted the fascist state to a soft landing on the plains of a more or less conventional parliamentary democracy. He had done so while maintaining a nearly perfect continuity of personnel in the upper reaches of the civil service, judiciary and armed forces, except where it had been necessary to find posts for former bureaucrats of the defunct vertical syndicates. The new constitution guaranteed the principle of private property, ac-knowledged the army's role in 'protecting the constitutional order', gave the monarch supreme command of the military, and obliged any government to maintain relations of cooperation with the church. Such was the settlement for which the Spanish left exchanged its republican birthright. In effect, once the reformist course had won the day in the political establishment, the PSOE and PCE leaderships simply fell in with its scope and timing. The Communists, despite their lower electoral support, played a more central role in this process, both because their historical record identified them in popular eyes as the main antagonists of the regime, and because they had a greater capacity for independent action in the shape of their larger and more militant membership, and control of the Workers' Commissions. The acceptance by the two main parties of the left of Suárez's handiwork was justified on the grounds of the overriding need for a liberal-democratic regime in Spain, after the tyranny of the past forty years, and the claim that any attempt to moot the terms set by Franco's heirs would risk military intervention and the cancellation of all prospects of civil liberties. In other words, there was no other responsible or realistic course that the PSOE and PCE could have taken.

Such arguments – not dissimilar from the case made by the PCI for its course in Italy of 1943–47 – lack conviction, as even observers sympathetic to the political settlement have not failed to note.[4] If the Communists and Socialists had refused to go along with it, they would have exerted strong pressure on the right to accept real compromises rather than pious phrases, since it had neither the political will nor the medium-range capacity to settle matters by a show of force. Instead the PCE and PSOE sought a social accord that would trade wage restraint for welfare and civil-service reforms, in the famous Moncloa Pact reached with the UCD in late 1977. Its results were highly favourable to business, vindicating its basic decision to phase out the trappings of Francoism. The number of strikes, which had been the highest in Europe, soon fell towards the West German norm of the time. On the other hand, unemployment started to soar as employers took advantage of trade-union flexibility to circumvent the job-protection legislation introduced in the early years of the dictatorship. The PCE was left to praise the Moncloa accords as a model of enlightened social partnership for the years to come. The PSOE, though no less responsible for them, preferred to adopt a lower profile and wait for the unnatural situation to unravel. Throughout much of 1977 and 1978 Suárez skilfully cultivated an image of discreet understanding between the UCD and the PCE, while Carrillo conjured up visions of an epoch of collaboration between the bourgeois and workers' parties, which would carry Spain to the very threshold of socialism. For its part, the González leadership of the PSOE kept its sights fixed on a German type of political system in which the Socialists and the Centre would loyally alternate in the roles of government and opposition. In the meantime, it could well allow Carrillo his hour in the sun setting the pace for the successive compromises of the left.

Three months after a referendum had approved the new constitution, rounding off the period of transition, Suárez called new elections for March 1979. On the eve of the ballot, he then turned on his loyal Socialist and Communist allies of the previous three years, warning of the menace their Marxist affiliations posed to the democratic order and the sanctity of the family. The period of collaboration with the PSOE and PCE had been very productive in drawing the teeth of working-class radicalism, while isolating the right-wing opponents of political reform. But whatever Suárez's own attitude may have been, the notables of the UCD had never imagined that a pact with the workers' parties could form a stable and dependable basis for their rule. The red-baiting campaign of March 1979 therefore served two purposes: to draw an unambiguous line under the *pactista* experience; and to absorb into the UCD some of the hard-right constituency of Alianza Popular, the party led by Manuel Fraga, once Franco's minister of the interior. These aims were largely achieved, although the elections did not mark a net advance for the right as a whole. The UCD was returned with 48 per cent of the seats in the Assembly, comfortably assuring Suárez another mandate.

On the left, the results confirmed the predominance of the PSOE over the PCE that had been revealed in the elections of 1977 – the Socialists again winning about three times as many votes (30.4 per cent) as the Communists (10.7 per cent). But the nature and direction of the new Spanish Socialism still remained unclear. The PSOE had not played any significant role in the underground struggle against Franco's dictatorship. After the war, while the Communist Party was energetically rebuilding an organizational structure within Spain, the exiled leadership of Rodolfo Llopis, based in Toulouse, grew increasingly remote from – indeed, often morbidly suspicious of – the opposition to the regime emerging inside the country among the working class and intelligentsia. It was not until the late sixties that new forces were drawn into the party. In Seville, a young labour lawyer, Felipe González, and a theatre producer, Alfonso Guerra, both of whom had been abroad, started to work closely together to create a local PSOE milieu. Their partnership, to which Guerra brought formidable organizational skills and González outstanding persuasive gifts, soon made its impact. At the 24th PSOE Congress in Toulouse in 1970, the forces of the 'interior' succeeded in gaining full control over their own structures and committing the emigré apparatus to responsibility for their actions inside the country. Two years later, Llopis had been marginalized and the *renovadores* were in effective charge of the party. At the 26th Party Congress in 1974 – only a year before Franco's death – González was elected the new secretary-general. He was then thirty-two, and the party's total membership stood at no more than four thousand.

Outside Spain, however, lay important allies. The Socialist International in general, and the German SPD in particular, were determined to nurture a modern social-democratic party in Spain that would be capable of challenging the Communists after Franco's death. In 1974 a steady flow of funds came on stream from Bonn, enabling the Socialists to field an impressive network of local offices throughout the country by the time Franco died in November 1975. A year later, the PSOE held its first congress in Spain since the Civil War, and adopted a new programme, which seemed to define it as the most radical Socialist party in Europe – a 'class party with a mass character, Marxist and democratic'. Rejecting 'any path of accommodation to capitalism', the programme envisaged 'the taking of economic and political power, the socialization of the means of production, distribution and exchange by the working class'. Seventeen years after Bad Godesberg, this was scarcely what the SPD would have wished. But the PSOE, now re-legalized, had been recruiting from radical layers similar to those then swelling the ranks of the PCE and the far left; negotiations with Suárez had yet to begin in earnest; and the prospects for González's leadership depended, much as they did for Mitterrand's PS in France, on the dynamics of rivalry with political forces to its left. The lead taken by the PCE, not yet compromised by its later manoeuvring with Suárez, left the *felipistas* with little choice for the moment but to swim with the stream.

The satisfactory results of the first free election since the Civil War gave no cause for regret at this choice. In 1977, with a platform little different from that of the Communists, the Socialists won 29.4 to their rivals' 9.3 per cent. Two years later, however, the PSOE had only increased its vote by 1 per cent – despite having absorbed the small Partido Socialista Popular, led by Enrique Tierno Galvan, which had won 4.5 per cent in the previous elections. The setback of March 1979 set off a sharp polarization within the party. For a month later, when joint PSOE–PCE lists won a majority in the municipal elections in Madrid, Barcelona and Valencia and 27 of the 50 provincial capitals, left Socialists contended that radical traditions of cooperation with the Communists offered the best way forward. The González–Guerra leadership, on the other hand, argued that the PSOE's Marxist image had proved an electoral millstone at the national level. The 28th Congress in May 1979 was the scene of a historic confrontation within the party. When González and his allies proposed the deletion of references to Marxism in the party platform, the assorted forces of the left mounted a vigorous counter-attack and won a convincing majority against the tabled changes. González riposted by resigning as general secretary, throwing his critics – who signally lacked, indeed scarcely aspired to, the coherence of an alternative leadership – onto the defensive. Behind the scenes, moreover, the representatives of the SPD and SI made it clear that their political and financial resources had been invested in Felipe's charisma and would not be readily available otherwise.[5]

In the course of the summer the PSOE apparatus, under Guerra's forceful command, turned the situation around by introducing a new system whereby congress delegations were selected en bloc at regional level rather than by local branches. This allowed the maximum pressure to be concentrated at strategic points – in a few cases of recalcitrance the regional congresses would be suspended for alleged irregularities. When an extraordinary national congress convened again at the end of September, not an echo was heard of the May revolt as the delegates voted by acclamation for González's reappointment. Marxism was conceded a place in the party's repertoire of ideals, but with no greater privilege than 'committed Christian socialism, or socialism springing out of anthropological positions' of an 'ecological, Krausian or humanist' variety.[6] Such openness did not, however, extend to more profane matters. The main work of the congress was to sweep every last *crítico* from the party executive, which thereafter exhibited a degree of monolithism with few parallels in Western Europe.

Crisis on the Right

At the same time, the UCD was beginning to show early signs of the dizzying crisis which would lead to its collapse at the polls in 1982, when it won no more than 7 per cent of the vote and eleven seats in parliament. There were a number of dimensions to this breakdown, some of a circumstantial or even personal nature, but the most important involved structural features of the Spanish political scene which continue to operate to this day.

Founded a month before the June 1977 ballot, the UCD was initially conceived as little more than an electoral alliance between Suárez's *franquista* reformists and a galaxy of fourteen minor parties ranging from Christian, Popular and Social Democrat through 'Social Liberals' to regionally based formations in Murcia, Galicia, the Canaries and Estremadura. Many of these had already functioned as a kind of democratic showcase under the Franco regime, never sinking roots beyond a tiny stratum of local notables. Faced with the prospect of oblivion in the 1977 elections, they opted to throw in their lot with the old layer of state bureaucrats with which they had grown familiar in the sixties and early seventies. On their side, the *franquistas* needed the modern-sounding names of the proto-UCD parties in order to cover their tracks before the electorate. But being also aware that they alone could provide a charismatic leader for the campaign, they were able to divide up the list in such a way that they received a third of the UCD seats in the first parliament of the transition. Immediately thereafter, Suárez embarked upon an ambitious project to turn the UCD into a centralized political party with a unified membership structure – a project which, after serious resistance from some of the constituent sectors, came to fruition in the autumn of 1978.

As it turned out, this drive to force the pace of homogenization was to break the back of the UCD. So long as the debate over the constitution closed its ranks against the Popular Alliance, Suárez was able to exercise firm control and to paper over any cracks that appeared in the facade. But once the constitutional referendum and the March 1979 elections had relieved the pressure from the right, the full force of centrifugal tendencies began to reassert itself. Suárez realized that if the UCD was to establish itself as a hegemonic party in the country, the facts of electoral competition with the PSOE now dictated a shift to the 'left' on such issues as divorce, fiscal reform and modernization of the state apparatus. The very composition of the UCD, however, as well as the conservative dispositions of many of its key supporters, stood in the way of this design. Suárez was not deterred. Both political calculation and personal inclination determined this trained administrator to press ahead.

The first plank was tax reform. Under Franco Spain had one of the most notoriously inequitable and ineffective fiscal systems in Europe. Suárez pushed through the first graduated income tax in the country's history, and somewhat increased other charges on rentier and entrepreneurial wealth. Though far from radical by north European standards, indeed still leaving a constant deficit in public revenues to be covered by emissions from the Bank of Spain, this measure won him the enduring hostility of Spanish employers. The formation of a Spanish equivalent of the CBI – the CEOE – was their response. Business antagonism to Suárez was strengthened by the rather mild dose of inflation of these years, judged by the employers too lenient to wage-earners. Divorce was a second divisive issue. Illegal under Franco, it continued to arouse obstinate opposition among notables within the Cortes, attached to traditional Catholic values, and concerned to insulate the rural population from the rising tide of secularism. After much internal jockeying Suárez's government did pass divorce legislation that was among the most progressive in Europe, but at the price of a revolt by a sizeable section of UCD deputies.

Meanwhile, the nature and extent of the autonomy to be granted to historically dissident regions of the country was proving a third area of acute tension within the UCD, as in Spanish politics at large. Here too Suárez showed himself resolute and dexterous, negotiating accords with Basque and Catalan nationalists that gave relatively wide powers of self-government against the opposition of centralizers in his own party and Fraga's Popular Alliance. The passing of the Basque statute did not satisfy ETA, however, the level of violence increasing in its wake. Conservative resistance to regional devolution thereupon hardened, while the two examples of it already ceded had a snowball effect in other provinces, which were soon demanding equivalent autonomy. When Suárez next reached agreement with the Andalusian authorities (led by the PSOE) for a local statute, the UCD council disavowed him – only to be repudiated in its turn by the party's electorate in Andalusia, which rejected its call for abstention in the ensuing referendum.

The incoherence and confusion revealed in this episode proved, in fact, to be the turning-point for the government. Suárez's skills as a state-builder and broker were not matched by abilities as either a party leader or a parliamentary tribune. Fanned by personal rivalries and the conceit of local oligarchies, divisions over policy intensified in the UCD, fatally undermining Suárez's project of forging a unified centre party. Suárez himself made little attempt to create a modern mass-membership organization, or even a personalized political machine, remaining aloof from the factional disputes within the party. His appearances in the Cortes were sparse and unimpressive, and his liaison with the palace declined – perhaps reflecting his private opinion of the calibre of his deputies and sovereign alike. The result was his increasing isolation at the summit of the state, while intrigue and manoeuvre ran riot among the assorted 'barons' of the UCD. In these conditions Suárez appeared to lose his sense of direction and to lapse into apathy. By the spring of 1981 it was clearly only a matter of time before the party broke up.

Underlying the surface of this trajectory, there were deeper reasons for the eclipse of the UCD. In Western Europe there are really only two examples of a dominant bourgeois party of secular origin. The Conservatives in Britain are, of course, the oldest and most successful. Gaullism in France is a much more recent creation, which has never had the same monopoly of representation on the right; the RPR today shares its electorate with the much more amorphous UDF. Scandinavia lacks any conservative ascendancy. Elsewhere, in Austria, West Germany, the low countries and Italy, it was Catholicism that typically cemented the foundations of modern bourgeois politics. In the early seventies Spain was widely thought to be a future candidate for this pattern and a number of formative currents in the UCD, including the influential Tácito group, designated themselves as Christian Democrat. It is probably fair to say that the central ideological contingent within the UCD was always more or less vaguely Christian Democratic in inspiration. But wherever its lines be drawn, it was never hegemonic over the party as a whole. Suárez himself was of a decidedly lay bent, as the divorce issue showed; and many of his ministers defined themselves as 'Social Democrats' or 'Liberals'. The rapid disintegration of the UCD (triggered by one of its Catholic factions) was thus, by way of contrast, to throw into sharp relief the absence of a broad and vigorous Spanish Christian Democracy.

Why did a society traditionally famed for the force of reactionary bigotry and Catholic fanaticism so signally fail to generate its own DC? Part of the answer is that, since the nineteenth century, Catholicism itself has never been as pervasive as in Italy, while popular and liberal aversion to clerical culture has been correspondingly stronger. Furthermore, the Spanish church of the late 1970s was not only more controversial but also more divided an institution than its Italian counterpart of the late 1940s and 1950s. Its hierarchy had been intimately associated with Franco, who had the right of nomination to bishoprics, and some of its prelates outdid the Caudillo himself in gnarled repressive zeal. But its middle ranks were affected by the Second Vatican Council, and some of the lower clergy by progressive nationalist (in Euzkadi) or even socialist ideas. The church as a whole anyway lacked the tradition of voluntary mass associations of the laity so characteristic of Italy.[7] It was thus in no position to intervene monolithically in the fluid post-Franco scene. An uneasy hierarchy proved reluctant to tie itself too closely to specific political organiz-ations, preferring to diversify its leverage on the social questions that really concerned it. But this leverage itself had been greatly weakened by the cultural secularization attendant on the long boom, and the revolts of the late sixties and seventies. The historical moment of 1945–50 when the DC, MRP and CDU took such abundant root in the soil of continental anti-communism and provincial piety had passed. There could be no Hispanic repetition of this experience. But in its absence, the UCD lacked any compelling ideological identity or organizational dynamic. Its miscellaneity condemned it to a short life.

There was a further obstacle to its consolidation, however – one that also presents itself to successor formations today. The oldest and strongest centres of a true industrial and commercial bourgeoisie in Spain have been located on the geographical periphery, in the Basque lands and Catalonia. Under normal conditions, these would have represented the heartlands of capitalist hegemony in the state as a whole – the regions which historically enjoyed the largest concen-trations of industry, the highest per capita income, and the densest strata of intermediate classes (above all, a numerous and articulate petty bourgeoisie) between capital and labour. But in Spain, they have been precisely the prime antagonists of central power, each the hearth of an intense national sentiment at variance with Castilian rule and culture. The political consequence, once Franco's especially oppressive dictatorship over these provinces had ended, was the re-emergence of nationalist parties with commanding local authority. On the ground, the Basque National Party (PNV) and Convergencia i Unió (CiU) are not comparable in all respects – both class configuration and linguistic situation differing significantly between Euzkadi and Catalonia.[8] But in the framework of Spanish politics as a whole, their structural role is very similar. Both are genuine mass organizations, with a large inter-class membership and wide cultural penumbra. Each is securely dominated by a local bourgeoisie that is traditionally more enlightened in outlook than elsewhere in the peninsula. Suggestively, both too are infused with Catholic spirit. The PNV is actually a member of the European Christian Democratic Union. The CiU is less overtly clerical in connection, but its leader Pujol makes no secret of his attachment to the church. These, in other words, are the nearest things to real Christian Democratic parties in Spain – just as one might expect, as organic expressions of proud local possessing classes. But their very strength has so far been a net *subtraction* from the total potential of the Spanish centre and right, as the 'natural' bastions of a self-confident bourgeois politics have become jutting redoubts for the most part turned against it.

The first clear sign of what this would mean came with the regional elections which followed Suárez's negotiation of autonomy statutes for Euzkadi and Catalonia in March 1980. The UCD was humiliated at the hands of the nationalist parties in both regions, ending up in fifth position in the Basque country and fourth in Catalonia. By the turn of the year, the party was in virtual fission and Suárez was on the point of resigning as prime minister. Within the next twelve months fifteen 'Social Democratic' deputies had exited from the UCD, in many cases finding their way into the new-style PSOE. They were followed by Suárez himself, who withdrew to form a Democratic Social Centre that would win no more than a minuscule 2.9 per cent of the vote in the autumn 1982 elections, and by right-wing Christian and Popular Democrats moving into the orbit of Fraga's Popular Alliance. Meanwhile another ex-*franquista*, Leopoldo Calvo-Sotelo, had taken over the leadership of the UCD in February 1981, but his efforts to freeze the crisis by means of lowest-common-denominator politics merely left him at the head of a party and government operating in a social vacuum. It was to fill this vacuum, at the moment of Calvo-Sotelo's investiture, that Lieutenant-Colonel Tejero's ragged band of Civil Guards burst into the Cortes and attempted to rally the forces of the old order. The royal *non placet* brought this spectacle to an end within twenty-four hours. The pre-modern social and ecclesiastical forces which had underpinned the Civil War regime were no longer available for a military dictatorship.

The disintegration of the UCD on the right cleared the way for the advance of Spanish Socialism towards centre-stage. But there was another condition for this too – the simultaneous auto-destruct of the PCE to its left. Spanish Communism had entered the post-Franco epoch with a strong hand. It was the only party to have built up and maintained organized resistance to the dictatorship, whose jails were filled principally with its militants. It led the largest independent trade-union network in the country, the Workers' Commissions. It exercised predominant influence over the new and rebellious intelligentsia that had emerged during the 1960s. It had a mass rank and file which no rival could boast, claiming some 200,000 members in 1978. Yet within a few years it was in ruins: split three ways and stunted to a mere 4 per cent of the electorate. How did this happen?

Carrillo's first and most basic blunder lay in his eagerness to secure legalization of the PCE from Suárez, in exchange for abandonment of the party's historic identity as the fulcrum of resistance to Franco's dictatorship and its royal appendage. The folly of this haste was soon demonstrated. In effect, the PCE leadership managed to combine an underestimation of its real potential, which would sooner or later have forced legalization on any post-Franco government, with wild illusions that it might immediately score 30 per cent of the vote once legalized. The 1977 elections, in which the PCE got less than 10 per cent, were a rude awakening. But in a *fuite en avant* of misjudgement, Carrillo then outdid González in extolling the Moncloa Pact as the formula for a 'government of national concentration' in which the PCE would work shoulder to shoulder with the UCD. Such a line could only benefit the PSOE, letting it pose as both more radical in words and safer in deeds.

Meanwhile, belying the bland Eurocommunist image that he sought outwardly, Carrillo's leadership within the party was a roughneck autocracy under which the newer generations, recruited from the resistance within the country, increasingly chafed. In July 1981 a group of 'renovators' attempted to democratize the internal regime at the party's 10th Congress, and were promptly purged. Organizational tension soon intersected with regional frictions, as the Basque and Catalan affiliates of the PCE strove to assert their autonomy from the centre. In the autumn of 1981, a majority of the central committee of the Basque party revolted against Carrillo, and were expelled. Soon after fell the hammer-blow of the 1982 elections, which prompted many of Carrillo's erstwhile supporters to rebel against his personalism. Obliged to make a tactical withdrawal, Carrillo installed a young Asturian miner, Gerardo Iglesias, whom he assumed he could control, as secretary-general in his stead – only to see this understudy swing over to the line of 'renewal' against Carrillo. The veteran Ignacio Gallego had meanwhile led a secession to form an ultra-orthodox

PCPE, mainly based in Catalonia. Then Carrillo himself mutinied against the new official leadership, walking out with significant support in Madrid and Valencia. The result was that by 1983 three separate organizations, each denouncing the other and all claiming the same heritage, existed in Spain.[9]

Eurocommunism was little enough of a recipe for political success in Italy or France, but nowhere was its price so high as in Spain. This was chiefly because its implementation there involved a much more drastic and demoralizing break with cadre traditions – both recent and revolutionary, in the underground. But it was also because the PCE had no layer of homogenized collective leadership such as that which steered the PCI through its vicissitudes after the sixties. Carrillo was a promontory within his organization in a way that Marchais or Berlinguer was not. The discrepancy between democratic ideology and bureaucratic practice was thus much more sharply felt inside the PCE, and there was little time for generational or regional annealing once the fatal consequences of 1977 set in. Whatever the historical limitations of the PCE, even in its best days under Franco, the moral immolation of the party to a futile *realpolitik* and an unworkable autocracy was a disaster for the Spanish labour movement. One obvious result was that the PSOE no longer had to fear sanctions to its left.

The PSOE Victory

The decks thus cleared on either side, the PSOE victory in the elections of October 1982 was one of the most decisive in the history of European socialism, and more generally of European parliamentarism. With 10,127,392 votes, or 48.4 per cent, the Socialists scored nearly double the total of their closest rival, the Popular Alliance, and – profiting from the premium created by Suárez – took 57.7 per cent of the seats in the Congress of Deputies. Their advance was remarkably uniform across the country. In Andalusia, for example, the PSOE vote in Cadiz soared from 30.2 per cent in 1979 to 63.8 per cent in 1982, in Granada from 35.8 per cent to 57.9 per cent. But in some of the least pro-Socialist rural provinces of Castille and Galicia, the percentage rise was no less dramatic – climbing from 17.9 per cent to 38.4 per cent in La Coruña, for instance. Only in the Basque heartlands of Guipuzcoa and Biscay, and in parts of Catalonia, did the party's increase fall below 10 per cent.

A historic breakthrough of these proportions – at least for the workers' parties – has usually been accompanied by an important strengthening of their grassroots organization and overall presence

Table 8.1 Votes and Seats in Spanish Elections, 1977–82

	Votes (%)			Seats (%)		
	1977	1979	1982	1977	1979	1982
UCD	34.8	35.0	6.8	47.1	48.0	3.4
AP	8.4	5.8	26.5	4.6	2.6	30.3
CDS	–	–	2.9	–	–	0.6
PSOE	29.4	30.4	48.4	33.7	34.6	57.7
PCE	9.3	10.7	4.0	5.7	6.6	1.1
PSP	4.5	–	–	1.1	–	–
CiU	3.7	2.6	3.7	3.1	2.3	3.4
PNV	1.7	1.5	1.9	2.3	2.0	2.3
Others	8.2	14.0	5.8	2.3	4.0	1.1

Source: Calculated from Ministry of Interior figures, as reproduced in J. M. Maravall and J. Santamaria, 'La transición política en España', *Sistema*, November 1985, pp. 97, 118. It has not been possible to give a consistent breakdown of the figure for other parties, which conceals some not insignificant results such as the 3.1 per cent for five far-left groups in 1977.

Note: AP: Popular Alliance, led by Manuel Fraga; CDS: Democratic Social Centre, the party founded by Adolfo Suárez in 1982 after his break from the UCD; CiU: Convergencia i Unió, the main bourgeois-nationalist party in Catalonia; PNV: the Basque Nationalist Party.

within society. This did not happen in the case of the PSOE. Its membership figure, already falling towards the end of the seventies, slipped back from 101,000 in 1979 to 97,000 in 1981, while the number of UGT *afiliados* showed a parallel decline from 1,460,000 to 1,375,000.[10] If the Socialists nevertheless succeeded in almost doubling their vote between 1979 and 1982, this was essentially due to the collapse of the PCE and UCD. With no serious rival on its left, and with the right regrouped around Fraga, the Socialists found themselves virtually alone in the broad spectrum of centre-to-left politics. On the one hand, they were able to project an image of discipline and self-confidence, in stark contrast with the surrounding disorder. On the other hand, the UCD's failure to address the problem of soaring unemployment, and its drive in autumn 1981 to steamroller the country into NATO, had broadened receptiveness to the PSOE's offer of moderate change. The rise in electoral participation from 67 per cent in 1979 to a more typical European level of 80 per cent in 1982 was another major factor in the PSOE victory, as millions of new voters reinforced its domination of the centre ground.

    Not unnaturally, the *felipistas* presented October 1982 as a final vindication of the 1979 turn away from left radicalism – a turn so evident that during the election campaign Suárez's new-founded populist CDS could demagogically claim to be to the left of the PSOE on issues like nationalization and state intervention in the economy. It might be argued, however, that since the PSOE/PSP, PCE and far-left vote already totalled 46.3 per cent in 1977, less than two years after Franco's death, a united left would have had every chance of profiting from the break-up of the bourgeois centre anyway. By diluting its social programme, and rejecting any concessions to political unity, the Socialist leadership ensured that the 1982 victory would consolidate the PSOE as, so to speak, a left occupant of the centre, rather than extend the reach of the left to new sections of the population. Yet it would be wrong to underestimate the mixture of appeals which the party had to make to secure its triumph. Two of these, in particular, continued to sound a radical note. The first was the commitment to halve unemployment, and the second was the pledge to call a referendum on Spain's membership of NATO, opposed by the party in the Cortes and the streets alike. Among the most popular of the promises made by the PSOE, these were to provide significant bench-marks of its evolution in power.

The González government took office with an undertaking to create 800,000 jobs during its mandate. This was not a casual promise made in the heat of the hustings. The PSOE election manifesto prominently defined the lowering of unemployment as 'the main challenge facing Spanish society in the next few years' and 'the priority objective of Socialist policy'. Nor was this public commitment quickly relinquished, despite later claims that the real scale of Spain's economic crisis became apparent to the party as soon as it had to rule. In the summer of 1983, Guerra – now deputy prime minister – was still proudly repeating in an interview: 'Whatever the Cassandras may say, I can tell you that the government is prepared to confirm its promise of creating 800,000 jobs in the life of this parliament.' The text continues: 'Guerra pointed out that it was a difficult undertaking, but "we knew that when we gave it".'[11]

Seasoned politicians have usually been more wary of quoting a precise figure. In reality, however, economic policy was not in the hands of Guerra but of Miguel Boyer, a banker of the *beau monde*, determined to pursue a course of orthodox rationalization capable of winning the confidence of international financial markets. In 1982–83, when unemployment was rising more or less sharply throughout Western Europe, a major programme of job creation would have run directly against the tendencies of the time, involving a challenge to the whole drift of capitalist development in the eighties. Unlike the Socialists in France, the PSOE – forewarned by the fate of the French experiment, already unmistakeable by the winter of 1982, and acutely conscious of Spain's weaker position as a national economy – never really attempted one. The UCD had left a legacy of low growth, high inflation, fiscal deficit and negative balance of payments. Boyer's cure was tight money and increased taxation, to disinflate the economy and restructure Spanish industry by weeding out declining or loss-making sectors, and attract foreign capital to upgrade the country's technological stock, prior to entry into the EC. To this end, the government early embarked on a privatization drive to increase the relative weight of multinational enterprises in Spain. The giant Rumasa group, nationalized on the brink of collapse in January 1983, was restored to profitability and handed back almost in its entirety to private capital; while the Instituto Nacional de Industria (INI), the state holding company set up by the Franco regime, sold off its assets in a wide range of industries, from textiles to tourism, including a 51 per cent share in the key SEAT and ENASA motor companies, bought respectively by Volkswagen and General Motors. The prize deal, however, was to be the crossing of Companía Telefónica Nacional de España and American Telephone and Telegraph to create AT y Microelectrónica de España, producing microchips at a new Tres Cantos plant north of Madrid: one parent a leading US multinational, the other a private Spanish communications monopoly – the role of the state in the marriage being to endow it with about a third of the initial 35 billion peseta investment.

On the other hand, the old core industries of the peninsula were scheduled for decimation. By early 1986, official programmes for their reconversion were projecting redundancies of a third of the workforce in steel, half in heavy electrical equipment, 60 per cent in ship-building, a fifth in textiles, and even losses in motor vehicles.[12]

The results, in conventional bankers' terms, were not unsatisfactory. The first González government certainly improved the performance of Spanish capitalism. Inflation, whose reduction was one of its main policy goals, fell from over 14 per cent a year in 1982 to 8 per cent in 1985. The gross domestic product grew at an annual rate of around 2 per cent – close to the EC average for this period. Exports rose substantially, while imports held steady, returning the external account to surplus. On the other hand, the price of this success was in large measure paid by Spanish labour. Instead of creating 800,000 new jobs, the PSOE in power presided over the destruction of another 500,000. Unemployment, which had been 5 per cent back in 1976, and already 17 per cent when González took office in 1982, rose to 22 per cent by 1986, when Spain entered the European Community – far the highest figure in the EC. Over half of the 16–19 age group, and 38 per cent of 20 to 24-year-olds, were already without a job in 1983, and the numbers of those who – lacking any public relief – had to depend upon the vagaries of parental humour or scratch around in the underground economy for the bare necessities of life, increased remorselessly. Against this background, initial UGT support for the government's policies of wage restraint and industrial reconversion soon waned, along with union strength itself. By the spring of 1985, the federation's president Nicolas Redondo was declaring: 'What is certain is that this version of market economy, which is presented to us as the only one possible and the universal panacea, is bringing to our country nothing other than greater unemployment, greater inequality and greater poverty.'[13] Redondo, one of the historic leaders who had reorganized the PSOE along with González and Guerra in the mid seventies, had seen UGT membership fall by nearly a half to 700,000 since the Socialists had come to power. Union discontent could not be entirely ignored by the government. In the spring of 1985 Boyer loosened fiscal policy, to give some breathing-space to the job market. But, extolled as the saviour of Spain's finances by the business community, he overplayed his hand by demanding the job of deputy premier with powers over all spending departments – resigning when González refused to displace Guerra in his favour. He was succeeded by Carlos Solchaga, the minister of industry responsible for 'reconversion', guaranteeing continuity of policy. In the following year – 1986 – the economic conjuncture finally altered, as the impact of the American boom coincided with Spanish entry into the EC, setting off a period of rapid accumulation.

Socialist Atlanticism

The final year of the first Socialist administration, nevertheless, was dominated less by the state of the economy than by security policy. In 1981 Calvo-Sotelo's failing and inchoate UCD government, in a rare display of initiative, had suddenly negotiated Spain's rapid entry into the political structure of NATO, with the eventual aim of full military integration. Spain had long been an important link in the chain of American military bases girding the globe. But the US treaty with Spain did not represent an optimal arrangement for Washington. In 1963 and again in 1968, Franco bargained hard over the terms of its renewal, demanding financial and diplomatic concessions from the US which suggested that it would always remain open to a Spanish government to disturb the balance of what it might regard as largely, if not solely, a business arrangement. Moreover, under Franco the Spanish armed forces were organized, equipped and deployed for the purposes of internal repression – on a parsimonious budget, at a low level of military technology – so that the manpower reserves of Western Europe's fifth largest country were practically useless for NATO planning. Full integration into the North Atlantic Pact was obviously preferable, but both Franco's own isolationism, and Benelux and Scandinavian objections to the admission of his dictatorship, prevented this. The advent of parliamentary democracy in Madrid lifted these obstacles. Entry into NATO now formed a natural part of the overall drive for a Euromodernization of Spain sought by business and mainstream opinion. But as the Calvo-Sotelo cabinet pushed Spanish membership through the Cortes, the PSOE launched a vigorous campaign – along with the PCE and the rest of the left – against it. The result was a major shift in public attitudes. Whereas in 1979 polls showed that 58 per cent of Spaniards still had no definite view and only 15 per cent were mildly or strongly against, those opposed to Spanish entry into NATO had risen to 43 per cent by September 1981.[14]

But once the PSOE had won the elections of 1982, it started to take another tack. Now the González government allowed that, although it was not in principle favourable to Spain's membership, it could not now lightly countenance withdrawal. Military expenditure climbed rapidly under the defence minister Narcís Serra, absorbing a larger share of the budget than under Franco, with a big programme of weapons acquisitions – fighters, aircraft carriers, jump jets – from the US. By the spring of 1983, the government had formally reversed its position. Its spokesmen now explained that Spain's national interests required it to play its part in NATO's defence of the West; the PSOE had been mistaken to imagine there was any alternative, for Spain's entry into the EC was indissociable from membership of NATO. Once, the PSOE had insisted that 'to relate the two things to each other is simply wrong in principle. To horse-trade in public about such basic decisions shows a singular lack of political and diplomatic sense – it is a way of tricking the people.'[15] Now, it sought to persuade Spaniards that NATO and the EC were to all intents and purposes one, striving to convert an understandable popular desire to overcome Spain's relative isolation from the life of the continent into acceptance of the necessity of the Atlantic Alliance. Such was, in fact, the conviction of Felipe González himself – for whom modernization of Spain had come to mean a drive to make it a country like any other of its size in the world of Northern capitalism. 'Normalcy' was the goal; NATO one of the tickets to it.

Yet despite the change in its strategic options, the PSOE continued to be stuck with its promise to hold a referendum on Spanish membership of NATO. After three years of prevarication, during which González and Guerra must have spent long hours weighing their tactical choices, they in the end concluded that to repudiate such a clear commitment involved too great a risk of political discredit. Despite the lack of popular enthusiasm for NATO, moreover, there were good grounds for thinking that the PSOE could force a decision in a plebiscite its way. To its right, Fraga's Popular Alliance was more vociferously pro-Western than the government itself. To its left, Spanish Communism was so split and shrunk that it seemed to pose little political threat. Within the Socialist ranks themselves, virtually all opposition would soon be silenced, as González announced that any party member campaigning against the government's position would be subject to disciplinary action. With the two major political parties – government and opposition – united on the basic issue, commanding 80 per cent of the Cortes, and proportionate radio and television time, the chances of a 'No' vote looked slender.

In fact, PSOE calculations came close to misfiring. The breadth of resistance to NATO among ordinary Spaniards proved greater than expected. Popular perceptions of the global role of the United States, the first power to befriend Franco after the Civil War, could not be shifted so easily, at the height of Reagan's *contra* operations in Central America. Distinct from these sentiments was the tradition of Spanish neutrality, which had kept the country out of two world wars even under governments of authoritarian reaction. An informal coordinating committee (CEOP) and ad hoc Civic Platform – uniting Christians, pacifists, feminists, human rights groups, Communists, the far left – confounded officialdom by the energy with which it mobilized these feelings on a peninsular scale, launching a massive and imaginative campaign of demonstrations and meetings, which put the administration on the defensive from the start.

A week away from the referendum, opinion polls still showed a majority for withdrawal. To prevent this materializing, the government mustered every rhetorical and practical resource at its disposal. The two leitmotifs of PSOE propaganda were the argument that a vote against NATO lacked any credible administration to implement it and would throw the country into turmoil; and that were it carried through, hundreds of thousands of Spaniards would lose their jobs. A relentless television blitz, twenty-eight million letters sent from the prime minister to the electorate, £3 million spent by the PSOE on press and radio advertising, and a final address to the nation by González himself, intoning the word 'peace' without let, eventually had their effect – many working-class voters responding to the simple appeal of party loyalty at all costs. But despite everything, nearly seven million Spaniards – 40 per cent of those who voted, and an actual majority in the most advanced regions of Spain, the Basque lands and Catalonia – stood out against NATO.

Victory in the referendum, nevertheless, paved the way for the PSOE's second term of office. Economically, although González had presided over rising unemployment, inflation had fallen and – after three bleak years – growth was now picking up. The ministry of economy could claim orthodoxy had paid off. The general decline of belief in any economic alternative to the logic of a capitalist recession – a pervasive feature of the West European scene in the eighties – worked to Socialist advantage in Spain. Socially, the government could point to educational expansion and modernization, if little else: a very restrictive abortion law and public financing of church schools were witness to the modesty of its goals – welfare had scarcely been enlarged at all. Politically, on the other hand, the PSOE could legitimately maintain that it had 'consolidated democracy' – a claim with undoubted electoral resonance. If the original architect of the new parliamentary order had been Suárez, it was González – a much abler politician, if less notable state-builder – who reaped the credit for its stabilization. The retirement of the army to its barracks was more a consequence of the collapse of the *tejerazo* than of minister Serra's personnel policies. But the rapid extension of regional autonomy throughout Spain, without obstruction from Madrid, was a significant PSOE achievement. Entry into the European Community, negotiated from 1983 and accomplished in 1986, was without question an institutional turning-point.

There was also another sense in which the González government earned the reputation it sought: at ministerial level as such, PSOE rule had proved strikingly stable by comparison with its UCD predecessor. Cabinet posts became fixtures for their occupants, with a few notable exceptions, and party discipline absolute – in contrast with the roulette-wheel of appointments in Suárez's days, unsettling even to loyal supporters. Within the administration at large, the PSOE assured the rapid social promotion of younger Spanish professionals and technicians – in no other Western country of this period was the generational political turnover so swift and sweeping. Beneath this stratum, and to some extent regardless of policies, popular attachment to the name and memory of the party persisted. These assets – the career open to middle-class talents, the image of a militant past – did not yield a deep organizational anchorage in Spanish society as a whole: with no more than 150,000 members, the PSOE had the lowest density of any major party, left or right, in Western Europe. But its advantages over its domestic opponents were more than sufficient. Presenting itself to the country as a regime of enlightened competence, against a right still led by Fraga – a Galician Strauss widely distrusted outside his own rather marginal fief – and a centre confined to Catalonia and the Basque country, Spanish Socialism won a second term of office in autumn 1986 without much difficulty. Its vote – 44.4

per cent – still towered above that of the Alianza Popular, at 26.1 per cent, and the party once more gained an absolute majority in the Cortes.

Growth Fever

The climate of the second González administration differed markedly from the first. In 1987 the Spanish economy accelerated rapidly, to a growth rate of over 5 per cent, and for three golden years Spain registered the fastest boom in Western Europe. Integration into the European Community unleashed a sudden avalanche of foreign investment, attracted by cheap labour, stable government, and abundant sun. Between 1986 and 1990, ten billion pesetas worth of capital poured into the country, or ten times more than in the previous five years – towards the end, the volume of direct investment virtually doubled from one year to another. At the same time, the drop in world oil prices cut manufacturing costs by the equivalent of some 3.5 per cent of Spanish GNP. Profits soared, as Solchaga uncorked a massive programme of privatization. The stock market hit an all-time high, amidst a frenzy of financial mergers and real-estate speculation – land prices in Madrid quintupled in the eighties. Spanish cities were the scene of a consumption boom without precedent in the country's history.

The new prosperity did not, however, spell out tranquillity. If the austerity of the first PSOE government was not substantially disturbed by social unrest, there was an abrupt change with the plethora of the second. The origins of the alteration of mood can be traced back to the political mobilization against NATO of 1986, which had lasting effects on the Spanish scene. The campaign had been very successful in the schools, and it was the new levy of students who now startled the government with the militancy of their demonstrations against it in late 1986 and 1987, forcing José Maravall – the minister of education and PSOE's most distinguished intellectual – to offer his resignation, which took effect a year later in the face of a teachers' strike. Meanwhile, the labour front had shifted. Here too the impact of the referendum campaign made itself felt. Confronted with the scale of the opposition to NATO, dwarfing its own diminutive vote, the Communist Party sought to preserve the potential for a broader radical politics it had revealed by creating an electoral cartel, Izquierda Unida, to regroup the different forces that had organized the campaign. The new front, assembled in the spring of 1986, included Gallego's breakaway PCPE, several small left-liberal formations, and ecological and peace groups. A year later the Communist trade-union federation, the Comisiones Obreras – now headed by a younger leader, Antonio Gutierrez –

moved towards rapprochement with the disaffected UGT, in common hostility to Solchaga's neo-liberal line.

The result was a mounting trade-union campaign, demanding that the PSOE government acquit its debt to the workers who had elected it, after the years of austerity, and make a 'social turn' in its economic policies. After protracted negotiations proved fruitless, the combined union movement declared a twenty-four general strike against the government. On 14 December 1988, the entire country came to a halt in what was not only the most imposing stoppage in Spanish history, but the most effective strike action in Western Europe in the eighties. As the economy lay paralysed, and television went off the air, González contemplated resignation. Panic was short-lived, but the lesson was not. Realizing the political danger it was in, the Socialist government yielded. The 'social turn' was made, and fast. Under the UCD, spending on health, pensions and unemployment compensation had increased by a full 1.5 per cent of GDP in the year 1980–81; under the PSOE, it had risen by just 0.4 per cent in the five years 1983–88. Now, with the union pistol at its head, the González government discovered it had the resources after all: in 1989–91, social spending jumped by over two billion pesetas, or 1.6 per cent of GDP.

The switch came just in time, while the boom was still rolling. The effect of the two was enough to return the Socialists to power again, by a narrower margin, in the elections of October 1989. The PSOE lost a million votes, but the right made no gains. The novelty was the success of Izquierda Unida. Now led by Julio Anguita, the popular mayor of Córdoba, who had replaced Iglesias as secretary-general of the PCE in 1988, the IU polled 9.2 per cent, effectively recovering the level of support attracted by Spanish Communism in the time of the transition. This was enough to ensure no hasty reversion to social minimalism by the PSOE. In 1990 the unions achieved a long-standing goal, when they forced the government – after years of resistance – to accept indexation of pensions. On the other hand, the official cult of enrichissez-vous – Solchaga boasting that 'Spain is the country in Europe, perhaps in the world, where the most money can be made in a short space of time' – now started to boomerang against the PSOE, as increasing evidence of corruption in the penumbra of the party came to light. Most of this was illegal financing of the party through intermediates paid for fictitious services by interested business groups, rather than personal enrichment, and was not confined to the Socialists – the right was also implicated. But when Alfonso Guerra's brother, Juan Guerra, was found to have profited from dubious facilities in Seville, the clamour for the head of the deputy prime minister – never popular with the mainstream press – was vociferous. Although no one suggested that Guerra himself had gained from his brother's activities, massive public pressure built up against him, much of it orchestrated from behind the scenes by Solchaga. The prolonged crisis over his position marked a turning-point for the PSOE. The fortunes of the party had been built in good measure on the close bond between González and Guerra over a tumultuous quarter-century, the former assuring the electoral appeal and the latter the organizational skill that were together essential for its success. As late as the autumn of 1990, González was declaring that he would himself resign if Guerra were to do so.

The deputy premier, however, had never been trusted by Spanish business or bourgeois opinion at large. The hostility towards him was not due to any fundamental difference between himself and González on the general economic or security strategy of the PSOE, once in power. But in the division of roles between them, Guerra was responsible for the party as an organized presence within society rather than as a cog in the machinery of state. Here he was ruthless in handling leftists and stifling dissent, playing a decisive part in enforcing the change of line on NATO. But his very identification with the party apparatus made him a less certain quantity at the centre of a government whose logic was to free policy as much as possible from the constraints – however long-range – of the militants and voters of the PSOE and the pressures of organized labour. Boyer and Solchaga both sought his removal as a brake on their own power, since he had on occasion opposed initiatives of the finance ministry with explosive social potential, such as Boyer's pension reform. By position, holding both the vice-premiership and the effective control of the party – a rare combination – Guerra came to embody one of the central tensions of any social-democratic regime. By temperament, he was more 'ideological' than most of his colleagues, playing a prominent role in financing and organizing Programma 2000 – a much-publicized project to modernize the strategic thinking of the PSOE, which engaged the energies of party intellectuals in substantial research as well as the organization of thousands of public and internal debates. The Programma ended up as an inoffensive document extolling the 'social market', while also recalling the need for welfare and full employment, adopted and forgotten by the party at its 32nd Congress in 1990. Yet for all its outcome, the process of discussion still projected an image of the party, and its full-time apparatus, as a living entity relatively autonomous of the government. There were thus good reasons for Guerra to be distrusted by established opinion. González, who had greatly depended on him, struggled to the last to keep him in place. But in January 1991 Guerra – like Chevènement in France, if less publicly –

258   MAPPING THE WEST EUROPEAN LEFT

opposed participation in the Gulf War. This consummated the breach
for which capital had been pressing: as Spanish warships sailed for the
Straits of Hormuz, González let Guerra go. His departure was widely
seen to be a watershed in the evolution of the Socialist Party.

Economically, meanwhile, Solchaga was trying to cool down the
overheated growth of the late eighties. Spain was taken into the EMS at
a high exchange rate, and a tight credit squeeze imposed. By 1991,
investment was in a steep fall and a thousand jobs were being lost a day.
But as recession loomed again, the PSOE could no longer claim the
achievements of the early eighties: for inflation remained high, the
budget was in deficit, and the trade gap widening. As in France, the
high interest rates required to maintain parity with the post-unification
deutschmark depressed employment and damaged exports, while
availing little against speculative attacks. In the autumn of 1992, after
costly and futile defence, the 'hard' peseta crumbled amid the general
European monetary turmoil. By early 1993, after months of mounting
crisis, the PSOE's coherence and even Felipe González's own staying
power seemed in jeopardy. When the government called elections for
June, predictions of Socialist defeat were widespread.

For by now the right had rallied. After the fiasco of the AP in the
1986 elections, Fraga had resigned as its president. But his successor –
a tyro from Andalusia – had his weaknesses without his strengths, and
in early 1989 Fraga took over the reins again when the party fused with
Liberals and Christian Democrats to create the Partido Popular. This
time, however, his dauphin José Maria Aznar, a dour young tax
inspector, proved more effective, leading the new formation into the
elections of October 1989, and taking over as president in the spring of
1990. Under Aznar, the PP distanced itself from the *franquista* past,
studiously cultivated an image of responsible moderation, and started
to recruit widely among Spanish middle-class youth. By the campaign
of June 1993, Aznar was at the head of a well-organized party with a
vigorous mass following, enjoying a new benevolence in the country's
mainstream media. González, by contrast, seemed drained of energy
and lustre, and was trounced in the first television debate between the
two. In the traditionally personalized atmosphere of Spanish politics,
now tricked out with the latest American techniques, much depended
on the performance of the party leaders. But the PSOE leader
recovered his stamina, finishing the campaign strongly on television
and at mass rallies, warning of the historic dangers of the Spanish right
with a political urgency long since unheard in his official discourse.

The result was the fourth and least expected Socialist victory at the
polls. The PSOE won 38.7 per cent of the votes, after absorbing
Euskadiko Ezquerra, the small group of independent socialists in the

Table 8.2 Votes and Seats in the Spanish Elections, 1986–93

	Votes (%)			Seats		
	1986	1989	1993	1986	1989	1993
AP/PP	26.2	25.8	34.8	105	106	141
CDS	9.3	7.9	–	19	14	–
PSOE	44.3	39.6	38.7	184	175	159
IU	4.7	9.1	9.6	7	17	18
CiU	5.0	5.0	4.9	18	18	17
PNV	1.5	1.2	1.2	6	5	5
Others	9.0	11.4	10.8	11	15	10

Basque country, just 1 per cent below its 1989 total. But in doing so it gained nearly a million new votes, on a much higher turn-out – by any standards an impressive performance. The Partido Popular, netting no doubt most of the former constituency of the virtually defunct CDS, increased its share to just under 35 per cent. The Izquierda Unida, which had been expected to encroach on the Socialist vote, rose only slightly, to 9.6 per cent. The results gave the PSOE, benefiting once again from disproportional representation in the Cortes, a legislative plurality easily converted into another González government, with tacit Catalan nationalist support.

The Stamina of the Left

Thus twelve years after its triumph of 1982, apparently defying the rules of electoral gravity, the PSOE remains in power. What explains this remarkable success? The election of 1993 in effect highlighted the three main reasons. Firstly, the fundamental balance of forces in the country has favoured the left. The Spanish right has remained penalized by the legacy of Franco, in two senses. On the one hand, the very continuity of Súarez's transition to democracy meant that there was never any clean break with the past for Spanish conservatism, of the kind that occurred in Germany or Italy after the War, or in Portugal in the mid seventies. The shadow of suspicion still lingers over it for millions of Spaniards, who responded to González's calls to alarm in the polarized atmosphere of the last week of the campaign. On the other hand, the right also continues to be weakest where bourgeois politics should otherwise be strongest, in Catalonia and the Basque country – subtracted by national movements which have grown steadily stronger at the local level in the past fifteen years. The accord with Pujol's Convergencia i Unió which has installed González in the

Moncloa once again is symbolic of the consequences. In this vital respect – the division of bourgeois forces – the hegemony of the PSOE in Spain resembles that of Social Democracy in Scandinavia. On its other flank, as in the Nordic countries too, there is a substantial force of more radical character, derived from the Communist tradition. Together they compose a left that can win half the vote in a general election, with no need for the kind of 'alliance with progressive bourgeois' in prospect in Italy, or Germany. 'Hell!', one PP leader remarked in June, 'this country really is still on the left!'[16] In fact, ever since 1982, a government of 'union of the left' was not only always a mathematical possibility, but probably corresponded more closely to the aspirations of most PSOE voters than González's actual understandings with the bankers. But such an alliance would, of course, have meant a much more radical *cambio* in Spanish society than the PSOE leadership ever envisaged – closer to the alternative perspective, however lacking in detail, offered by Izquierda Unida.

If union of the left was never considered, but alliance with the centre was never necessary, part of the reason has lain in the role of Felipe González himself. No politician in Western Europe has so completely dominated national life since de Gaulle. González's power has been earned by a rare combination of skills – the ability to communicate, to manoeuvre and to administer, with a popular mixture of fluency and firmness. But it has also rested on the exceptional position of the prime minister (or *presidente*, as he is known in Spanish) in the Spanish constitution, whose prerogatives are greater than those of any other West European head of government. González effectively combines most of the powers of the French president and prime minister in the constitution of the Fifth Republic. Personally directing day-to-day administration, with a cabinet appointed by himself, whose members need be neither members of the Cortes nor of his own party, he is under no obligation to appear before parliament, once invested by it, and can only be removed by a 'constructive motion' which includes the name of a replacement.[17] In such a system the scope is evidently enormous for the *presidente* to operate what is in effect a presidential regime, rather than to act as a prime minister accountable to a parliamentary majority. The Cortes becomes a sounding-box, and the cabinet a cipher. Ministers have little or no power of their own, and scant collective contact with González himself. Guerra once tersely remarked: 'The Council of Ministers does not discuss politics; they are matters for the party leadership'.[18] Since his departure, the latter too has become increasingly impotent. The PSOE leadership, acutely aware of its electoral dependence upon González, has lacked the will and perhaps any real desire to control the actions of the government;

while González, never seriously challenged on policy, has refrained from provoking any confrontation with the party apparatus. The trend towards a charismatic personal rule above the party that has raised him up is evident. But if González has concentrated ever greater power in his hands, he has never lost sight of his original constituency. For all the neo-liberalism of his macroeconomic policy, it is a mistake to think – as is often said on both left and right – that González has simply pursued a Spanish equivalent of Thatcherism. If the union movement retained its militancy and self-confidence far more than in other European countries, this was due not only to the relative security of its position in major workplaces but also to the fact that it continued to share elements of a common tradition with the prime minister and the majority party in parliament, carefully tended in manner by González – whose ability to maintain working relations with trade-union leaders, even in the midst of sharp conflicts, has surpassed that of Wilson or Callaghan. Nor has this just been a question of style. In substance, the Socialist leader has known when to retreat, to preserve the social basis of the PSOE appeal.

Here has lain the third reason for the survival of Socialist rule in Spain. In 1992, nine months before the elections, the tenth annversary of the first PSOE victory was celebrated, to the accompaniment of many retrospects. What was the balance-sheet of the decade? Spain had grown faster than the average country of the European Community, and per capita income virtually doubled. The resultant rise of living standards had naturally redounded to the advantage of the party in power. The fruits of relative prosperity had been unequally divided. Much as in Italy, fiscal returns showed that employees typically paid higher taxes than employers, while real wages fell as a share of national income and their purchasing power increased only half as much as the average for the EC. Unemployment, 16.2 per cent in 1982, was back up to 17.6 per cent in 1992, heavily concentrated among young people and women, and rising sharply: less than half those out of work receive any form of dole. In the interim, some 1.3 million jobs had been created, although total employment was still less than it had been in 1972.[19] A third of the new work positions were in the bureaucracy, which jumped in size by nearly a quarter (due above all to the growth of regional administrations) – a force PSOE leaders themselves lamented their failure to reform.

Socially, the proudest claim of the party was – in Guerra's formulation – to have universalized rights to schooling, health and pensions.[20] There had indeed been a major expansion of education, where spending may have as much as doubled as a proportion of GDP, giving Spain one of the highest rates of scolarization in West Europe – as much as a third of the

20 to 24-year age-group are in some form of higher education, although its quality has fallen as numbers have risen. Health coverage was extended to some five million new persons, but medical resources to treat them did not increase proportionately – Spain has half as many hospital beds per thousand inhabitants as France. The spread of pensions, however, has been received as an incontestable benefit: under the Socialists, nearly two million Spaniards started to draw them for the first time. Their purchasing power fiercely defended against inflation by the trade unions, pensions were the PSOE's trump card in the 1993 elections, as González warned of the danger that the right might cut them. In the second half of the eighties, there was a greater increase in infrastructural investment – on motorways, railroads, airports, dams – than in social spending, despite the 'turn'.[21] But it could no longer be said that the PSOE had not created the elements of a welfare state. What might be said is that most of what it had achieved could have been done by any enlightened government of the right, in a capitalist country of a medium level of development. But since no such right existed in Spain, the PSOE's claim for historical credit has understandably won enough popular acceptance. It has held an electorate that has no idealized vision of the party. In late 1992, asked whether they believed the PSOE's denials of corruption, 80 per cent of its own voters did not. More striking still, asked which social group or class had benefited most from ten years of Socialist rule, over 40 per cent of PSOE supporters said 'the rich', as against 16 per cent who said the workers or lower classes – while no less than 55 per cent said it was these who had suffered most.[22] The loyalty that exists to the Socialist record is a clear-sighted one.

Prospects

The fourth González government, elected in a recession, has from the outset turned to the right. Dependence on Catalan toleration in the Cortes has its logic, not necessarily unwelcome to the prime minister. The new cabinet contains no fewer than seven 'independent' – i.e. technocratic – ministers, not recruited from the PSOE. Solchaga himself has been shifted from the treasury into the Cortes, as leader of the Socialist delegation there, to reduce Guerra's influence in the party. In the PSOE apparatus as a whole, the *guerristas* are being marginalized, although they have continued to hold out with some success in their southern strongholds. The decks are being cleared for conflicts to come. For the government is now on a collision course with the unions over the position of organized labour within Spanish society, since its principal objective has become 'flexibilization' of the workplace to

make Spanish capitalism more competitive. It aims to abolish protective regulations dating back to Franco's time, to enable cheaper
redundancies on new catch-all grounds, and simpler procedures for
relocation and regrading, as well as a reduction in real wages over the
next three years. As this new offensive – or 'class option', as the
Communist leader Julio Anguita has called it – generates strikes and
other forms of resistance, more strain than ever before will be placed
upon relations between the government and its original constituency.
If the new course has continued an underlying trend of the past
decade, in attuning Spanish government policy to the imperatives of
international markets, the conditions for doing so have changed
sharply for the worse. The price for the speculative fever of the late
eighties, when Madrid outbid all other European capitals as a
catchment centre for hot money, temporarily covering a flood of
consumer imports, is now a large public deficit and a falling external
account – one that has moved from a small surplus in 1985 to a negative
balance of $11.4 billion in 1989, $15.9 billion in 1991 and $24.0 billion
in 1992.[23] Three devaluations within the past year, with a stance
shifting in the same space of time from the most severe pro-EMU
rhetoric to the virtual abandonment of any convergence ambition,
leave the impression of a ship swamped by the forces summoned to
sweep it forward.

In this situation the spectre of unemployment, never laid to rest, has
returned to haunt the Socialist Party. As the jobless total again soars
over 20 per cent, approaching three times the OECD average, it is not
clear that even a major stimulus to the economy – more ample than the
modest interest-rate cuts so far introduced – will be able to restart any
of the motors of growth of the late eighties. Multinational investment is
drying up as German firms look eastwards; new hi-tech industries have
hardly offset the collapse of traditional sectors that is likely to be
speeded up in the European single market;[24] construction is deep in
the grip of recession; and financial services, where many new jobs were
created, face very uncertain times. All the government now appears to
offer is a programme of substantial cuts in living standards and
security, in the hope that this will make the country more attractive to
investors.

Against this background, the Partido Popular continues to position
itself for the inheritance. The party leadership has taken the first steps
in breaking from Fraga's ambivalent relation to the past: Aznar openly
embraces the traditions of Second Republic liberalism and – not
altogether consistently – has aligned the PP with Christian Democracy
in the European political arena. He has also proved to be a more able
political manoeuvrer than the Galician warhorse, entering into the

spirit of parliamentary debate and ideological competition and remaining open to ad hoc deals on particular issues or eventually even a broader coalition. He also has age on his side, just over forty in a shadow cabinet which itself averages only fifty. Nevertheless, despite its success in eliminating the CDS as a competitor on the right, the PP has not succeeded in breaking into the new working-class layers necessary for victory at the polls; and in the present economic climate it is doubtful whether its programme of tax cuts, privatization and assistance to small businesses could win it new ground. It has played a relatively cautious game over European integration, painting itself in more national colours than the PSOE – in this respect more in tune with the Spanish employers' federation than with the big banks that have been so crucial to PSOE management of the economy. The ease with which the PSOE has entered into an informal understanding with Convergencia i Unió since the elections indicates how problematic it still is for the bourgeois centre-right to assemble a feasible alternative to Socialist rule. The ambitions of the Catalan nationalists are as yet by no means satisfied, and there are likely to be difficult passages between Felipe González and Jordi Pujol. But given the importance of European integration in Pujol's economic and political strategy for Catalonia, an entente with the PP's Castilian centralists remains improbable.

For the foreseeable future at least (which is not as long as it used to be), the cry of PP exasperation still rings true. Spain is likely to remain a 'country of the left' – although by no means necessarily 'of the PSOE'. The Italian experience demonstrates how rapidly a political order can be transformed now that the constraints of the Cold War have been removed. Numerically, the PSOE has strengthened itself as an organization since the mid eighties,[25] but socially it is not so deeply rooted that it has an indefinite lease on power. The storms of financial scandal which washed over the fourth González administration in the spring of 1994, engulfing both the monetary and security branches of the state, and sweeping Solchaga himself overboard, have already gravely threatened it. The leverage of Pujol's Catalan bourgeoisie over the government has increased proportionately. If the González regime continues – as it shows every sign of doing – to try to raise itself above its core electorate, other social-democratic experiences are a reminder of what its fate is likely to be.

Notes

1. For a stock-taking at the end of the sixties, see Richard Soler, 'The New Spain', *New Left Review* 58, November–December 1969.

2. José Maria Maravall, *La Política de la transición*, Madrid 1985, p. 68.

3. The notion of a 'buffer zone' is shrewdly developed by the Chilean analyst Carlos Huneeus in *La Unión de centro democrático y la transición a la democracia en España*, Madrid 1985, pp. 27–32 – a fundamental work for this period.

4. See, for example, Raymond Carr and Juan Pablo Fusi, *Spain: Dictatorship to Democracy*, London 1981, pp. 226–7 – two authors above suspicion of any ultra-left enthusiasm.

5. See R. de las Cierva, *Historia del socialismo en España, 1879–1983*, Barcelona 1983, p. 263.

6. J.L. Cebrián's interview with González in *El País*, 14 June 1979, cited by A.G. Santesmases, 'Evolución ideológica del socialismo en la España actual', *Sistema*, November 1985, p. 67.

7. The point is well made by Huneeus, in a penetrating discussion of the whole question of Christian Democracy in Spain, op. cit, pp. 175–90. There was no Spanish counterpart of the Partito Popolare in the twenties.

8. For a vivid description of the contrasts, see Ronald Fraser, 'Spain on the Brink', *New Left Review* 96, March–April 1976.

9. For a somewhat extended discussion of this process, see Patrick Camiller, 'The Eclipse of Spanish Communism', *New Left Review* 147, September–October 1984.

10. See J.F. Tezanos, 'Continuidad y cambio en el socialismo español', *Sistema*, November 1985, p. 24, quoting congress reports. Figures for the period between 1976 and 1979 are generally much less reliable.

11. M. Fernandez-Braso, *Conversaciones con Alfonso Guerra*, Barcelona 1983, p. 196.

12. See the sector-by-sector survey in the *Financial Times*, 20 January 1986.

13. In *ABC*, 10 May 1985.

14. Survey data of the *Centro de Investigaciones Sociológicas*: see Angel Viñas, 'Coordenados de la política de seguridad española', *Leviatán*, no. 17, autumn 1984, p. 13.

15. See the official PSOE pamphlet *Cincuenta preguntas sobre la OTAN*, Madrid 1981, quoted here here from the lengthy extract in *ABC*, 8 December 1985, p. 26.

16. *El Pais*, 14 June 1993.

17. See Paul Heywood, 'Governing a New Democracy: The Power of the Prime Minister in Spain', *West European Politics*, April 1991.

18. See *Perfil de una década*, special supplement of *El País*, 28 October 1992.

19. For these and other data below, see the comprehensive survey edited by Soledad Gallego-Díaz, Andreu Missé and Joaquín Prieto, *Perfil de una década*.

20. See Guerra's introduction to the volume he edited with José Felix Tezanos, *La Década del cambio*, Madrid 1992, which in effect represents the official PSOE account of its accomplishments: pp. 16–17.

21. Compare the tables in Francisco Fernandez Marugan, 'La Década de los ochenta: Impulso y reforma económica', in *La Década del cambio*, pp. 177, 185–188.

22. *Perfil de una década*, p. 22.

23. Sources: for 1989, Keith G. Salmon, *The Modern Spanish Economy*, London 1991, p. 18; and for 1991 and 1992, *Financial Times*, 2 April 1993.

24. Industrial production fell by 0.9 per cent in 1991 and 1.0 percent in 1992, and is expected to decline further in 1993.

25. Membership of the PSOE grew from 117,000 in 1982 to 309,000 in 1991: José Felix Tezanos, 'El Papel social y político del PSOE', *La Década del cambio*, p. 46.

Notes on the Contributors

Tobias Abse is Lecturer in Modern European History at Goldsmiths' College, University of London, and author of *Sovversivi e fascisti a Livorno: Lotta politica e sociale* (1991). He is currently preparing a book on the Italian political crisis of 1989–94.

Perry Anderson is Professor of History and Sociology at UCLA, and author of *Passages from Antiquity to Feudalism* and *Lineages of the Absolutist State* (1974); *Considerations on Western Marxism* (1976); *In the Tracks of Historical Materialism* (1983); *English Questions* and *A Zone of Engagement* (1992).

Patrick Camiller lectures in European Politics at the University of North London.

Ådne Cappelen is Research Director at Statistics Norway.

Niels Finn Christiansen is Senior Lecturer at the Centre for the Study of Workers' Culture, University of Copenhagen. His recent publications include *The Organization of Class Society 1900–1925* (1990), part of a general History of Denmark, and a biography of the Danish Social Democratic politician and classicist *Hartvig Frisch* (1990).

Jan Fagerberg is Senior Researcher at the Norwegian Institute of Foreign Affairs.

Jane Jenson is Research Affiliate of the Center for European Studies, Harvard University, and Professeuse titulaire in the Département de science politique, Université de Montréal. She is co-author of – among other books – *Mitterrand et les Françaises: un rendez-vous manqué* (1994), *The Politics of Abortion* (1992), *Absent Mandate: The Politics of Electoral Change in Canada* (1990), and *The View from Inside: A French Communist Cell in Crisis* (with George Ross) (1985). She is also co-editor of *The Feminization of the Labour Force* (1988), and author of numerous articles on politics and political economy in Canada and France.

267

Peter Mair is Professor of Comparative Politics at the University of Leiden. He is respectively author and co-author of *The Changing Irish Party System* (1987), *Identity, Competition and Electoral Availability* (1990), and *Representative Government in Modern Europe* (second edition 1994).

Lars Mjøset is Research Director at the Institute for Social Research, Oslo.

Stephen Padgett is Jean Monnet Senior Lecturer in European Politics at the University of Essex. He is co-author of *Political Parties and Elections in West Germany* (1986) and *A History of Social Democracy in Postwar Europe* (1991). He is co-editor of *Developments in German Politics* (1992) and editor of *Adenauer to Kohl: The Development of the German Chancellorship* (1994). He is also co-editor of the journal *German Politics*.

William E. Paterson is Salvesen Professor of European Institutions and Director of the Europa Institute, University of Edinburgh. His most recent co-authored books are *Government and the Chemical Industry in Britain and Germany* (1988), *Governing Germany* (1991) and *A History of Social Democracy in Postwar Europe* (1991). He is co-editor of *Developments in German Politics* (1992), and of the journal *German Politics*.

Jonas Pontusson is Associate Professor of Government at Cornell University. He is the author of *The Limits of Social Democracy: Investment Politics in Sweden* (1992), co-editor of *Bargaining for Change: Union Politics in North America and Europe* (1992), and currently engaged in comparative research on industrial restructuring and political change in Western Europe.

George Ross is Morris Hillquit Professor in Labor and Social Thought at Brandeis University, and Senior Associate at the Minda de Gunzburg Center for European Studies, Harvard University. His recent books include *Workers and Communists in France* (1982), *The View from Inside: A French Communist Cell in Crisis* (with Jane Jenson) (1985), *Unions, Crisis and Change* (with P. Lange and M. Vannicelli) (1982), Volume I of the Harvard Center for European Studies series on trade-union responses to economic crises, *The Mitterrand Experiment* (with S. Hoffmann and S. Malzacher, eds), and *Searching for the New France* (with James Hollifield). His *The Cyclist: Jacques Delors and European Integration* will be published in 1994.

Bent Sofus Tranøy is Research Scholar at the Center for International Climate and Energy Research, University of Oslo.

Index

269